NEGATIVE C...

'How truly she is a writer shows ...
moment-by-moment pleasure tri...
Hilary Mantel, *The Guardian*

'Michèle Roberts ... stares at a moment of apparent failure and plucks from it a ripe success. Only a born writer can replenish the truth like this.' **Andrew O'Hagan**

'There is much to savour in this most valuable and wondrous diary. Michele Roberts is a writer who has always excelled at embodying the joy of female intellectual and earthly appetites.'
Deborah Levy

'Funny, wise and all-embracing.' **Carmen Callil**

'A memoir that perfectly captures the writer's life and how your identity is bound up in your work.' **Karen Campbell**

'Brave, naked, defiant and exquisitely written.'
Julie Myerson, *The Spectator*

'A wonderful writer: one in possession of immense feeling.'
Rachel Cooke, *The Observer*

'Raw and glittering ... Superb.'
Christina Patterson, *The Sunday Times*

'Roberts writes with wit and honesty.' *The Independent*

'Bracing and galvanising ... Roberts' prose is winning.'
Susie Boyt, *Financial Times*

Michèle Roberts writes novels, short stories, poetry and essays. She lives in London.

Also by Michèle Roberts

NEGATIVE CAPABILITY

A Diary of Surviving

Michèle Roberts

SANDSTONE PRESS

First published in Great Britain by
Sandstone Press Ltd
Willow House
Stoneyfield Business Park
Inverness
IV2 7PA
Scotland

www.sandstonepress.com

This edition 2020

Sandstone Press is committed to a sustainable future. This book
is made from Forest Stewardship Council® certified paper.

MIX
Paper from
responsible sources
FSC® C020471

Hardback ISBN: 978-1-913207-14-4
Paperback ISBN: 978-1-913207-51-9
ISBNe: 978-1-913207-15-1

Cover design by Nathan Burton
Typeset by Iolaire, Newtonmore
Printed and bound by CPI Group (UK) Ltd, Croydon, CR0 4YY

To Sarah and Jenny

Contents

CHAPTER 1

APRIL

One Day In Orchard Street, London

Yesterday ended in disaster. Very late at night, I decided to write down everything that had happened, the only way I could think of coping. So here goes.

Yesterday I woke up at seven thirty in my white-painted wrought-iron bed, felt lazy, decided to have a lie-in. Almost immediately, above me, the neighbours' bed began creaking. This went on for ten minutes or so, then stopped. Angus and Bettina got up and thumped to and fro on their wooden floor. I got up too. While coffee brewed, I went out into the back garden bearing yesterday's coffee grounds – slug deterrent – and slices of used lemon – cat deterrent. The local cats like to shit in my flowerbeds and I like to swear at them, if I spot them, and chase them off. A dog fox ran along the bed at the far end. When I shouted at it and waved my arms it leaped the fence into my neighbour Mike's garden. I deadheaded a few primroses, admired the hellebores' pale pink flowers, the violets and wallflowers in bloom, counted three spikes of lily-of-the-valley poking up and went back inside. I decided not to do yesterday's washing-up, left it still piled in the sink. I preferred to get down to work straight away.

Usually in the mornings I work on rewriting my novel, revising it line by line, page by page. I am determined to get it published, even though the Publisher rejected it several months ago, she and her reader finding it overall 'too intense... too heavy' though in part 'stupendous'. Failing is part of writing, though not all writers admit to failing ever. Fail again, said Samuel Beckett: fail better. Accordingly, I had begun to rewrite the novel, expanding it, doubling it to inhabit two separate timescales, letting one strand of story haunt another.

Yesterday morning, however, I had a review to finish writing, so put my novel aside. I was in the middle of a spat with a friend, Susan, so felt pleased I had a commission to be getting on with, which might take my mind off hurt and anger. Nothing like work for giving back a lost sense of proportion.

Susan is younger than I am, beautiful, multi-talented, brave, cool. Recently, a particular piece of behaviour on her part had felt like a punch to the belly, knocking me off-balance. I'd protested, trying to explain my upset. After that I kept silent. Not being in touch felt right; peaceful; a relief. I had then made the mistake of replying to an email from Susan gaily inviting us to meet. So now I was involved in an exchange of explanations. Part of me felt I had to see them through, that it might be worth it for the sake of the friendship, part of me felt I'd been hooked back into something dodgy.

Thank heavens for deadlines. I went on with the work I had begun last night, the piece that I was due to send off this morning: a thousand words on Vera Brittain's *Testament of Youth*. I drank strong Italian coffee from my big breakfast cup. Two cups of coffee every morning: a ritual, an addiction, a pleasure.

I wrestled with language for four hours, finding it pleasanter than wrestling with Susan. Writing about the language of Brittain's memoir, her weird, conflicted style alternating between pomposity and succinct brilliance, I worked out what I thought about her treatment of her subject: war. Initially she seems to have wanted to join in, to have resented not being allowed to. After the deaths of her fiancé and brother, the carnage she witnessed as a Red Cross volunteer nurse, she became a pacifist. Bravely she got on with the job: trying to patch up men smashed to red pulp. Brittain's soldier patients had been forced to be brave on the battlefield, but now, in terrible pain, many of them lost control and screamed in wild abandonment.

Thinking about the soldiers' suffering, I made a crass egotistical connection, remembered that I haven't gone back to the dentist, because I haven't yet screwed up sufficient courage. Last time, when Denis-the-dentist sprayed water into the tooth cavity, just washing it, the water jet hurt the sensitive tissue there and I screeched and jumped and the nurse put her gloved forefinger on my lower jaw to hold my mouth open and I wanted to clamp my mouth shut and of course couldn't or I'd have bitten her. The pain and the helplessness combined with the rough whirring and grinding of the drill as Denis smoothed the edge of the newly fitted tooth, the drill clamped to me like a dog shaking its prey, revived the trauma of going to that sadist, Mr Watts, when I was young, as he drilled away with no local anaesthetic and often hit a nerve and I couldn't scream because he was still drilling. We had to go to Mr Watts for twelve years and for twelve years I lived in silent terror of the next visit, the next bout of pain. Unthinkable to complain, to ask to go to a different dentist who might not hurt us. We were drilled in obedience and then Mr Watts took over.

Jim, my ex-husband, knowing I feared dentists so much, had recommended Denis-the-dentist's group practice: don't worry, Mimi, they'll sedate you for treatment if you ask them to, they'll knock you out cold. Handsome, burly Denis listened, on my first visit, when I tried to explain to him how scared I was. He said, yes, dentistry used to be medieval. He picked up my hand and studied my wet palm: look at you, sweating with terror just as I'm about to inject you with the best drugs on the market!

Thinking about those childhood experiences of terror, how trauma lodges outside time and outside language, helped me think about war trauma. My own tiny pain helped me think about others' huge ones. Gave me a way in to writing about Vera Brittain's experiences tending young men dying in agony.

My basement flat's workroom, serving also as sitting room and dining room, fronts the street, mostly free of traffic thanks to the gate erected by the council at the park end. The tall window lets in plenty of light. I went on writing, rewriting, cutting, rewriting. Halfway through the morning, Tommy, one of my neighbours, walked past my window, slowed to catch my glance, and waved, and I waved back. We do this every day. He is a big, curly-haired man, a trained butler who gets evening work at City parties. Once he brought me back a table decoration, a short-stemmed nosegay of white tulips, which would otherwise have got thrown away at the end of the evening. As a New Year first-footing present he left on the doorstep a potted amaryllis bulb, which is currently in enormous pink bloom. One day, knowing I was sad, he left me a heather in a pot. He brings me abandoned plants people have chucked onto the pavement next to the rubbish bins: you're the plant doctor! When we meet in the street, we stop for brief chats. He is droll, and dry. We make each other laugh.

I worked all morning to the sound of my upstairs neighbour Bettina's brother practising guitar overhead, strumming clumsily and thinly wailing out of tune, then in between songs thumping back and forth. He comes to stay with Angus and Bettina often. The new wooden floor they've put in (three months of loud machinery noises) relays the sound just as much as the old MDF one did. I managed, some weeks ago, to knock on the door and ask the brother to turn down the TV and not to shout into his mobile. I felt able to object to loud daytime TV and overloud phone conversations but I don't like to hurt his feelings by criticising his guitar-playing.

At twelve noon I emailed the review to the editor who'd commissioned it. She emailed back to say she'd respond with any queries later in the day.

I felt better. I had achieved something: got work sent off on time. I decided to go out. Run errands, do some necessary food shopping, get some fresh air. I smartened myself up, hunted for my scarf. I arranged it 1940s style, as demonstrated by a Parisian friend: simply crossed over in front in a loose V, tucked inside your jacket, leaving your throat clear. That's how men in film noir wear their scarves. *Chic comme chez chic!* Perhaps, also, it disguises the lack of a shirt. Hard-up villains can't afford clean collars, not until they have done murder, got away with the swag.

I wondered about putting on lipstick (trousers rolled? Daring to eat a peach?). I rarely wear it, enjoy it when I do. A sudden flag. Red alert. See me! Years ago, at the hairdresser's (what an antique word – should I say hair salon?), I read a sentence by Pattie Barron, a magazine beauty editor, which stuck with me. She wrote sternly that lipstick (indeed all make-up – *putting on your face*) signalled women's good manners, a form of courtesy to others. Our unpowdered noses and unblushered cheeks would apparently send people screaming for cover. Now Pattie Barron writes the gardening page for the *Evening Standard*'s property section on Wednesdays, and she still likes to consider colours and makeovers, to create corrective illusions, pleasing effects. *Pace* Pattie, you don't dig and mulch and plant your garden so much as just buy things to pop into it, much as you'd pop on some eyeshadow. Pattie's colour scheme for this year's town gardens is pink, purple and white and I am trying it out. I own two lipsticks, both bright red. Recently, my young neighbour Anny, a government researcher, meeting me in the street on a lipstick day, seemed taken aback: Michèle! I didn't know you ever wore lipstick, I never wear it myself, it seems fraudulent. I laughed at her: femininity is a masquerade! Etcetera. She grinned back. We waved goodbye, parted.

Chilly out: sunshine and a bitter wind. I shoved my hands into my pockets. No gloves. I lost one, and the other stayed at my house in France to act as a pan-holder; both my pan-holders there (dark blue check; quilted) had become covered in black mould after the winter rains made the house damp and slimy. No foundations: the house stands on rock. The old stone walls suck up the damp, then in spring it ebbs back down, and inside the sitting room another patch of green-painted plaster falls off at skirting-board level.

I wandered along the thronged main road. Hearing West African people speaking French I wanted to greet them, talk to them. French was my mother's language. I grew up bilingual. Mum stopped speaking to us in French after we reached the age of seven, she told us later, since she worried that hearing two languages would confuse us. Also I think she felt loyal to my father's language, to England her adoptive country. As an immigrant she was keen to fit in. She spoke fluent English, and tried to act with middle-class English decorum and restraint, but sometimes when she was angry with my father her French accent would return and her grammar would crack, she reverted to a younger passionate self, and that charmed me, because I caught a flash of her as a person not only my mother, even though that also frightened me because the rows could sound severe to children listening quaking in their bedroom overhead, and when she jumped into the car and drove off I was convinced she'd left home never to return, though she always did eventually.

While she and I were going through our years of not getting on, we communicated – or failed to – only in English. I was repudiating her Catholic values, and her love of Molière and Ronsard, in favour of feminist heresy and political authors such as Simone de Beauvoir. Mum had spent a year at the Sorbonne, and would describe going dancing and then having onion soup in the morning at Les Halles, and I fantasise she might have bumped into Simone, and compared how coming from similar bourgeois backgrounds they were both training as teachers though planning on going in different directions, but no, that could never have happened, they'd have regarded each other with suspicion and incomprehension.

For years Mum and I saw each other's hatred more than each other's love and I, certainly, needed to keep those feelings well apart and did not understand how they shimmy back to back, each a shadow of the other. Years later, when Mum and I had forgiven each other, wanted to spend time together, I'd sometimes address her in French, and the resulting conversation would bring us close, as though we'd stripped off disguises and could recognise each other, accept how alike we actually were as well as different. French words handed back and forth between us might ostensibly be to do with memories of the past in Normandy, for example going swimming at Etretat and exploring the tunnels inside the arching cliffs, memories that we could now re-create, adding fresh opinion and comment, but also they stood, on a deep level, for the caresses and physical playfulness that had been impossible when I was small and Mum was so busy, with four children under seven to care for.

Roland Barthes once said that writing was playing with the body of the mother. I don't think most English male writers would think that. Too reductive! Childish and absurd! Hurrumph! Bollocks! Perhaps Barthes meant that writing enacts a wish, invents a return to a lost paradise. I never dwelt in that paradise, but I can long to believe in it, want to create it through writing, then realise I'm inventing a different country (not *mon continent*, as in 'correct' French, but *ma continent* as the French-Canadian writer Nicole Brossard puts it). Perhaps Barthes meant that too. Anyway, somehow I understand his metaphor better when I read and speak in my mother-tongue.

I went into the corner shop on the main road to buy the *Guardian*. The young man behind the counter greeted me with smiles. Every morning we say hello to each other, how are you, briefly discuss the weather. His parents came here from Mumbai. He doesn't speak much English, he's shy too, so our conversations include lots of hand gestures and exaggerated smiles or frowns. He works long hours. He told me once that on Sunday all he does is sleep.

Once outside the shop again I felt lazy, and cold, with the wind scouring my face, so I jumped on the bus rather than walking to the post office. In East Street Market I bought a bowlful of red and orange peppers for a pound, a bowl of cour-gettes ditto. There you are, young lady, shouted the handsome Turkish stallholder, such an easy way to please me, so of course I gave him a smile.

The vegetables sold in the market are not super-fresh and don't keep. But they are cheap. I had resolved three days back to become much thriftier. Since the Publisher had rejected my novel my hoped-for advance had not materialised, so my income (OK at the moment) would nosedive after my current teaching (a weekly evening class) finished. I needed to train myself to stop impulse spending. When I'm unhappy and rest-less it is all too easy to trawl the charity shops and buy picture frames for pictures I haven't yet painted; or antique-ish plates and pots (just to rescue them, it feels like) from the East Street Sunday junk stalls. I am very fortunate: I own my flat outright so don't have to pay a mortgage; bits of freelance work come in; dribs and drabs of royalties on previous books. But next year I may be quite poor, in my own terms.

Many people round here are much poorer than I am. We newly arrived, cosily off, middle-class homeowners are called by some locals the incomers. I'm an immigrant. As Mum was. At the same time I feel connected to this district. My English ancestors were farm labourers in Kent, who moved up to this area of south-east London in the nineteenth century to find work. I lived in a communal household down in nearby Camberwell in the mid-1970s, also my ex-husband Jim's family worked locally, in East Street Market. I've known the neighbourhood for a long time.

So far I have afforded to keep on La Lièvrerie, my house in France. That makes me really wealthy, in my neighbours' terms. Mine, as a young woman starting out as a writer, was an elected, chosen poverty, not an enforced one. The neighbours I've become friendly with are gracious and accepting and we stop to chat when we meet.

I greet passers-by on my street, and the women nod back, whereas the men, the ones of my age that is, often slow down, fire off questions: where d'you live? You got a job? You married? You got kids?

One huge, middle-aged white skinhead, walking his pitbull dog, both looking very fierce, calls to me across the street whenever we pass, hello, darling. One youngish black man shakes his beaded braids at me when we meet late at night in the 24-hour grocery, catches me in a hug. One tall young black man, after three years of being greeted as he lolled dreamily in his doorway, now hails me as I go by. Last week he enquired: you a mum, then, or a grandma, or a policewoman? One older white man, a retired photographer, newly moved in to the nearby sheltered housing unit, has pestered both my neighbour Val and myself on the bus, on separate occasions, as we discovered when we compared notes. Val has named him the Groper. He fondled my knees, ooh these are pretty stockings, black polka-dots eh, invited me home with him to peruse his album of photos of Twiggy. He came to the Christmas carol singsong last year at the Tenants' & Residents' Association House. I opened the door to him. Without saying one word he immediately lifted his camera and began photographing me. He dawdles along the street, said camera dangling at his crotch, swinging like a loose penis. Whenever he spots me he fumbles for his camera, I dash past and he protests: I want to photograph you, why won't you let me photograph you?

Leaving East Street, I went to Morrisons across the road to buy milk and wine. Just inside the entrance, one of their male employees was helping a woman squeeze her bulging plastic carrier bags, full of shopping, into her wheelie bag. They were blocking access to the trolleys. I waited a few moments, then said: excuse me, could you move just a tiny bit? He glowered at me: can't you see there are more trolleys over there? I thought I saw him thinking: pushy middle-class white woman. I apologised: oh I'm sorry, so sorry, I didn't see them. I scuttled off. At the vegetable racks a young white woman with a thin, tired face and big hooped brass earrings was shouting at an older one: see these fucking organic beetroot? See what they fucking cost? Fucking middle-class wankers, must make them feel so good to buy fucking organic beetroot! I backed away in case she started shouting at me too. Fucking middle-class incomer! You don't belong here! Fuck off!

Why was I feeling so pathetic and wimpish? I realised anew how raw I felt over the debacle with Susan. This in turn had revived how smashed-up I'd felt when the Publisher rejected my novel. The passing of time had not made me feel any better. The pain kept re-erupting, fresh as could be.

After the publication of my previous novel, then two pamphlets of poems, and an artist's book (made with my friend Caroline Isgar), I'd started work on a new novel, set in the present, narrated by a woman, which was drifting along, taking its time, when suddenly the idea of a different story, set in the nineteenth century, narrated by a man, leapt up through it and disrupted it. I write about the unconscious, I write in it and from it, and I could see that these two narratives, one begun and one potential, co-existed in related layers, vertically, like the unconscious and the conscious mind. I saw that I could rearrange them horizontally, putting one next to the other, I could combine them into a single story, into coherent narrative time, by intertwining them. That experiment didn't work, or, at least, at that time I couldn't make it work. It felt inert, somehow. Accordingly I discarded the chapters set in the present and started again, with the newly arrived story.

Two images inspired it. They just swam up out of a waking reverie. I began with nothing more than a desire to make sense of them, translate them into words. The first image was of a dark door outlined with gold, as though the room beyond were bathed in firelight and candlelight. The second image was of a man following a woman up a dark staircase at night, she holding a lit taper in her raised hand. I simply had to follow the man up the stairs, follow him into that lit room, find out why he was there and what would happen next.

I found out by writing, not by thinking; the story flew along just ahead of me, it flew out of me, but also it seemed to have pre-existed my finding it. It embodied two aspects of imagination: making up something out of nothing; also finding something hidden, that was there all along, only you didn't know until you stumbled on it. My male narrator was a passionate, troubled, difficult man, but I felt intrigued by him, loved him. The story seeming almost to write itself, so forcefully, I believed in it. When I finished it I believed I had written a good novel. Accordingly I'd sent it off to my agent, for her to forward to the Publisher.

My agent phoned me a week in advance of the meeting requested by the Publisher, to warn me, to tell me the situation was not good. The novel was not wanted. I wasn't being offered a contract subject to a rewrite. No, the novel had been turned down flat. My agent sounded, as ever, cool and detached. Her call crushed me. I'm a writer: that's my identity and always has been, a solid core. Now I felt that my inside was a fragile, hollow eggshell that had been struck with a hammer, splintered, smashed. Nothing of me left. The day after my agent's phone call I collapsed at Val's, at her house in Plum Street, she having heard that I was going through a bad time, so she rang me and summoned me round, come and have a drink and tell me all about it, and I cried my eyes out for a few minutes while she plied me with wine and good advice. I remembered that Joan Armatrading song about a child needing comfort. In fact like that child I wanted *more* comfort, I wanted to let out my misery for longer, but Val steered me to listening to her matching tales of sorrow, which brought me out of my self-absorption, and I calmed down.

We got on to talking about relationships, past and present. I told Val how a year ago I'd split up with my lover Jack, after five years together, and that the wounds still sometimes twitched. Val said that one reason intense, passionate love affairs were so difficult was that they re-evoked childhood conflicts and needs that we could not always cope with. I agreed. Before things went wrong between us Jack and I had enjoyed a heady mixture of poetry and sex, however the passion and intimacy also created a desire in me to be his one and only, what my friend Nell Dunn calls the Queen Bee, and indeed for a while I assumed I was. Perhaps that desire was strengthened by the fact I hadn't been a Queen Bee in childhood: I was one of twins, the two of us squidged in between my mother's favourite child, our elder sister, and her adored son, our younger brother. Sitting talking to Val I remembered reading Marion Milner, the Freudian psychotherapist who wrote on art, who'd posited in one chapter of *On Not Being Able To Paint* that the infant was (temporarily at least) King Baby, the sole focus of his mother's attention, and I'd thought: no, not if you're a twin, lady, you have to share her. I had to share Jack, since although separated from his wife, who had left him and gone to live in a different city, he had not got divorced, and it turned out in the end that she had remained the Queen Bee all along. A while after I told her of the break-up Susan had said, oh you'll find another lover in no time, you're so good at flirting! This needled rather than consoled me.

Talking with Val in her sitting room scented with frankincense, letting my hair down (Victorian women in novels, at night, brushing out their hair, chatting), I'd made myself vulnerable to her, which was scary. I'd told her how I felt a complete failure on all fronts. I couldn't write a novel the Publisher wanted, I couldn't remember that I'd written books in the past people had liked, I couldn't sustain a love affair, I couldn't feel any confidence about myself or any aspect of my life. To some of my friends this would seem ridiculous and neurotic, I shouldn't be thinking like that, so I felt a failure about that too.

Standing in Morrisons staring at the *fucking organic beetroot*, I decided I must stop remembering for a bit, concentrate on being in the present. At least I'd got out of my flat. When you spend most of your day in isolation, writing, a trip to the supermarket hurls you back into the world. Morrisons is basic, cheap and cheerful. The cashiers know many of the customers and pause to chat. Dandies of all ages and shapes barge around in eccentric outfits. A man in a knitted suit of rainbow-striped wool. A man wearing a crisp beige suit with a yellow shirt, cream brogues, a fedora, an orange silk scarf tucked into his breast pocket. Young women in breast-popping halter-necks and tiny shorts curving in half-moons over their buttocks. Other women concealed under black robes and face veils. Elaborately curled wigs and long fake nails and bristling fake eyelashes. Beehives and bouffants and braids. Morrisons caters for everyone, offering sacks of basmati rice stacked on pallets, Polish sausage and pickled cabbage, Chinese and Vietnamese spices, jerk paste, Caribbean fruit loaves, frozen pizzas, the occasional organic chicken breast hiding on a top shelf. Jack, who lived in a leafy white suburb of south-west London, shopped at his local Waitrose, a vast, air-conditioned temple to gourmet savoir-faire. Artisan breads hand-woven by Sicilian peasant grandmothers. That kind of thing. You could spend fifty pounds in a blink.

Morrisons, where the peasant grandmothers shop, is much friendlier than Waitrose. A woman tapped my sleeve, flourished a piece of paper: where will I find juniper berries? What are they? This Jamie Oliver recipe says I've got to have juniper berries. A passing shelf-stacker, appealed to, shook his head: not sure we stock those. I said, go to Waitrose! A white-haired shawl-wrapped woman in a wheelchair, parked by the bulk-buy loo rolls, caught my eye and hailed me: I've been abandoned! She was joking in order not to feel embarrassed. She waved her hands in their pale blue woollen gloves: my daughter's gone to the cigarette counter, she'll be back any minute, don't you worry, love, I'll be fine.

My new life of thrift meant I did not buy yet another armful of saxifrage plants for only £1 each. I bought a packet of cod marked down to £2. That would do for two suppers. I made for the checkout. Just being in a queue was a comfort: I had a place, braced by other people. My women writer friends have braced me during these past months of living with the Publisher's rejection, during what has felt like a shipwreck, my craft driven onto the rocks.

In public I behaved bravely and cheerfully. I wasn't going to tell the gossips who buzz around at literary parties that my novel had been turned down, I wasn't going to give snipers and snoopers a chance to pity me or delight in my misfortune. In private I heard that familiar sneering voice: we told you so, your novels are too literary, too difficult, too experimental, too serious, too poetic, too unironic, too female, too ex-Catholic, too uncool, too everything, why can't you write a bestseller, why should anyone bother listening to you, why aren't you a proper intellectual, don't you know the novel is dead, why are you so ambitious, why do you go on using metaphor, why can't you just write nice middlebrow feminine stuff in a nice plain style, you're a failure, you're no good, why not just give up now, just admit it, you're a has-been a washout just drop dead. When I felt strong I would shout back: I'll survive this, just you wait and see, I'll be rediscovered when I'm ninety, you'll call it a comeback but I'll have been writing away all along, I refuse to give up so just fuck off and leave me alone! When I didn't feel strong I would curl up in my chair and read favourite sustaining novels and shut the voices out that way. Often aided by a sustaining glass of wine.

When teaching writing I advise students to make a relationship with this inner self-hating voice, if it pops up, so that it won't stop them writing, to make it into a character in a story, yet sometimes it is hard to take my own advice, easier to feel weak and hopeless. Do the stakes get raised the longer we go on, the more novels we write? Mrs Elton boasted to Emma how well-primed she was with inner resources, but I seemed to have none to fall back on. My past successes counted for nothing. There was only this smashed-up present. Over the past few months I'd plunged into the black pit, hauling myself out when necessary in order to do my teaching, see friends and family. At the meeting with the Publisher I had pretended I felt fine. Perching on a café chair in her elegant office at the publishing house, my agent seated alongside, as the Publisher gazed at me sweetly and murmured how so, so sorry she was to turn down my novel, I was damned if I was going to reveal my upset. That was strategy: showing I minded would have done me no good.

I suddenly felt able to say to the Publisher that I knew how I could rewrite the novel, I could go back to my original plan that I'd abandoned, let one story haunt the other.

She smiled approvingly. A ghost story, yes, that sounded good. I knew she meant well. Not her fault if marketing persons now required writers to turn into brands and to provide suitable works Tesco et al. would snap up and shelve alongside the cornflakes, that Amazon would sell online for peanuts, exemplifying the shift from aesthetic value mattering as much as sales figures to sales figures being the only marker of excellence. This had happened when publishers agreed to scrap the Net Book Agreement, which used to protect book prices, therefore authors' royalties. In those olden days, literary novels, highly esteemed by readers and critics as they might be, did not necessarily sell in tens of thousands and were subsidised by the bestsellers; we weren't all expected to sell like J. K. Rowling. Now each book's sales could be called up online in a twinkling and each book had to earn its own keep, stocked for two weeks in Waterstones if you were very lucky then out. That was modern business, sneered the internal voice, so stop whingeing, traditional publishing is dying anyway, just self-publish your book online.

Out in the street my agent said: that meeting went very well. I smiled hypocritically at her and fled to the bus stop. I tried to console myself: at least the waiting was over. No more hanging on for months in silence until agent and Publisher's reader and Publisher found the time to read my work. Three whole months had gone by in that state. Agony. Like being a starving baby howling for food that never came.

I concentrated on standing in the checkout queue at Morrisons, listening in to and watching all the dramas going on around me. Every single person in the store was the centre of his or her world, going through who knew what struggles and sorrows. Toddlers kicked and wept and their exhausted-looking mothers berated them, the saintly women cashiers smiled wearily and made jokes with regulars, a crew of schoolchildren swept by endearingly and noisily showing off, people flirted, preened, slumped, scowled, argued. I loaded my shopping into my little leather rucksack. Rather than get back on the bus, I walked home down the main road from Morrisons, telling myself not to be lazy, that I had to keep fit, take exercise, stay healthy. In fact the walk provided the treat of looking at shop windows: vast double beds moulded in gold plastic rococo swirls stuck with fake jewels and strewn with nylon leopard skins; blingy gold jewellery; sarsaparilla dispensers; wig emporia advertising Virgin Brazilian Hair; Ayurvedic pharmacies.

Back at home I picked up the mail from the mat and opened it. A threatening reminder of my unpaid bill from the gas and electricity supplier. Also a letter from an acquaintance in North America, dated a year back, originally misdelivered it seemed, which frequently happens round here, because the postie has now to deliver more post in less time and so in her haste often doesn't sort things properly, and so neighbours have to redeliver each other's post. This is fine if they are kindly reliable people like Sally and Tommy but not so good if the letters go to the same number as mine in the neighbouring street where the inhabitants are more laissez-faire and probably feel pissed off at the thought of having to walk round the corner to help someone they don't know. We do not complain about the faulty service to the Post Office, not wishing to get the postie into trouble. She has a gammy leg and swings gamely along the street with her bright red cart and calls me darling because after four years she has got to like me, not least I think because as soon as I catch her flash of red on the pavement I run up to take my mail, if there is any and if she hasn't already delivered it to the people in the next street, to save her having to heave her bad leg down my area steps and back up again, and because I give her a box at Christmas, if I see her that is.

I still couldn't face doing the washing-up, or any housework, so I went out into the back garden for a bit, just staring at it, then came in, read the *Guardian*, thought about the situation in Ukraine, remembered accompanying Jack to Kiev on his lecture trip. I read another article, felt rage over what the government's up to, cutting benefits and vilifying the unemployed, slashing support for vulnerable groups, deporting people seeking asylum. All these struggling people were being labelled failures. They detracted from the bright shiny Tory diktat of Everybody Can Make It. Those who didn't or couldn't had to disappear or be disappeared. I escaped from my rage by daydreaming over the paper's centrefold photograph of a huge, galleried, book-filled ancient reading room.

I made lunch, a Spanish-style dish of a few cod scraps gently cooked in olive oil with red peppers, sultanas, some leftover spinach, flavoured with garlic and paprika, served on a bed of chopped watercress. That last bit wasn't Spanish, but I like inventing new versions of dishes. I drank two glasses of white wine, thinking: to hell with it.

I took a siesta for an hour. I got up and checked my email. Susan had sent a new message, saying she still couldn't understand what I was so angry and upset about. I decided to answer her. I wrote about recognising that I projected my mother onto her, not the real-for-herself mother (who'd done her best, after all, and who'd died seven years back) but the mother-in-my-head, the one who was very critical and whom I was always trying to please. (My mother used to put me down for being successful as a writer. I feared her envious attacks. Hence Susan's joky digs over the years at my worldly successes had riled me more than they should.) I told Susan I knew that my making the projection was unfair and unhelpful. I apologised for it. What I didn't say was that Susan's 'jokes' provoked, I felt, such projections on my part. So my grudge still lodged at my heart and I still felt childishly grumpy and hard-done-by.

I sat and thought about how hard it is to deal with these childhood wounds when their scars burst open, when childhood pain re-erupts, how ashamed I feel that as an adult I can still turn back into that hurt child, that hurt young woman. But I do. That's how my unconscious works: it takes no notice of time. My friend Pat Kavanagh used to insist to me that after a certain age people simply had to have got over their early difficulties, their family problems. Too neat. Old griefs re-erupt when they need to. Anyway, I haven't managed that maturity, that wisdom. Only some of the time. Better to acknowledge that. Glance at the scars. Try to look after myself better. Also, better recognise that it's not just as a child but as an adult that I feel angry with Susan.

A second email was from the newspaper literary editor. She really liked my review. I cheered up.

My friend Nell Dunn rang. She is always honest, always kind, always sympathetic to other writers' travails with publishers. She was warm and funny. She told me a tale of going somewhere on the bus and taking her small dog Iris with her. While she sorted out her bag and newspapers she popped Iris on the seat next to her. The man behind her said: you shouldn't put a dog on a seat! Quick as a flash Nell replied: she's not a dog, she's a baby! She took Iris into her arms and dandled her and the man said no more. Nell said: why did I say that? I haven't a clue! She whooped with laughter. Then she told me a grimmer tale. A computer had been delivered to her house that morning, addressed to her lover Dan, who has been dead for four years. BT declined to take the computer back and wanted Nell to pay for it. She was pretty upset. We discussed what she should do. In the end I suggested she contact the Consumer Champions at the *Guardian*, and she said she would.

After Nell rang off I sat remembering our joint holiday last September. Nell had invited me to join her, also Carmen Callil and Jane Martineau, two other mutual friends, for a week's trip to Italy, renting a house in a hilltop village near Cortona. Knowing I was broke, the three of them very kindly insisted on paying my share of the rent. The former wine *fattoria* was so vast you could get lost in it when making your way to bed at night up its various staircases and down its ill-lit branching switchback corridors, ill-lit partly because the wall-set lamps were weak and the light switches hard to spot and partly because the metered electricity was super-expensive, so at first Jane and I kept turning the lights off when we all went to bed. This was tough on Carmen as the passage from her bedroom to her bathroom was gloomy and of course in the darkness the light switches were invisible and the polished tiled floors slippery and treacherous and if Carmen had slipped and fallen she would perhaps have lain there in the labyrinth, lost, for days, while we hunted for her with torches. So we compromised: some lights stayed on while others went off.

On arrival, late at night, we'd picked rooms pretty much at random. Carmen snagged a smallish one: this is all I need! My room, the most distant, opening onto a bathroom-cubicle set in a tower, was huge, with a vast bed, several buffets and cupboards, lots of sporting memorabilia, pictures of racing cars, photos of young men in mortarboards, magazines on male health and fitness. Jane slept badly in her (smaller) room, which looked over the narrow front street and the building works going noisily on opposite from dawn onwards, so I offered to swap with her.

My new room, with a frescoed ceiling, had three doors opening off it. Its main door led through an anteroom to a *salone,* and thence to a staircase down to the ground floor. A second, obscure door, flat in the wall and covered in the same blue chintz-style paper, opened, when unbolted, not into a cupboard as I expected but onto a narrow staircase. I tiptoed down this one night to explore, feeling brave as Mrs Bluebeard, foolish as Catherine Morland. It turned at right angles, debouched into a dark, vaulted hallway, which I crept along, first in one direction then another. Doors at either end: one gave onto the garden and the other onto the street. The third door in my bedroom opened onto a blank brick wall. I imagined an errant daughter bricked up behind this, as a punishment for allowing her gallant to creep up the secret staircase from the garden, and allowing another gallant to creep in from the street, and then hosting a threesome. Such a big bed! Pity to waste it, as one of my lovers used to say of his early morning erections.

In fact the creepiest aspect of the place was revealed by Carmen's discovery that the family owning it had been supporters of fascism during the 1930s. A large black and white framed photo in one *salone* showed a lean, cold-faced man in full military uniform, epaulettes, heavy belt, knee-high boots, the lot, posing stiffly in a brocade-covered armchair, a crimp-haired bejewelled woman in backless evening dress fawning at his feet. The inscription on the back, complete with dates and names, made the family's loyalties clear. Appalled, Carmen googled the man in uniform and discovered he'd been an active pro-Nazi, who'd escaped being put on trial after the war despite having 'served' in Ethiopia and overseen the incarceration and slaughter of African people. Other photos, early colour-tinted ones, showed a family couple at a ski resort, mountains in the background, the husband and wife managing to look, with raised keen profiles and sweptback blond hair, like heroes at an Aryan sports rally. The fascist taste in oil paintings ran to studies of nude nymphs, with splayed legs and coy expressions, and clumsy still lives of fruit and veg.

This discovery of the family's bad history blighted the holiday to some extent. Powerful memories of reading Primo Levi's account of concentration camp brutalities leaped up, also the images of Nazi methods of torture and death in Rossellini's *Roma città aperta*. On the other hand the disclosure brought me closer to my friends, since we all had to deal with it, talk about it. What else did we talk about? Books, art, sex, milk thistle, mosquito bites, our childhoods, frocks, shoes, people we all knew, publishing. We had group conversations and tête-à-tête conversations. One cold night, tipsy, I embroiled Nell, sitting by the wood fire, for which I'd foraged kindling, in the fascists' main *salone* hung with banal paintings, in a heated discussion of class differences and class privilege. More of a monologue actually. I think I'd suddenly got overcome by worries about my insecure financial future as an impoverished failed writer. Nell's background was posh, though she had bravely rejected it as a young woman in order to forge her own bohemian life and to write novels, and in my tipsiness I made her stand in for the rich people I was suddenly envying, not least the fascists I suppose, to my extreme shame. Nell listened, she kindly and sweetly heard me through my speech, she forbore to remind me that in most of my Londoner neighbours' eyes I was the rich, privileged one, she forbore to remind me that she, Jane and Carmen had so kindly paid for my rent in the fascist *fattoria*, she was tolerant, she said she believed in the good faith between us, and all that made me love her even more, because we could open our hearts to each other, tell our truth to each other, acknowledge our difference, without fear.

Italy in early autumn had been blue and hot and sunny. Here in springtime south-east London the sky beyond my workroom window now clouded over, turned coldly grey. Rain spurted down. I made a cup of tea, which I drank from my gold-rimmed 1950s French porcelain cup, sat down at my laptop, told myself to get back to work. Accordingly I went on redrafting part of a chapter of my novel and trying to take my agent Lily's advice into account.

Once I'd finished the new version of my novel, a few weeks back, I'd sent it to Lily. I'd completely reworked it. I'd tried to remove the over-intensity the Publisher had disliked, and I had intertwined the nineteenth-century story with the modern one I'd formerly abandoned but had now put back and rewritten, linking them with a ghost motif.

Lily hadn't liked the rewritten novel at all. At our meeting at her office she plunged straight into what was wrong with it. She considered my male narrator 'a whinger' and declared 'I don't like whingers!' She didn't like some of the sex, particularly the male narrator's memory of a particular childhood sexual fantasy. She hadn't realised, although they shared a name, that the male character in the prologue and the male character in the first chapter were one and the same person. She hadn't understood the ending.

I was depressed by this interview, cross about it too, since she'd kept me waiting quite a while just to hear in the end that she was awarding me *nul points*. The inner voice sneered: see, you're not special. Your writing's nothing special, either. Tee hee! However, I realised as I stood sadly and grumpily at the bus stop at the top of Chelsea Old Church Street that Lily had in fact said two helpful things. The novel was too long and needed cutting, and the ghost story was too subtle and needed emphasising. At that very moment the Groper appeared from the direction of Chelsea Arts Club, where doubtless he had been showing his album of photographs of Twiggy to any woman who'd let him within reach, and recognising me leered and pointed his camera and lurched towards me, so, absurdly flustered, I leapt on the bus that had just drawn up and was carried swiftly away to Piccadilly, quite the wrong destination. I changed buses, got on the 12 and got home.

I'd had a good angry moan to writer friends about that difficult interview with Lily, and then had started rewriting yet again. I was still at it. Working on this particular chapter, sitting at my laptop in my workroom, took several hours, which fled past without my noticing. Bliss: forgetting myself.

I turned on Radio 3, poured myself a glass of white wine and made supper: fusilli with sliced courgettes fried in olive oil, with chopped rosemary and garlic. I suddenly wished I'd organised myself to go out. It felt too late now, too dark and cold outside. I felt unsettled, not knowing what to do, that I was rattling and kicking around the place. I felt lonely. Not quite as bad as the mad loneliness I used to feel when Jack went off with his family for family weddings and his relatives were clearly allowed to think he and his wife were still happily married and living together, so obviously I, his lover of several years, didn't exist; it wasn't his going away I minded so much, I didn't expect to be invited to his daughter's wedding, since I hadn't been allowed to meet her, or to his cousin's daughter's wedding, but I hated feeling powerless, blotted out. Yes, like an abandoned baby. Howl as much as you want; no one will come. The inner voice sneered: how pathetic to feel like a baby, how repulsive, how self-indulgent and stupid. Misery fell back onto me, and I cried.

Enough! I decided to take my mind off bloody misery, to read one of the clutch of novels I had bought on my last visit to the London Review of Books bookshop. I am trying to read more foreign novels, particularly by women. Far more male writers than female ones get translated; you have to hunt for the great women authors of abroad. One exception to this rule was Serpent's Tail, who for example published *The Passport* by Herta Müller many years before she won the Nobel Prize. Pete Ayrton, its founder, had published early stories of mine in various anthologies, and had become a friend. I liked to tease him that his female authors constituted a list called The Perverse Feminine, for example Catherine Millet on her pursuit of the penis at all times and in all situations, or Kathy Acker on sex and drugs and violence, and indeed such books did well and brought their authors cult status.

Last night I'd found *Why the Child is Cooking in the Polenta* by Aglaja Veteranyi entrancing: poetic, harsh, moving, elegiac. Tonight's reading was *The Notebook* by Agota Kristof, set in Hungary during WW2. Crisply and simply written, no emotion allowed to show, a story of twin children's survival, very powerful, shocking and disturbing, full of cruelty, perversion and abusive sex. A bit too much for me in my present state. I skipped the middle, read the ending, slammed the book down, picked up *Jane Eyre* instead. Over the lonely, freezing moor Jane plods, starving and sad, but determined, brave, her self-respect intact.

I remembered reading Jean Radford's essay on the novel, published back in the 1970s, which pointed out that Jane's pilgrim's progress, from Gateshead to Lowood School to Thornfield to Moor House, finally to Ferndean the house in the forest, shows her searching for a home. When Bettina and Angus regularly made such a noise overhead I felt I didn't have much of a home: they crashed in and occupied my flat. I felt pushed out.

Now I remembered that I had felt like that before, forty years ago, when the house where I rented a room got collectivised overnight. We were all radicals, libertarians, active in local politics. One weekend, while I was away, the owners of the house, a married couple, decided that no one would have a room of their own any more: you'd just sleep on any spare mattress you could find knocking around. An end to bourgeois possessiveness! I returned to discover that my room was now the library. I think the owners did this so that they no longer had to share a room and therefore could feel sexually free. For a while I went along with the new set-up. I was over-compliant, hiding behind the false, goody-goody self I'd developed in childhood, desperate to please my mother, believing that my misbehaving would increase her depression, migraines and sleepless nights; I had to be good so that she wouldn't suffer more. In the same way, I tried to please these new 'parents' who'd chucked me out of my room, but after a while I felt so angry and unhappy that I fled. I thought I'd dealt with that painful experience but here it was jumping up again.

In *Jane Eyre* the moon is homeless Jane's mother, and Jane addresses her as such. I've been observing the moon, coming home or going out, on these recent clear nights. Evening skies of sapphire darkening to indigo, apple green at the horizon, then up swings the moon. Watching the moon sail above inner-city rooftops connects me to La Lièvrerie, where I watch the moon rise every night the clouds allow.

My friends Sarah and Jenny have both, in different years, given me lunar calendars for Christmas, blue scrolls precisely patterned with swelling and diminishing white crescents and

29

circles. We three watch the moon from our vantage-spots in different parts of the country. We live far apart, but email connects us; also our plans for our joint book that has evolved out of our ten years old writers' group, a book Lily has declined to represent, and which we are sending out ourselves to possible editors. So far: failure to find one. Sometimes I see the three of us as three poles leaning together to form a tripod, a pot of stories dangling between us over the fire. At other times I see us as a tripod of bamboo sticks bearing froths of sweet peas, such as Grandpa used to grow in his back garden. We're strongly individual, but also we come together, we bend together, we make something between us as well as making things when we are apart. We support each other. We support each other to go rambling off like sweet pea tendrils! Jenny and Sarah have helped me survive the Publisher's rejection. They threw me a lifebelt of consoling words, by telephone and email, when I was drowning.

Angus and Bettina had returned home promptly at six and begun clumping to and fro overhead. They were still at it. Their sitting room is above mine. Why do they so rarely sit still? They pace, they thud back and forth, the floor creak-creak-creaks. I can't help trying to imagine what they are doing. Exercising? When they have sex in their sitting room, as opposed to their bedroom, the floor creak-creak-creaks in just one particular spot and I hear Bettina squeaking, so I put music on to drown them out. Loud Handel arias at the moment. But this constant walking to and fro is odd. A few months ago they went through a time of having noisy rows, Bettina sobbing and reproaching Angus on and on and on, at the same time pounding to and fro, finally shouting at him and slamming doors. Thrice this happened in the middle of the night and woke me up, and I lay listening and fretting. Some time after the worst, noisiest overnight row Angus came to my front door to apologise for the disturbance. I'm not a bad man, I want you to know, I've given up drinking now, Bettina has some issues, we're going to Relate.

So the rows had stopped, but not the thudding to and fro. Then, in mid-evening, the guitar-playing had begun again and was continuing. I got up from my chair and put on a CD. Beethoven piano quartets. Complicated, heavenly, rapture-inducing music. So often I've worried that if I have the radio on too loud or play music too loudly I'll be disturbing Angus and Bettina. I think they disturb me more often than I disturb them.

At 11pm I heard new sounds upstairs, which at the moment are repeated each night, and which I have worked out is Angus and Bettina unfolding a sofa bed or its equivalent for Bettina's brother. Much stomping and creaking. I went to bed. So did Angus and Bettina. Creak-creak-creak.

I lay and listened. No choice but to listen! Sex going on upstairs, in the bedroom above me. No sex in my life. Sex going on in my imagination. Sex going on in that unpleasant novel I'd read earlier. Nonetheless, the amorality of the sex in that novel – look, you can do whatever you like, no holds barred – plus the unwilling voyeurism induced by the noises above, plus the power of my own sexual longings, all joined to turn me on. I touched myself, came rapidly, repeatedly.

Drowsing, I slowly realised I'd somehow floated loose from conscious thoughts, I didn't know where I was, what the date was, what was happening. I'd entered a fugue state, I'd entered the unconscious, my own unconscious, layers and layers of memory shimmering and sparkling all round me, images I couldn't quite see or grasp, fishes flicking beneath the sea, I just knew they were there, memories of everything that had ever happened in my life it felt like, showers of brilliants behind transparent veils. Timelessness. The eternal present. I was lost in it, bewildered. Adrift. Had I gone mad? What should I do? What could I do?

The experience had no words in it, just sensations, thousands of lost memories gleaming tantalisingly just below the surface of my oceanic mind, tiny sparkling lights in a web of connection outside time.

I managed to grasp that the tumult and torment of the day just past might have something to do with this state. I couldn't contain it. My mind had exploded. How to recompose it?

The only thing I could think of doing was to make a narrative. Write. I hung onto this idea as onto a rope thrown to me where I was drowning in the sea. I would put the split, spilt, scattered images of the previous day back into time. The hours of the day, arbitrary in my present diffused state but meaningful for making a helpful pattern, would form a backbone to the narrative, and I'd marshal events and feelings towards that. Comb them back into connection with a central core. I would connect everything within that chronological order. The day was like a prone body with a spine, and broken-off ribs and other bones could be drawn towards it, swept towards it by my writing, could reassemble themselves. A new, reordered body could be made out of complete disorder. Out of the destroyed pieces of myself I could make something. I could put myself back together again.

Reassured, I was able to turn over, pull the covers round me, and fall asleep.

I dreamed that I was in my English grandparents' back garden in Edgware. Adam Phillips, the psychoanalyst-writer, was sitting, reading a book, on the 1920s rustic wooden bench made of criss-crossed branches where Nana and Grandpa would sit together on summer evenings, the sweet peas twining overhead. I sat nearby, sorting out a large bunch of fireworks, mainly rockets, which I planned to let off at a children's party later on.

Then I woke up this morning, at 7.30am.

My dreams often make simple visual puns. Recording this dream in this narrative present, this writing present, I think the dream was suggesting I needed to see a therapist. Well, I saw one! There he sat, calmly reading a book. I'd summoned him to a place connected to my beloved, benevolent, trustworthy grandparents. If I were to explode like a rocket, at least helpful figures would be nearby. Perhaps, though, I wasn't a brilliant, shining shower of stars but a damp squib sputtering out.

Never mind. Get up and write about it.

CHAPTER 2

MAY

One Day In Bloomsbury

Whom am I addressing in this diary? Diaries are private documents, written for the author alone. The diarist writes to herself. Perhaps keeping this diary will compose a self for me, a future self, a possible self, a strong self I've lost touch with. In any case, I need to keep on writing it. If I don't, I may lose myself in that strange, timeless, scattered state again. So here goes.

Yesterday morning, the weather being sunny, I drank my breakfast coffee outdoors in the back garden, sitting on one of the white iron French café chairs that I bought on a whim in a Herne Hill junk shop soon after I moved in.

That hot summer day, to visit my friend Christie Hickman in West Dulwich I'd walked from Walworth down to Camberwell, then through the Peckham backstreets lined with splendidly neo-Gothic and neo-classical mid-Victorian cottages and villas, then up and down the hills towards Brockwell Park, my route taking me past groups of pretty 1920s low white cottage-style council houses curved in half-moons around 'village' greens, and from the hill tops affording views across the outskirts of south-east London towards the Kentish Downs, also peeps at narrow hedged lanes with no tarmac or pavements, ancient surviving bridle paths perhaps, that curved away downhill. I went past rows of opulent Edwardian semi-detacheds. The glory of vernacular architecture! Avenues and crescents swooping up and down slopes, turreted mini-castles sprouting towers and porches and gables, all fronted with gardens frothing with creepers and flowers. Arriving in Herne Hill, I spotted the chairs in a shop on the corner, immediately bought them, asked the owner to deliver them next day, then continued on my way to see Christie, and went out to supper with her in a palatial local Victorian pub with bars the size of ballrooms.

The café table at which I drank my morning coffee came from the Walworth Road junk shop where I also bought a little chest of drawers. When I tried to bargain for this nicely painted but flimsy piece, the sheepskin-coated, cigar-smoking seller earnestly said: but it's Sheraton-fronted, d'you see? I felt abashed. I did see. I paid what he asked and he graciously delivered it that afternoon.

These Walworth gardens run back to back in green corridors, some gardens collectivised, like next door's, for all the council tenants who live in layers in one house, some privately owned by the basement flat dwellers like myself, some, like Val's, owned by a single owner-occupier of a house. Foxes treat the whole lot as their territory. They have made Val's back garden a playground, they gambol on her lawn and piss on her choice plants and kill them, and the big vixens, protecting their cubs, terrorise her, so that she can only advance very cautiously, wielding a broom, to her shed at the far end under the overhanging sycamore trees, where the foxes hang out when not prancing at her back door.

We are not allowed to cull them as they are not classified as a nuisance, though you could argue they are savage vermin, tossing the rubbish about and attacking children and defying gentle people like Val to enjoy smelling her roses, but I have been tempted several times, after catching a dog fox relaxing sunbathing on top of my parsley plants, to put down poison. Poisoned Mars bars are the thing, one of Val's friends told her after a Google search. Val was horrified when I suggested she actually do it. A nasty death, I guess, probably more painful than being shot.

How satisfying however it would be to shoot then eat a fox, as you might eat other creatures you considered predators. For example the French farmers hunt, kill and eat wild boar, and they do this not for brutal fun but because the boar, no respecters of electrified wire fences or notices saying Dear Boar Kindly Keep Off S.V.P., rampage through the young crops digging them up half-eating them flinging them about, and so have to be dealt with. Once, years ago, I asked my neighbour Grégoire if I could accompany him on a Saturday morning wild boar hunt. He looked aghast then said no. Men only. My dear farmer lover, who also hunted, said it was pretty boring really, mostly just hanging about behind bushes in the rain waiting for boar to jog past, which they sometimes declined to do, and only being able to chat in whispers.

Grégoire's other form of hunting could not be excused as socially responsible. He raised flocks of baby partridges in a large dark shed, released them once they'd grown up, then shot them. You could not call the partridges predators. Myself I wouldn't eat them, in the same way as I never now eat hare – though in the mid-1980s, living in Italy, I did enjoy pappardelle in hare sauce – since hares occasionally lope past my door in France, and also I love seeing them leaping across the fields with ears flying, and in spring boxing each other. I only wish I could eat the London squirrels that gnaw my fragile new clematis seedlings, and especially the slugs that chomp my foxgloves to shreds; I wish I could coat the slimy beasts in seasoned crumbs, drop them into boiling fat, serve them garnished with parsley, the non-foxy bits that is.

People eat snails, those other destroyers of garden plants, after all, for example Paulette my earth-mother neighbour in the Mayenne, the queen of foragers, does, and London gourmets do too. Well, the right sort of snails, the big brown and cream *escargots de Bourgogne*. A while back I read in the *Guardian* that there was a shortage of these; perhaps they all took refuge in the Mayenne ditches. On rainy mornings crowds of snails lounge out and about, sometimes pausing lengthily to couple, but then people like Paulette come along with buckets to collect them.

I ate snails at L'Escargot in Dean Street in my childhood. Alec Gaudin, the owner, was a friend of my mother's family in Normandy, and when Mum got cut off from them, teaching in Wales for a year as a French *assistante*, when war broke out in 1939 and Normandy was occupied by the enemy, Alec would send coded messages via the Free French Radio: *Monique mange toujours des escargots*; and villagers with illegal radios would pick these messages up and nip round to my grandparents' house, pretending to the German soldiers billeted there that they were just popping over to recite the rosary, to tell my grandparents that all was well with their daughter. After the war, the Gaudins would invite Mum and Dad to Sunday lunches at their bungalow on the river in Henley-on-Thames, and once, Mum reported over one of our dinners by candlelight with a bottle of claret, late in her life, when we had forgiven each other and loved one another again and enjoyed each other's company and she liked to tell me stories of the past, Dad got very turned on after a particularly tasty lunch and while the Gaudins took their siesta, insisted on having sex with her behind a bush in the garden by the softly lapping waves.

Occasionally, before the Gaudins retired in the early 1960s, we children would be taken for Saturday lunch to the restaurant, whose dining-room lampshades were strung with snail shells, and offered the aforesaid escargots to eat, and we'd be shown down to the kitchen to see the frogs' legs being prepared, laid out in rows on oven trays, and we'd clock the Gaudin labels on the bottles of vermouth lined up on the bar, and be given empty cedarwood cigar boxes, still smelling richly of tobacco, as presents, and Alec would throw the plates back at the waiters if they weren't hot enough.

Escargots in garlicky butter were fashionable in Hampstead bistros in the early 1970s, alongside red-checked tablecloths and candles in Chianti bottles, and certainly more recently chez Paulette, so why not slugs? I like the idea of eating my enemies. I wrote a story about a stalker once, published in *Playing Sardines*, who did just that, fuelled by rage at being rejected. Now I'm older I can admit my own capacity for rage, which I could not do when young, striving so hard to be good, as I have said. Mostly I turn my murderous wishes into comic short stories or novels featuring violent death and so feel relieved of worrying I am a psychopath and then can also smugly lecture my students, the women particularly, the older ones especially, on the importance of recognising our aggression, which feels taboo for many of them, if we are to write well. Conventional ideals of femininity exclude aggression, even if all you do with it is put it into your prose.

Feminism enabled me to understand that, the 1970s kind, less so the feminism of the female modernists I admired as a young writer. For example, Virginia Woolf wanted to free women from inherited Victorian notions of correct feminine behaviour and thinking, she is wonderfully witty in her essays about those constraints. At the same time, despite allowing herself to write angry feminist polemic such as *Three Guineas*, despite being bitterly critical of women's exclusion from higher education and most professions, she thought that female anger when expressed in fiction or even when fuelling fiction detracted from the androgynous calm and detachment that she considered great art required. She feared anger and found it dangerous, as many women still do, taught as nice little girls to repress it and then finding it bursting up in nightmares or indeed in what's called madness. Surely her own madness had a lot of repressed anger in it?

It is neighbours who can be the cause of anger in cities, and indeed also in the countryside. The people who cared about Virginia Woolf's health, Leonard and her doctors, felt she should lead a calm life with not too much excitement. In Sussex, at Monk's House, she and Leonard lived in a detached house, other people at a distance (except for the poor put-upon live-in maids whom Alison Light wrote about so brilliantly in *Mrs*

Woolf and the Servants, who were just too close and therefore irritated super-sensitive VW) and even when in London, in a terraced house in a square, she did not as far as I know have to deal with difficult neighbours having back garden parties with thunderous music continuing half the night or tossing dirty nappies out of their front windows or letting their dogs shit just where a pushchair needed to pass or screaming in S-M agony until dawn. The people Woolf met at parties seemed to her bad enough. Next day she would revile them in her diary.

Recently I'd been rereading her diaries, and I'd been wondering whether the way she could so easily feel overpowered and invaded by other people, need to retreat from them and then revile them to her secret companion, was connected to the fact that she hadn't been able to recoil from her nasty half-brother George when he sat her on the ledge by the hall mirror in her parents' Kensington home and explored what she called her private parts, nor when he came creeping into her bed to repeat his probings and strokings. She wasn't able to express her anger to him. His aggression overpowered her. (Later, in an essay in *Moments of Being*, she wrote about her ambivalence towards mirrors and I wonder whether that's connected to horrible George too.) I also wonder whether the terrifying prospect of being invaded by enemies in 1942 (German pilots were regularly bombing the nearby coast) reactivated that childhood trauma and contributed to her final breakdown and her suicide.

One of my aggressive fantasies is provoked by neighbours' behaviour, in particular their planting of leylandii trees which were fashionable back in the 1970s and so people put them in without thinking and now they, like urban foxes, terrorise us, and so I long to get them hacked down overnight and the resulting debris just left in those neighbours' gardens for them to clear up.

I have to live in the shade of such a tree. Having drunk my breakfast coffee I watered the flowerbed darkened by my neighbour Mike's towering leylandii beyond the fence at the far end of the garden, which not only keeps half the garden in shadow all day long but also sucks up all moisture and goodness so that it is hard to grow anything at all near its enormous trunk. From time to time through a gap in the fence Mike spots me sweeping up the sour-looking brown twigs that rain daily from this tree, mulching my poor plants to dry death, and approaches and calls through the gap for an amiable chat. He is a council tenant, a pensioner, so cannot afford to pay the council to have the tree cut down, which other neighbours besides myself would love him to do. Sam, with the back garden next to Mike's, spoke to me despairingly recently over the fence about the way that the leylandii roots stop anything growing in his garden too. He has given up and left the space as a tract of dry earth that not even passing cats will shit in.

The roots have also unsettled the beautiful old brick walls dividing our plots. A section of bricks has fallen from my next door neighbour Tanya's garden into Sam's, though Tanya is partly to blame, being pretty clueless about gardening, letting ivy get its teeth into the ancient walls and help tug them down, letting ash saplings turn into trees rather than rooting them up at weed stage. Another of my aggressive fantasies concerns climbing over the wobbling brick wall and rooting up her ash tree which dominates my garden on one side. Wild sycamores and ash sprout all over the local streets in people's front gardens. Soon we'll be forest again.

Mike waters his leylandii, since nothing else grows in his garden either and he seems to enjoy watering, and tells me about the ballet he has seen recently at Sadler's Wells, or his cheap weekend break in Morocco. He mumbles, rather, and can be hard to understand. When I first knew him he kept mentioning wonders, wonders, pointing back towards the blank wall of his ground-floor flat, and I assumed he meant miracles occurring in his kitchen, an angel appearing perhaps to announce the immediate demise of his leylandii, but then I realised he meant windows, windows, and was complaining about how the council had not thought to provide him with enough light. Yesterday morning he appeared, indeed like an angel of the Annunciation, and told me that the council is relenting, our local Tenants' & Residents' Association having put in an impassioned plea on behalf of the group of affected neighbours, and will indeed have the tree cut down, since it has been assessed as not being of major aesthetic value for the neighbourhood, and moreover the council will do the work without charge. At some point in the future as yet unspecified.

Back indoors I did no writing. I'd emailed my rewritten novel (third completed version) off to Lily-the-agent a couple of days previously. I was already beginning to feel anxious about her response, but I felt lightened, too, freer: at least it had gone.

I had cut it by 30,000 words. When you're in the mood, cutting is satisfyingly aggressive; like pruning an overgrown bush, or attacking a leylandii tree. First I wielded my saw and shears, then my secateurs, finally tiny scissors for nipping out a last word here, a last word there. I was compressing and condensing, rather as dreams do, using image rather than narrative description. A single image could replace a whole paragraph. Of course I thought I'd pruned before, but I hadn't pruned sufficiently. I know sometimes when I'm writing I'll forget myself, get carried away by language and reach a state of ecstasy, of lyrical outpouring. For example I'd described a character's perception of her garden on a spring morning, after she's had lovely sex, in terms of her rapture at the effects of golden light on plants. That would not do! Away with it!

In other parts of the novel I'd put in too much of the male protagonist's inner feelings between his bursts of speech. The unspoken feelings often contrasted with or fleshed out the speech. I had considered that my incredibly subtle deployment of authorial irony undercut the protagonist's apparent sincerity. But now a lot of his silent thoughts had to go, I had to trust the reader to deduce what wasn't being said – or just allow them not to care about it at all. I had wanted to explore characters' sexual fantasies and sexual feelings. Explicit sex too. Lily-the-agent didn't like too much inwardness, particularly because Joseph the male protagonist (who I'd insisted to her was troubled rather than the 'whinger' she called him) had some private hostility towards women. Well, yes, he did. That was the point. The novel showed him finding a way through that. Rewriting, I had to create a balance between staying true to my own vision of this novel, and attending to my sense of what readers (Lily and the Publisher at least) might find a bit too much, a bit too longwinded. So I had replaced many of the protagonist's silent thoughts with his gestures, presenting him more from the outside. Since his remembered childhood sexual fantasy was key to the story, I refused to remove it, but tried to underline that it *was* a fantasy. Ho hum.

Anyway, I had sent off the novel to Lily and would just have to wait for her verdict.

I slung on a red T-shirt and a pair of leggings, and made more coffee. It felt strange to have a free day, not to be writing. Usually, seven days a week, I get up and immediately start writing, but this morning I broke with that routine. I did some cooking for the lunch party I'm giving here for friends in two days' time. I had previously pot-roasted a chicken. Now I stripped off the flesh, with which to make a *chaudfroid* later, and put the carcase in a saucepan with a carrot, an onion and a bouquet garni, a glass of white wine and some water, and simmered it for an hour. I would use some of this stock (some reserved for the *chaudfroid*) to cook a *salade de lentilles* of small green lentils, with chunks of bacon added. Real bacon, not the supermarket sort plumped up with water. When the lentils were done, you added a glass of red wine while they were still warm, some vinaigrette and some chopped fresh tarragon and parsley. As a first course I planned to serve asparagus. We would have a green salad, some cheese, some fruit. I thought of Mrs Dalloway saying she would do the flowers herself. Well, my little back garden, the part not in leylandii-induced darkness, was full of roses and clematis in bloom. We'd cram in round the table under the blossoming climbing rose and have a Blooms Day.

Yesterday turned out to be a Bloomsbury Day. Nick Murray, the writer who runs Rack Press, had emailed to let me know there was going to be a blue plaque put up by the Marchmont Society in Woburn Walk, to commemorate Dorothy Richardson, who'd lived there during 1905-6. The unveiling ceremony would be held this afternoon. He couldn't go, as he'd be away, but would I like to? Certainly I would. I'd read *Pilgrimage*, DR's four-volume magnum opus, in my late twenties, when Virago reissued it as one of their Classics, with an introduction by Gill Hanscombe. I'd reviewed it for *Gay News*.

I greatly admired it. You enter one woman's mind, a fine-spun golden net she flings out to capture the whole world, as she works, dreams and loafs, and you stay there. You enter her city of imagination, mapped onto a London drifting with yellow-grey fogs and lit by flaring gaslights. Virginia Woolf considered that Dorothy Richardson had invented the woman's sentence, undulating, free-associative, a sentence that wound rhythmically back and forth and indeed continued unbroken, it seemed to me, for those four volumes of *Pilgrimage*. Wonderfully shameless, to write at that length. Reviewers were raving about Knausgaard writing copiously about his own life, but DR got there first a hundred years ago (though she called her work fiction).

I put the chicken stock in the fridge, to complete its cooling. Tomorrow I'd scrape off the layer of golden fat which would have risen to the top and solidified, and reveal the set jelly underneath. The fat could be used for roasting or frying potatoes, at some future date. Or not.

Elizabeth David remarked somewhere that it was really unhelpful to serve fried potatoes to anyone trying to lose weight. I'd have to offer them to a very thin friend. I once met a very thin art dealer, who was staying with my artist friends Tom and Caroline in their house in the Mayenne near mine. On a scorching hot day this needle-person, dressed in a tiny long-sleeved black Lycra frock, cooked the rest of us a bubbling brown gratin of *pommes dauphinois*, sliced potatoes layered and baked in rich double cream, dishing us up big fat helpings then herself toying with a single green bean and watching us quizzically as we politely dug in. I wanted to prick her with my fork. Next day I felt ashamed of my mean response, since I knew that women with anorexia were terrified of their own needs, which they projected onto food, which they then felt attacked by and had to push away, but I still resented her efforts at social control and could not summon any sympathy at all.

I went up into the street and watered the marigolds and fuchsias I'd planted around the plane tree opposite my front door. My neighbour Dick loitered along to watch. Some people think it's daft, what you do, he said: planting up round the trees, but I tell them, leave her alone, her lot are improving the neighbourhood, I remember how it used to be, full of drug dealers. We went on chatting. He mentioned his age, and I mentioned mine. For some idiotic reason I added that it was my birthday in a couple of days' time. Well then! he said, and gave me a smacking kiss on the lips. I was taken aback, and then felt foolish.

For lunch I made a salad of green beans, more than one, plus tomatoes and hardboiled eggs. To go out and celebrate female modernism I donned the bright pink linen coat my niece Helen gave me, which makes me feel jaunty, also as though I am channelling the late Barbara Cartland, who of course was not a modernist. Not a feminist either. When I interviewed her for *City Limits*, thirty years back, she was obviously annoyed that the magazine had sent a female journalist and over the daintily spread much-doilyed tea-table reserved her eyelash-fluttering for the male photographer, whom she constantly pressed to eat more cucumber sandwiches. She looked like a pink meringue in her big pink turban and bouffant pink frock. Underneath, you could sense from the hints she dropped, the anecdotes of childhood that she told, she was a small, sad girl. She'd revenged herself on her cold parents by earning masses of money from writing romances about perfect love. She'd triumphed. But she didn't like women.

In her world, you were supposed to put men first; if you strove to be the approved type of super-feminine man-pleaser, you hadn't to like women *too much*, or you'd be reviled as a *lezzie*. Unnatural; deformed; ugly; predatory. At my all-girls secondary school I loved my girlfriends with passion. Was I a lezzie? I liked boys too. The eccentric, non-macho ones. Part-time lezzie? At Oxford, devoted to my friend Sian, I discovered that a couple of Balliol boys saw us as lezzies in need of conversion and laid bets on who'd fuck us first.

I caught the 68 bus, got off at Holborn Tube, took a back-street route north, twisting and turning and doubling back. I got lost once or twice, which pleased me, meaning I just had to trust my sense of direction and guide myself back on track. Most of the time in cities I don't get lost, I have a clear sense of north and south, but inside buildings I do, for example the BBC, a curving labyrinth on many floors, like a many-decked liner, with anonymous corridors and identical swing doors and staircases. Certain towns baffle me, when they are redeveloped, when formerly comprehensibly connected old streets are torn down and replaced by super-highways you can't walk along and by interlocking shopping malls. You get lost in these fake *piazze*, which I suppose is the intention: shop your way out.

Woburn Walk, running east-west just south of the Euston Road and now closed to traffic, remains a short, pretty street of terraced Georgian houses, set with some fixed benches in the middle, the few shops discreet and unobtrusive. A crowd about thirty-strong had collected, old and young, mostly women but a few men too. I felt exhilarated at milling about with other people in the street: liberation, freedom from having to keep to the pavement, able to spill out, take over public space, not to shop as on the fake *piazze* but simply to meet and talk. Perhaps that delighted feeling comes also from my years of going on demos, we the people swinging out onto the highway, stopping the cars.

I recognised Gill Hanscombe, whom I hadn't seen for many years after she went off to teach literature at Exeter University, but whose kindly, smiling face looked unchanged, also Jean Radford, still fiercely and intelligently beautiful. These days, whenever we bump into each other she says vaguely: who are you? Your face seems familiar. I tell her my name. I want to say, don't you remember? You invited me to contribute to the book of essays you edited on romance! Then we meet again, a few months later, and she's forgotten my name again. It wounds my vanity to know myself forgotten, though perhaps I am one of many. We've become part of Pound's poem. *Faces in the crowd: / petals on a wet, black bough.*

W. B. Yeats lived for a while in the house opposite Dorothy Richardson's, moving in at the same time she did. His plaque had been up for ages; English Heritage had installed many plaques to men but few to women. The Marchmont Society, a separate body, took responsibility for putting up plaques here in Bloomsbury. Now, thanks to the pressure exerted by locals such as Nick Murray, made aware of their omissions they had begun trying to rectify them.

Years ago I'd put up my own plaques to certain female writers English Heritage had neglected. For my inaugural professorial lecture at UEA back in 2004 I'd talked about the *flâneuse*, unrecognised by male writers, about the sexual double standard that named solitary male street-walkers as *flâneurs* and solitary female ones as prostitutes. I'd talked about women writers such as Jean Rhys, Virginia Woolf, and, yes, Dorothy Richardson, who loved walking alone in London and other cities. I'd talked about the looping, wandering female sentence defined by Woolf, and had wondered whether that was the same as *écriture féminine*, which the French philosopher Julia Kristeva found in James Joyce's work as well as in Richardson's. *Ecriture féminine* referred to a prose style that disobeyed what Kristeva called the Law of the Father, that's to say conventional grammatical rules of subject-verb-object, and approached poetry, the fluid babble of the child to the mother, thereby reclaiming our irrational, impulsive, emotional, unconscious selves subsequently repressed by authority figures with narrow notions of what growing up entailed. *Ecriture féminine* was not childish in a pejorative sense but newly adult, revolutionary.

In my lecture I had suggested that the sentence was itself

(herself) a *flâneuse*, just as the writer's mind could be. I'd made my own plaques out of the round lids of Brie boxes, inscribed them with names and dates in black felt tip, pierced holes at the sides and threaded string between them. I spent a day wandering around London, hanging these perishable plaques on certain front doors and railings. I commemorated Jean Rhys in Elgin Crescent in Notting Hill, Dorothy Sayers in St George's Square in Pimlico, Charlotte Mew in Doughty Street in Bloomsbury, and so on. A friend, Karen, an actor resting between jobs, accompanied me and photographed each plaque as I put it up. I had Karen's pictures turned into slides, which I showed as part of my lecture. I tried to offer the audience not only an intellectual experience but a sensual one too. As people entered, they heard k.d. lang singing and were offered brightly coloured sweets from a silver tray. Some of the academics looked a bit baffled, but the students got the point, in their cool way.

We Dorothy Richardson fans blocked Woburn Walk. Passing tourists paused, took photographs. People stood in groups chatting, waiting. A red cloth veiled the plaque, ready in place above the front door of Sutherland's antique shop. Ricci from the Marchmont Society fiddled with the sound system. He'd run a line into the shop, whose owner had obligingly made a socket available.

I looked up at the house opposite, the one with the plaque to W. B. Yeats, whose long first-floor windows, screened at waist-height by a small ironwork Juliet-style balcony, stood open. A dark-haired woman in a bibbed white apron appeared in this oblong space, the room beyond her in shadow. She hung a piece of thick ribbed silk, dark rose-pink, over the balcony railing. It looked like an animal carcase that you'd see hooked up in an old-fashioned butcher's shop. She began delicately manipulating it, carefully tearing at one end of it, cutting and separating it into pinkish-red streamers. Why was she doing this? What was she making? A costume for flayed Marsyas? For Actaeon torn to death by Diana's hounds? She stayed up there working, half in the street half out of it, seemingly oblivious of the small crowd of Richardson fans milling about down below. She must have been aware of us, our movements and chatter, but concentrated calmly on her work, cutting and teasing and pulling the thick silk fabric in her hands. I felt I was the only one of us aware of her. I tried to catch her eye but failed. Perhaps she was an extra in *Mrs Dalloway*. Perhaps she had risen up out of an early draft, she was a cut paragraph on Woolf's studio floor. A shimmering image from the early twentieth century, summoned by the modernist brouhaha in the street below.

With a click and a tick of the mike, the ceremony began. Ricci made a speech about the Bloomsbury Society and the Marchmont Society, and all the good things they do, followed by two other men, who spoke about Dorothy Richardson. One of these, an academic, said sheepishly that there really ought to be a woman making a speech too. I said loudly: yes!

Ricci then called on the renowned Richardson scholar, Professor Laura Marcus, to step forward and unveil the plaque. She raised her hand and pulled the cord and the red cloth tumbled satisfactorily down. Everyone applauded.

We were then marshalled to pose in a group in front of the plaque to have our photo taken for the local paper. The woman on the balcony opposite went on serenely tearing and cutting at her carcase of ribbed pink silk. I nudged the young women standing next to me: look at her up there! Look!

I chatted to Gill Hanscombe. She said, you've become so successful! I shook inwardly. She asked how I was. I lied. Oh, fine, fine. She told me, a touch defiantly, that she had returned to the Church. I did not ask her why. Did she want me to? Did I want to? That conversation would have taken more time than we had. I remembered Sylvia Townsend Warner's distress, recorded in her diary, when Valentine Ackland, her lover of many years, entered the Church as a convert, and vigorously, to Sylvia boringly and incomprehensibly, practised her new faith. Sylvia had devoted herself to Valentine and now Valentine was devoting herself to God. Rather than hide behind a façade of distancing tolerance, Sylvia wrote openly of her distress to the old friends who loved both her and Valentine. I admired her honesty. My old friend the novelist Paul Bailey had recently gone through a period of religious belief, being received as a Catholic, attending Mass in a church famed for its old-fashioned adherence to the Latin Mass, a conversion which had estranged me from Paul for the duration, since I couldn't understand why he would want to belong to an organisation both misogynistic and homophobic, though I knew perfectly well that many otherwise liberal-minded people did so, not least a couple of my dearest friends. As an ex-Catholic I did understand that organised religion offers structure in our chaotic lives, a sense of belonging and being loved, and for European Christians a way of connecting with the glories of traditional Western culture, not least its art and architecture, also a marvellous wraparound sensual experience, and crucially perhaps a method of transcending crude gender roles, for example allowing men to wear gorgeous scarlet frocks and red-heeled shoes, of course only if they become cardinals, their flamingo drag brilliantly discussed in a recent article by Colm Tóibín in the *LRB*. Similarly women, if they become nuns, can transcend, in their imaginations anyway, all the limitations of femininity imposed not least by the Church, and instead become super-women, glorious virgins, powerful unto death and beyond.

I didn't discuss my misgivings with Paul, just sulked that he'd done something I disapproved of. He left the Church after a year or so, challenged me over my cowardly silence, and explained that really he'd gone mainly for the smells and bells and spells. He put it all self-deprecatingly and wittily, he is one of the wittiest people I've ever met, which is a major part of his charm, the generosity with which he will pour out funny stories, each one succinctly narrated, the punchline always delivered with perfect comic timing. He does not let his heart trouble get in the way of his pleasure in being a raconteur, or rather he uses the latter to cope with the former. For example, a week after Jack's heart operation, when he was still in hospital, having suffered complications including pneumonia, I was attending him down to the X-ray department in the basement one day, when we met Paul, also in a wheelchair, wrapped in blankets, awaiting his own go at the machine. Paul immediately started cracking jokes with irresistible gaiety, irresistible panache.

Anyway, here was newly Catholic Gill, that woman I'd so respected and admired years back for her staunch radical feminism, smiling wryly and affectionately at me. I asked after Gill's lover of many years, Suniti Namjoshi, tall and intriguing, a writer of sharp, witty animal fables and poems. Yes, she was fine. Though not, presumably, converted.

A lecture by Professor Marcus and a drinks reception followed at UCL. I skipped this, wanting to stay outside in the sunshine. I wandered off to the eastern end of the street, lured by the display of books outside the second-hand bookshop there, its name, The Maghreb Bookshop, flourishingly painted on a board hung above the entrance. Inside, from floor to ceiling, books packed a space not much bigger than a laundry cupboard.

The slight, grey-haired owner popped up from behind a rampart of volumes shielding his desk and asked if he could help. I replied that I was looking for old cookery books: did he have any? Only these, he said, gesturing at a stack of brightly jacketed large tomes by TV chefs. But do go through them and see what you can find.

He turned, picked up from behind his desk a saucer full of dates, held it out. Go on, please have some. I took one. He urged me to take more. Eating my handful of dates I squatted, turned over the pile of glossy cookbooks. Too big, too modern: show-off self-portraits of glitzy personalities toying with unconvincing-looking fusion fantasies; what my friend Stephen Hayward, a publisher of esoteric and entrancing cookery books, calls gastroporn; I prefer old-fashioned, small, Penguin-sized paperbacks with line illustrations.

The bookseller said: I haven't got room here for everything, the rest of my books are in the garage at home.

Was there a car-shaped space in the middle of the towers of books? Had Gill Hanscombe had a God-shaped space inside her such as Salman Rushdie once described?

The bookseller took me back out into the street and waved at the sign overhead: a student from St Martin's did that for me, and I am glad I am still here, I am fighting over the lease with the council all the time.

He had been so welcoming, offering me hospitality, that I wanted to buy something from him. I found a 1960s paperback that looked as though it would make a present for Caroline's husband Tom, who is not only a sculptor but also an alchemical wizard brewing plum brandy in his home-constructed still: a manual on making wine from home-grown veg and foraged fruit. I paid and left.

I walked down Burton Street, onwards south through Bloomsbury. Past Woolf Mews and Virginia Court, surely cynically named: dull-looking modern flats locked off behind iron gates that she would surely have deprecated. Thinking of her again, this time I made a connection to the LRB bookshop, which was nearby, just a little further down, in Bury Place, near the British Museum. They regularly host readers' evenings to introduce contemporary literary debates, panel discussions preceded by wine, and I remembered attending one recently on small press publishing. Nick Murray of Rack Press was on that panel, composed only of men, so duly in the q. and a. session I crossly asked whether they'd been able to find no female publishers to join in their conversation, such as the founder of the excellent Peirene Press, only I pronounced this name wrongly, *à la francaise*, and the belle-lettrist Nicholas Lezard, that evening sporting a moustache to support, as he explained, a men's cancer trust, put me right, in his reply stressing the correct pronunciation. I regretted annoying him, as I felt I had done, since I rather enjoyed his columns in the *New Statesman* and the *Guardian* and he would not know that, presumably putting me down as a boring ole feminista yawn yawn women banging on again about being left out.

During the discussion one of the LRB booksellers exclaimed that of course they would never, never stock self-published books, vanity publications, *oh mon Dieu*, and I thought hmmm, Virginia Woolf was self-published wasn't she, what else was the Hogarth Press she ran with Leonard, which published all her novels as well as those of other highly esteemed modernists? Yet of course the LRB bookshop stocked her books. Virginia Woolf did not have to cope with being told that if she did not sell in lorryloads she earned *nul points* nor did she have an agent disliking her discussions of subjectivity. She wouldn't have been ticked off about including sex, either, since she did not refer to it in her novels, only in her letters and her memoir pieces, which are all the livelier for it and indeed I prefer these, and her diaries and essays, to her novels.

I found myself wandering down Marchmont Street, which Woolf loved so much. It still has that certain shabby charm that she praised, it still has real shops such as bookshops. Gay's the Word still exists, for example. There, way back in 1978, I was awarded the Gay News Literary Award (for *A Piece of the Night*), that I shared with John Lahr who had just published his biography of Joe Orton. My Parisian friend Pascale (she of the artfully twined scarf) accompanied me, and was soon surrounded by lesbians admiring her tremendously chic frock. Twenty-five years back, I remembered, I had had lunch in the Italian restaurant, the Balfour, on the corner here, after a session with a hypnotherapist to help me stop smoking. I lay on a black leather recliner while this tiny woman, with an orange-red bouffant, sharply dressed in a black suit and high heels, led me through a series of visualisations. At one stage she asked me to produce an image of my unconscious and I said: I am a blue hyacinth. Awful cliché, my conscious mind immediately groaned. Nonetheless the hypnosis worked. I never took up a cigarette again and at that point I gave up smoking dope too, since the tobacco in the joints I rolled turned out to form a major part of the pleasure involved, and grass on its own was too strong. I had lunch that day, in the Balfour, with Philip Mercer, my boss at the City Lit, where I taught writing. A charming, clever man devotedly left-wing. Over our bowls of spaghetti I told him of my fears that I'd never be able to write again, since I so powerfully associated smoking with sitting at the typewriter putting words together, cigarettes functioning like semicolons, necessary pauses. In fact when I went home that afternoon I immediately sat down and wrote an entire short story. Without cigarettes I became dreamier, more liable to float off, a much slower writer. As though I were the cloud of smoke.

I walked to Covent Garden to meet Margi, my sister. We are twins; born in late May. Over the years we've worked out a way of celebrating our birthday that lets us acknowledge separateness and difference as well as togetherness. Each year we celebrate our birthdays on our own, with our own gang of people, and also we have a special joint celebration. This year we were meeting up to go to the ballet, Margi's favourite artform. Wayne McGregor's *Woolf Works* had had rave reviews: I'd suggested we should go and see it as our birthday treat.

First of all we were due to have an aperitif in Margi's favourite bar, Chez Gérard, whose first-floor balcony looks over Covent Garden Piazza. I arrived deliberately early, hoping to snaffle a table outside. On this sunny evening the balcony was already crowded, so I found two seats at a table in a corner inside and bought a bottle of Prosecco, Margi's favourite *apéro*. Waiting for my sister, I opened my new second-hand book, read a recipe for parsnip wine and people-watched. Smartly dressed office workers, the women in lots of make-up, tight skirts and high heels, the men with tousled, gelled hair and tight suits. A group of American tourists in sportswear settled onto beige leather pouffes. They sank down, plumf! clearly tired out from a day's sightseeing, then perked up and began joking and joshing.

Margi arrived, looking cheerful and pretty in a swishy knee-length frock and nipped-waist tweed jacket. She is thin and I am plump. Friends scold me for using that word: you are voluptuous! At least your shape goes in and out!

We are not identical twins but as children were dressed identically and often referred to not by our names but simply as the twins. My mother would insist to me in later years, when I'd been having a go at her: but we always treated you exactly the same! She was trying to reassure me she hadn't had a favourite. That wasn't the problem. I just wanted that much-vaunted equality to mean that our subjectivity could be recognised, each of us cherished for our separate individuality. Probably Mum felt that she did do that, and that I was the one making trouble (which I often did once I began trying to break away).

As a child I felt very close to Margi. In my late teens and early twenties, I stressed our differences. As adults, Margi and I developed our similarities as well as our differences. For example, although in childhood I'd been labelled as the intellectual one and Margi as the sporty one, she ended up taking several degrees and qualifying as a nurse-practitioner who could act as a GP and I ended up hooked on walking and swimming. Nowadays we share certain pleasures. We go to exhibitions together. We go to the theatre. To the ballet. We're there for each other: we are friends and when we rub each other up the wrong way we get through it.

Perching on our low seats in Chez Gérard's bar, Margi and I handed each other the birthday presents we'd brought with us, agreeing not to open them until our birthday. We wandered across the cobbles to the Opera House to collect our pre-paid tickets.

Margi had booked online, through a website offering special deals. She'd bought gallery seats cheaply, £30 each, a real bargain. When Margi had told me she'd saved money this way, I had felt worried, that this might be a dodgy site, a scam, but said nothing. No point complaining at a fait accompli. And I hadn't gone to the trouble of buying the tickets myself, had I? So shut up. Now at the Opera House advance-bookings counter Margi offered her printed-out confirmation of purchase. The box-office clerk shook his head as he checked his computer: I have no record here of your booking. He searched again and again.

The clock ticked towards seven twenty-two. The final bell rang; the last punters left the foyer. The clerk fetched the manager, a young man, with a short beard and spectacles, wearing a high-collared Chinese-style black velvet jacket fastened with tiny knobs of matching braid. The manager said in a very kind voice: no, your booking is not here. It's best not to book through those websites, you know.

The manager searched again. Seven twenty-five. No point making a fuss: what good would that do? We were in quiet despair. Margi said: well, could you sell us another couple of seats? The manager shook his head: sorry, we're completely booked out tonight. I said: thank you, we understand there is nothing you can do! Margi said sadly: it was our special birthday treat. I said to her: well, never mind, that's that, let's just go out to dinner instead.

We resigned ourselves, began turning away. Seven twenty-eight. The kindly manager must have received a radio call on an invisible transmitter, or perhaps he'd just glanced at a screen, because he suddenly said: here you go, and another young man was hurrying towards us: quick! Follow me! He scooted away and we ran after him, along a hushed, empty corridor. He flung open closed doors in the panelled wall, whisked us from darkness into shocking light, the hum and thrum of hundreds of people, like bees, the packed ground floor of the auditorium, the single notes of the orchestra tuning up, and pushed us into two seats at the end of a row in the orchestra stalls, practically the best seats in the house. He raced away. The lights went down. The orchestra started to play. I wanted to burst into tears.

Woolf Works comprised three ballets: one inspired by *Mrs Dalloway*, one by *Orlando* and one by *The Waves*. The first ballet magically integrated inventive lighting, backdrops of blown-up black and white photographs of 1920s London, music, exquisite dancing. Powerfully it summoned and reimagined the city, mysterious and seductive and bleak. The second ballet dramatised carnival, promenade. Perhaps because these are such normal aspects of ballet I wasn't particularly gripped, just appreciated the dancing. The third one seemed based on Woolf's life rather than her writing. Her formal invention went for nothing, or, at least, was elided with her psychological distress. The ballet ended with her suicide by drowning, cine images of waves rolling in and breaking, which I found jarring and annoying.

Never mind. In the two intervals we went outside and leaned against a column round to the side of the building, where people were smoking, and I fetched out from my little leather rucksack small bottles of Prosecco and tiny smoked salmon sandwiches. Crusts off. Well buttered. I had produced a version of these on a Eurostar trip two years back to visit our uncle and aunt near Avignon, and Margi's husband Richard has always remembered them. Some people get a bit nervous about butter but I think if you're going to have it then have it. We agreed that tomorrow I'd buy the kind manager a present, and deliver it to him by hand.

When the ballet finished, I walked Margi to Leicester Square Tube. We kissed and hugged goodbye.

I decided to walk some of the way home. I made my way south, towards Waterloo. Virginia Woolf took her train home to Richmond from here, after she'd strolled along the Strand and thought of Dr Johnson strolling there with Mr Savage or with Boswell. Those passages in her diary had inspired my short story, published in *Mud* (2010), about a *flâneuse* who goes to a Handel opera and then finds she has time-travelled and then meets Dr Johnson and Boswell, who take her for a tart and shoo her away. *Mud* had been shortlisted for the Edge Hill Prize, and

I'd gone along to the award evening, to hear it dismissed by the young male chair of judges as merely containing lots of literary games. Next to me stood Helen Simpson and Polly Samson, equally damned with faint praise. Back to *le salon des refusées*.

Following Virginia Woolf along the Strand, I wanted to stay with the pleasure I'd had, being tête-à-tête with my sister. My earliest memory concerns our closeness, sharing a double pram, propped up facing her, both the hoods drawn up, gazing up at the curved slit of light in between them. I'm convinced this is a real memory, but of course I can't be sure. Mum used to park us in this pram, down the end of the garden, in between feeds. Following the rigorous schedule prescribed by the nasty control-freak Dr Truby King, she was only allowed to feed us every four hours. She told me once: it was terrible hearing you screaming with hunger and not being able to do anything about it. Winnicott wrote somewhere that the baby who discovers she can't summon help eventually goes beyond being able to scream, into a sort of numb despair. Recently, when I caught myself calling depression the black pit, I wondered whether somehow I was referring to that pram, its deep black hold.

Nana told me once, while I was still a child, that when Mum found out she was going to have twins she burst into tears. I concluded she didn't like us, hadn't wanted us. She did, after all, once tell me she preferred men to women. She did once angrily say: you were supposed to be Jonathan and Jeremy! We knew how much she'd longed for a boy, after her first child, a son, died at three days old.

Much later, when she was in her eighties, Mum explained she'd been scared of getting us muddled up. I'd worried about this myself. Aged seven or so I tackled the problem by wondering about buses. Red double-deckers looked exactly the same but one was the 113, the other the 142. If you swapped their numbers, would they still be the same buses underneath?

I crossed the river at Waterloo, the dark water flowing between splatters of brilliant neon lights, then decided not to walk any further, I was too tired. I jumped on a bus instead. The trusty 176. It did what its number promised it would do and whizzed me home.

CHAPTER 3

JUNE

One Day In The Mayenne

Yesterday I woke up at dawn. Back in London the nights can be yellowish-grey beyond the curtains, only semi-dark, so that morning just fades in, but in here in north-west France the blackness is total, except for the stars that sprinkle it on cloudless nights or the full moon that shimmers at the beginning of the month.

My bedroom at La Lièvrerie is the converted grainstore, a big raftered space under the sloping roof, directly above the sitting/dining room, reached by a sturdy wooden *échelle de meunier* – a miller's ladder up which the farmer carried the sacks of grain. Down it I went and into the kitchen to make coffee.

Darkness shifted to pale blue and a red sun rose up at the horizon. I sat on the front step, looking across the strip of front garden and the lane to the orchard and meadow beyond. Birds sang. The air was cool and fresh. Gold from the east streaked low through the trees. Long thin shadows stretched along the dewy grass. The cherries shone scarlet. Just a few on the lower branches, most of them high up.

It's one thing to eat cherries, Paulette used to say, quite

another to gather them. Round, rosy-cheeked and smiling, she often arrived to visit on summer evenings after checking her hens in their enclosure higher up the hill. She would drive past the house, turn her van round on the green patch at the top of the lane where this curved out of sight to lead up to my neighbour Ambroise's fields and the forest, drive back down, stop outside my door. She would get out of her van, present her face to be kissed, and chat to me. Sometimes she'd give me a couple of eggs: there's your supper. She would inspect the garden and inform me what I'd done wrong. How will you learn to improve if I don't tell you? She would help herself to the wild cherries from the tree opposite my front door, tasting them then spitting the stones onto the ground. They're the sweetest and best, these little ones, you should bottle them in brandy.

Now Paulette has given up keeping chickens and grumbles about growing old. A neighbour's daughter, Annique, used to help Jim and me pick the cherries, darting up the ladder with a basket. Now she's given up country pursuits and plays rhythm guitar in a couple of tribute bands. Her English boyfriend Terry plays lead guitar. One day, soon after they got together, I invited them to lunch, Annique being someone I'd been fond of since she was a child. When I offered them a drink, Terry refused wine or beer: haven't you got any brandy? Unwillingly I opened a bottle of eau-de-vie, made from my friends Hilary and Bill's cider apples, and poured him a glass. He tossed it straight back. I remembered Grandpère's story of the American soldiers at the Liberation in 1944, invited in for a celebratory drink and served the best Bénédictine, preserved all through the war hidden under a heap of sand in the cellar. You were supposed to sip it, make it last, but the Americans seized the little glasses and knocked back the liqueur in one go then held out their glasses for more.

Larry rang up and said there was a *vide-grenier* (car boot sale) on at Saint-Apollinaire and would I like a lift? I said yes. I have no car at the moment. My former one, ancient and decrepit, finally died. With no way of getting to the shops, I'd arrived at my house (via Chantal's taxi from the little local station, always pleasurable trips because we discuss menus and she introduces me to the latest in mayennais fusion cooking) with my bag full of vegetables rather than clothes, remembering my antique dealer friend Tommaso coming to visit me in London once with a suitcase laden with salami, cheese, *pastasciutta* and olive oil: he didn't believe he'd get any decent food otherwise. By day he whisked me around smart Mayfair galleries I'd never dared enter, checking out the prices of Renaissance bronzes; by night he put on an apron and cooked gnocchi and *bollito misto* (boiled meats).

I met Larry through Jim, who after we split up bought a tumbledown cottage three kilometres from mine, and employed Larry among others for renovation work. English Larry is a carpenter and handyman, boyish-looking despite his brush of white hair. He once told a mutual friend that when his wife died (long ago), the roses blooming in his garden changed from red to white. He kindly came in to water my new rose bushes while I was away (the flowers remained pink). He refused payment. I'd buy him some of his favourite beer.

Larry arrived at 9am in his four-by-four, the roof down and the windows open. We sped to the village, then took the back way to Saint-Apollinaire along the narrow road curving between fields of ripening grain. Warm billows of air smelled sweetly of cut grass. We turned left at the Calvaire (a stone Calvary scene), plunged into the cool green darkness of the forest, emerged on the other side, followed the signs for the Hippodrome, where the *vide-grenier* was being held.

The stalls were arranged to one side of the race-course, stretching out in a long oval under the trees. They had sprung up seemingly overnight, as did the stalls for the fair held every year on the 15th August at my grandparents' village in France. This was a religious feast-day, marking the Assumption of the Virgin into heaven, but it was also a lay occasion of great importance, commemorating the Liberation in 1944. My Catholic grandparents in Normandy stressed the former meaning of the date rather than the latter. It took Ambroise and Bénédicte, my neighbours here in the Mayenne, to explain it. They took me with them to watch the celebratory fireworks in a nearby town, they spoke of the war, they pointed out the building in which women denounced as sexual collaborators had their heads shaved before being paraded to the throng.

The *vide-grenier* offered a cornucopia of treasures poured out onto blankets on the ground, onto metal tables. Salt pots, soup tureens, wine glasses, ladles, piles of plates. A surreal scene: indoor things laid out outdoors: massed, repeating patterns of round lids; a strobe of knives. Outdoor tools too: old aluminium watering cans, grain sieves, a birch broom. You saw these things afresh, made newly interesting because of being incongruously displayed on a tablecloth of grass.

Just past the entrance, at the very first stall, Larry and I were accosted by a thin, deeply sunburned, deeply wrinkled woman with frizzy dyed blonde hair. She wore a skimpy green vest and clutched a cigarette. She hailed us loudly and familiarly in English.

Passers-by turned their heads, clocking us as expats. E. M. Forster, in *A Room with a View*, mocked snobs like me. His Miss Lavish exclaims, 'Oh, the English abroad!' Like Miss Lavish, I hate sticking out as an English person. I always want to merge with the French background, to slink along seeming French. I am half-French, after all.

Then I realised the woman had been greeting Larry. He knows most of the expats, because he gets work from them, especially the ones who don't speak French. He said: hello, Ivy. She began recounting the tale of her recent operation for lung cancer: I'm still here! Her hoarse, cackling laugh made her seem witchlike. To avert a possible curse I bought from her a small lidded tureen in duck-egg pale green, and a 1960s beach basket of woven pink-dyed rushes to carry it in, for two euros each.

I remembered Sir Gawain in *The Green Knight*: he is courteous to the hag he's been forced to marry as the result of a mistaken vow, he recognises and respects her power, and so on their wedding night he is rewarded when she turns into a beautiful young woman. My ex-lover Jack had various texts on myth in his book-filled flat, and there one evening I read a feminist Jungian interpretation of the hag's story, to do with female perceptions of our creativity and power in middle age; how these shift and change. Jack was like Sir Gawain for a while, intermittently. One day, after a time of conflict (ours) and rage (mine) he said to me: I'd like to take care of you. He paused, then said: I think you should lose weight. Not just a hag but a fat hag.

The next stall along displayed boxes of kitchen stuff. I picked out two little open pots pierced with holes: moulds for draining cream cheeses, painted in cream-grey slip, with tiny balls for feet. I bought them for three euros each, also a salt pot for two. Larry said: something's only a bargain if you really need it, otherwise it'll just sit on a shelf gathering dust and taking up space. Think of Joe!

Joe is a sculptor, with a small house three villages away from mine. He frequently drives back from Emmaus (the used-furniture and junk depot run by homeless people) near Le Mans with a trailer full of beaten-up kitchen dressers, cupboards, sinks, doors, shutters, dismantled beds. He's even bought an old dentist's chair, which he poses on the lawn. He rescues things. He resembles Grandpère, who believed that you should never throw away anything made by human hand and whose *grenier*-workshop was accordingly stuffed to the roof. Rather like the garage of the book-dealer I met in May.

I certainly recognise that longing to possess. In my twenties and thirties, I longed for a home. However, having chosen to write rather than get a 'proper' fulltime job, I was unable to afford commercial rents let alone a mortgage. I lived in various communes, which I wrote about in *Paper Houses*. I wrote a novel (*In The Red Kitchen*) imagining a woman funding buying a house through selling sex. In *Daughters of the House* I reprised my wish for a home, on a grander scale. Whereas my French grandparents had lived in an ugly little 1890s redbrick cottage, I gave my two heroines an entire manor house to have adventures in. When that novel won the 1993 W. H. Smith Literary Award, a prize of £10,000, I rushed to France and bought a house with the money and never again felt envious of other women who had homes.

Near the box containing the cream-cheese moulds I spotted two old folding metal chairs with slatted wooden seats, grey-painted, and a yellow-painted square folding metal table. The dealer said, twenty euros the lot. Cheap! I did need garden chairs, but I decided to wait, to buy them on my way back, if they were still there.

Ten o'clock. The day heated up. Through stripes of sunshine and green shadow people thronged the sandy path. From a stall further along I bought for one euro a wood-handled knife with a thin, worn blade, such as vegetable-sellers at market use for cutting off onion stalks, and for a second euro I bought a sharpener block, which the man said was 'eighteenth or nineteenth century'. Hmmm. I remembered the sly antique-dealer at Sainte-Sévérine, the nearby hilltop village complete with castle and ramparts, who would try to pass off a bit of chintz as *toile de Jouy* fabric, therefore extra expensive, and who insisted in front of me to a group of gullible Parisians that a large black wire basket was for collecting snails, such a quaint and rare and unusual piece, therefore cost seventy euros, though I knew very well it was for collecting eggs, just a bigger version of the one Paulette had used. Nonetheless I relished the rogue dealer's lies, and the way that he sneaked looks at me under his eyelashes to see if I believed him. The *vide-grenier* dealer was more scrupulous. The knife, he explained seriously, was only twentieth century.

I halted in front of a stall displaying statues of the Virgin Mary. Did I really need another? The long beam-shelf in my studio bears my collection, found on bric-a-brac stalls. I remember my mother coming home exulting one day from a local church jumble sale, where she'd bought an elegant little Madonna in white Limoges porcelain, with touches of gilt, a cherry mouth and cheeks, for only half a crown (about twenty-five pence in today's money). She held out her find, wanting us to admire it. One of those transformative moments occurred: she was no longer my anglophile mother, submerged in English clothes and habits, but a passionate French person displaying a French treasure. Limoges china: the best! I inherited the little Virgin, and she sits on the high mantelpiece here at La Lièvrerie above the open fire.

The Virgin, whom as a child I worshipped as a goddess, represented, of course, my mother, although I only realised that in my twenties, five years after I lost my faith, when I began writing my first novel. The Virgin has her sweet, sentimental side, the one invented by and beloved of celibate male priests (Freud pointed out that she didn't bother with sex with adult chaps, she just loved her boy, oh Oedipus), but she also turns a severe face on wrongdoers, such as Communists, threatening them with flails and thunderbolts. When, some years back, the French government wanted to bury nuclear waste here in the Mayenne, under its granite hills, and a mass revolt occurred, with many demonstrations, aerial photos made into posters showing us all standing in a local field on white sheets we'd stitched together in a local textiles factory to read *NON*, tractors blocking the proposed digging sites, one sign that appeared in my village was a simple cardboard, handwritten one, hung on a bush at the side of the road, pleading: Spare Us Holy Mother.

To make that massive protest banner, local women donated their monogrammed linen sheets, the ones they'd sewed for their trousseaux. We joined them together into long strips, using the factory's treadle machines. Carefully we cut off the top edges with the raised monograms and later stitched these together in a white-on-white patchwork to be hung in a local village hall. Someone decided it needed jazzing up and therefore embroidered it with yellow ears of corn here and there. She did this very badly and ruined the patchwork.

My mother had just the one Virgin but I have about twenty. A chorus line of Madonnas. The compulsion to repeat? Over and over I return to the image of the mother in my writing, her tremendous force for loving and hating and the daughter's corresponding one. My mother my muse. When Louise Bourgeois had her solo retrospective at the Tate, and revealed how much her childhood difficulties with parents had inspired her, certain critics scorned her obsession with those archaic figures, but I felt vindicated. What mattered was making good work. Louise Bourgeois worked sometimes with fabric and tapestry. She would not have clumsily embroidered soppy ears of corn on a political patchwork.

From time to time I add to my collection of Extra Virgins. Now here was another, appearing deep in under the woodland trees, as Madonnas are often reported as doing.

Perching amidst stacks of stencilled soup plates and old earthenware rillettes pots, she was one of those brightly painted porcelain statuettes made in Brittany throughout the nineteenth

century, some produced in the Quimper factory and some else-
where. She stood about a foot high: a smooth, curved shape,
all flowing lines. She wore a high domed yellow crown like a
puffed cap, a dark blue veil over her long black hair, a white
robe patterned with semi-abstract flower sprigs in red and blue
interspersed with green dots, and under this, just visible, a skirt
striped in red, blue and black. With one hand she supported her
baby son and with the other she caressed his right foot. She had
big black eyes under strongly marked black eyebrows, the hint
of a smile. She stood on a blue plinth bearing the letters AV.
M. (Ave Maria). The plinth had been broken, then stuck back
together again, lines of glue showing. A triangular gap indicated
a lost chip of china.

She was an antique, therefore valuable, but knocked down
cheap because she was damaged. Thirty-five euros. Well, cheap
if you had the money. I wanted her. I offered twenty-five euros
for her, which the stallholder accepted. His faint smirk told me
I'd paid far too much.

Sunlight and shadow flickered on the sandy ground of the
path. The sun's heat reached in under the trees. I turned over
neat piles of linen drying-up cloths, each with a single red or
blue stripe down the side. Exactly like Mum's that she gave me.
You bought this cloth at market, pulled rippling off the bale and
cut to the lengths you wanted, then back at home you hemmed
each cloth, added a loop at the corner, sewed on a name-tape.
Mum's cloths, worn with age and very soft, bore a small square
cotton name-tag with her initials M. C. (Monique Caulle) from
before her marriage, embroidered in curly red script, and beside
that an oblong name tape printed with her married name,

Monique Roberts, in red capitals. The cloths reconnected me to my mother's skin. I don't remember her ever willingly touching me as a child; she flinched and went rigid if I hugged her; but she touched her cloths and later I could touch them and they caressed the plates I held in my hands. They functioned like the saints' relics that consecrated Catholic churches. A church was a maternal body: hence its sacredness and power. I'd explored that idea in various novels, for example *Impossible Saints*.

From another perspective, however, perhaps I was just being sentimental, pretentious and bourgeois, caring too much about bits of old cloth.

My fantasies of ideal wittily boho-chic interiors (which I never of course attain) are indeed bourgeois. Yet sometimes I choose to write from the perspective of the woman employed to clean the bourgeois house. My sympathies lie with her. Nana was a nursemaid before she married, working for a family in Harley Street, and told cheerful tales about servants' work and kept her 1920s semi whistling clean. My French grandmother employed a *femme de ménage*, Madame Duval. You saw mainly her back, bent over the sink, bent over the Hoover, bent over the ironing. She partly inspired my character Victorine in *Daughters of the House*, but since Victorine was also based on my aunt, who as well as teaching fulltime cared for my grandparents and did a lot of cooking, I gave her a certain power in the fictional family. Mum trained her three daughters (not her son) to do housework. Boring and repetitive dusting and polishing. I've always done my own housework (what little of it I do). I believe I should clean up my own mess. Why is it different outdoors? I pay Bertrand to cut the grass for me while I'm away and am simply glad I can afford it. The house represents the body-self. Only babies can't wipe their own faces and bums.

One way to cut down on housework is to own few things. Joe stashes his hoard in the barn, so doesn't have to dust it. He and Alice keep their furnishings simple: yellow-plastered walls hung with pictures from *brocantes*; a table; a few chairs. I still appreciate the cherry-wood buffet carved with swags and the straw-seated chairs my mother gave me from her parents' home. She and her brother were selling the cottage after my aunt's death, emptying it of its weird mix of beautiful, serviceable old kitchen things, ugly late-Victorian dinner services, kitsch 1970s ornaments. As a secretly arrogant child, I'd been certain that my taste was better than my relatives', that I could more surely distinguish beauty from ugliness, because I was looking objectively. My aunt had revered certain massive sideboards, certain insipidly decorated plates, certain cake-stands, simply because they were heirlooms. Just as she idealised her parents, so she conserved and cherished the past and its traditions, polishing them to a golden glow. The kitsch ornaments she'd bought herself or been given. My mother had a similar lack of taste, a similar respect for the past, but she combined it with a certain ruthlessness that allowed her to throw things out, and with a generosity from which I benefited. You want that chipped old blue enamel coffee-pot? Then take it. The coffee-pot went into my novel *The Looking-Glass*.

My mother loved me much more easily when I loved the same things that she did: French literature and architecture, Norman landscapes. She wanted me to be like her. My difference from her – my left-wing politics, my feminism – she found painful and labelled madness. The therapist I saw in my mid-twenties remarked one day: you really are your mother's unconscious, aren't you? So in my writing I have repeatedly explored mother-daughter conflict as well as identification. Sometimes this involves writing about the past. I know that nostalgia can be reactionary, as stern critics warn, if it sentimentalises and falsifies memory, but since mine returns me, ultimately, to the figure of the mother, the maternal body, I know that I have found my subject matter, and that I don't treat it in a reactionary way. It was so often absent; so often simply not there.

The sale of the family cottage kickstarted *The Looking-Glass*. Jim and I hired a van and drove the buffet, and the other bits and pieces, down to La Lièvrerie. My childhood summers in Normandy were over and gone; my grandparents and aunt were dead. No more trips to Etretat with its arching cliffs, pebbled beach marred with lumps of tar, upturned fishing boats, heaps of drying nets, smell of seaweed and salt. Swimming, exploring the rocks at low tide, clambering inside sand-floored caverns under the cliffs, we were free. Back inside my grandparents' tiny house, obliged to be quiet and well-behaved, I felt trapped. The buffet carried these meanings, carried them across. Lorna Sage's husband Vic once pointed out to me that in Greece a removals van will have Metaphor painted on its side.

We arrived back at La Lièvrerie and unloaded our new possessions. The following morning I began writing a novel with the words: it is the sea I miss most. Memories rose up and haunted me like angry ghosts. The novel circled around a composite figure based on Flaubert-Mallarmé, but also had a mother-shaped space at its heart, explored a young woman's loss of her mother, her semi-erotic yearning for a replacement.

My mother would have enjoyed the *vide-grenier,* the objects evoking memories of her own childhood, her life as a young married woman toiling over housework in a London suburb. She'd have been briskly unsentimental too. Thank goodness, Maman eventually had an American fridge; Grandpère worked in Washington just after the war and brought home a proper food-mixer as well.

On my way out, I bought the yellow metal table and the two grey slatted-wood chairs for the twenty euros the dealer requested. He threw in a watering-can for free. He had coal-black eyes in a fleshy face half-hidden by a grizzled black beard, black brows and hair. He explained he liked selling to the English: you look at a thing, you make up your mind, or you go away as you did earlier and then come back, you don't haggle, or at least not too much, you just buy it if you want it, whereas the French, and the North Africans, they haggle, also they don't make up their minds.

Larry drove me home. He gave me one of his newly printed business cards. French on one side, English on the other. Spot the misprint on the French side! Well, the expats won't notice, will they?

I saw that he was offering plasterboarding as part of his services. Great! I asked him to come and do a job for me. Two years ago, when the pine martens invaded my roof, for months I didn't realise how serious it was. I'd sit upstairs in my studio writing and hear small beasts racing round under the eaves and just assume it was mice imitating Les Vingt-Quatre Heures du Mans, I was busy, please God make them go away. Eventually, yellow patches appeared on the sloping plasterboarded ceiling: the pine martens' pee presumably. Patches of plasterboard cracked, then fell off. The water-boiler cupboard stank with their poo. Fluffy bits of insulation dropped down behind the central heating boiler.

Jean-Jacques, the roofer, came over to check the situation. He pointed out, round the back of the house, tiny gaps between the stones of the wall. That's where they got in. You see the grease-marks they leave? I offered him an *apéro*. We rang his wife Suzanne, the newsagent, and invited her to join us on her way home from work. She got lost in the maze of lanes, but at last appeared in her van. We sat in the garden, drinking and chatting, eating bread and pâté. They left at nine o'clock, as it began to grow dark. I felt very pleased they had wanted to stay, and grateful that while we waited for Suzanne Jean-Jacques had filled the holes at the back then put up his ladder and fixed some slipped tiles. He charged me forty euros and recommended an expert local man who'd do the plasterboard repairs. Accordingly I rang and made an appointment. The man had not appeared at the appointed time. His wife, when I phoned, was vague: he's still away, working, I'm not sure when he'll return. So the damp patches and holes in my studio ceiling remained, but I didn't care too much, because by then I'd discovered I preferred writing downstairs, in the big room next to the kitchen, with the door and window open onto the green garden, the branches of the cherry tree, the orchard beyond, and while I was writing I neglected all housework and house repairs.

Larry parked under the cherry tree, helped me unload my chairs and table and basket of stuff, and raced off. 11am. I laid out all my treasures and regarded them. I fetched pencils and paper and drew the grey pots. Then I made a *salade composée* for lunch: sliced potatoes and carrots, peas, green beans, a hardboiled egg, some anchovies.

With my lunch I drank some white wine. I drank too much, suddenly overwhelmed with anxiety so using the wine as a tranquilliser. Earlier this month Lily-the-agent had read my rewritten, shortened novel, and had advised me just to put it away because she now declined to represent it at all, as she didn't *like* it enough, she still didn't approve of the male protagonist – no longer 'a whinger' but still 'too selfish'. Not literary criticism so much as dating jargon. Just swipe it away. On to the next!

After a few days of despondency and despair I had emailed the Publisher to ask her to read it anyway, and she'd said yes, although she was too busy until September to do so herself, but her reader would look at it. So once again I was having to wait. So I soothed myself with three glasses of wine then took a siesta.

3pm. Too hot to garden. Instead, I propped the statue of the Virgin on a couple of books on the kitchen table and drew and then painted her. The drawing was just about OK; the painting less so. I turned the whole thing into a cartoon to send to my friend the novelist Patricia Duncker, a practising Catholic, also a Francophile.

She and I met through UEA. When I was headhunted for the professorship there, I didn't want the job at first. I applied for it only because I was so broke and had no income in view. Around that time a majestic, white-turbaned Sikh grabbed my arm in a street in Delhi, where I was attending a British Council literary conference, and demanded to tell my fortune. He took me round a corner, gazed at my palm and said, there is a man who has broken your heart. And soon you will come into a lot of money. My marriage having just ended, my heart was certainly broken but I pooh-poohed the idea of lots of money. Later on I realised that a university salary meant just that. After the interview, when offered the professorship as a fulltime post, I specified half-time. So Patricia, next on the shortlist, joined me and our professional relationship soon grew into friendship, which grew into love. Being with Patricia's exhilarating: like standing under a waterfall.

At about 5pm, when the heat began to lessen, I went outside, across the lane into the orchard, and picked cherries. The birds had pecked most of them, but I got a basketful of unblemished ones. I bottled them in the eau-de-vie given to me last year by Hilary and Bill, made from their cider apples, the eau-de-vie that Annique's boyfriend had tipped lustily back. You have to keep the jars in a warm place for six weeks, so I put them in my bedroom, on the chest under the Velux window. The sun shone through them, gold and amber.

I pruned the bushes in front of the house, wanting to make them low enough that when I'm sitting outside I can see the view down the hill and along this tiny valley, hedgerows and lines of mature trees, a single farmhouse in the distance, and beyond that the green-blue hills. I watered the roses, using my new/antique watering can. I got out the wheelbarrow and continued with a heavy task: carting earth away from the long low heap of *terreau* (compost) in the little green area at the top of the lane.

I should never have allowed the *terreau* to exist there, since that little spot is Didier's land. He parks his van here when he comes to check on his bullocks. The beginning of summer is marked by Didier leading his beasts up the lane past my house to their pasture. He runs ahead of them, shouting hey! hey! hey! and they lumber after him. When they're all safely on the other side of the barbed wire, trampling and bellowing, I go up to say hello, and Didier says, well, now you've got company, and I say, well, I bellow like that too sometimes. The word reminds me of Flaubert, writing to a friend after George Sand's death and saying that at her burial he bellowed like a calf.

Didier kindly lets my visitors park their cars on his little patch and in return I keep it neat and tidy, cutting the grass and hedge. However, bonfires being forbidden in summer because of the risk of fire, I'd been dumping pruned branches there for some time, in line with the barbed wire fence to the side, and they'd become covered with nettles and bindweed and settled themselves in as a low green wall. Also, Bertrand, cutting the grass in my absence, had taken to dumping great loads of grass clippings on top of this soft parapet, rather than on the compost heap down in the orchard. The low green wall of garden rubbish had turned into a substantial long, wide mound advancing well into Didier's territory, and Didier's son, arriving with a new herd of bullocks, had reproved me when I went up to apologise. I promised to clear away the mess. It was, yes, completely my fault.

I'd been doing an hour every evening. The top layers of recently cut grass were easy to remove with a pitchfork. I'd used these heaps of dried stalks to lay out a new island bed down in the orchard, weighing down the grass cuttings with short logs from the wild cherry trees I'd had cut down last winter. These logs lay about in large heaps, weathering. Another heap, apple boughs this time, lay in the meadow just beyond. I'd had the ancient apple tree there pruned, after its branches cracked under the weight of fruit and then broke. My neighbour Fernand puts his cows in that meadow every summer. I don't charge him anything, as I don't want a money relationship with him: he is Paulette's son-in-law and it would feel wrong. In any case the cows do the work of a lawnmower, one less job for me to fret over not doing myself. I'd begun shifting the lopped apple boughs last autumn, hauling them load by load up the hilly lane in a barrow, then stopped, and never got going again, feeling too lazy and hot to go on. The boughs had lain on the lane verge for far too long. I'd look at them and think: I really ought to move those; one of these days; then I'd wander off and read a book.

Once I'd forked up and carried away the top layers of grass cuttings from the mound, I found that those underneath had turned into pure, fine compost. I carted away six barrowloads and mulched the rose bushes and other shrubs. The mound hardly seemed dented. I poured with sweat. This felt like the labours of Hercules and Psyche put together.

I took a break, feeling hopeless and inept and cross and too hot. I slumped on the front step and drank water. A machine roared in the lane. Fernand appeared on a tractor, drove into the meadow and began spraying the thistles. After a bit he got down and walked over to the barbed-wire fence, so I went down to say hello. He is a cheerful man, bald, with a brown egglike head. He is compact and sturdy. We chatted for a bit, about the weather, the heatwave not doing the crops any good, they'd be scorched and not grow well. I invited him to come up to the house and drink a glass of white wine, and he accepted.

Michel, Bertrand's father, taught me that white wine was what you drank at work breaks. One day he'd come to help me cut the back meadow, insisting on doing it by himself, by hand, with a long-handled scythe. At mid-morning, he appeared at the door, and I offered him coffee, or water, or fruit juice. He shook his head. White wine! One glass, nice and cold.

Now Fernand sat in the garden with me, in the shade, and drank white wine, and elaborated seriously: it's the calories, you see, you need them for energy, but of course you mustn't overdo it in the heat. He looked up at the wild cherry tree: that's getting a bit too close to the electricity lines. He pointed down the lane to the heap of felled apple branches at the edge of the meadow. Who cut them? Jean-Luc? He should have brought them up to the house for you, I'll do it for you with my machine, won't take a minute.

His kind offer made it easy for me to ask him for help to shift the mound of *terreau* at the top of the lane. Fernand agreed immediately: the machine will do that, no problem. I knew I could not offer him money for the job, as that would have been insulting. Instead I asked him: do you still like whisky? He said, yes, I liked that bottle you gave me two years ago, good malt whisky that was. I said, well, I'll bring you another.

He began giving me news of his family. His nephew Joseph, Paulette's grandson, is now working for him. All the time he was growing up, Paulette was desperate to set Joseph up as a farmer. Her favourite grandson. She had wrested away from our neighbour Ambroise some fields that he was buying, going behind his back to offer a higher price and making an enemy of Ambroise as a result. Ambroise had gone to the village school with Paulette's husband, they had known and helped each other all their lives, but as a result of Paulette's treachery the two neighbours had broken off all contact, no longer spoke to one another. Ambroise had told me all this one evening, ten months back, when going past my door on his tractor he paused for a chat, as he often did. Apparently, Paulette had said to him: I don't care if you live or die!

Fernand, sipping his white wine, did not mention this dreadful story. He merely said: you know about the trouble Joseph had? We all knew. Joseph, living on his own, in charge of his own fields, struggling to make a go of things, no girlfriend as modern young women did not want to live in the countryside, had ended up by attempting suicide. Fernand said: he hasn't really recovered, he doesn't know how to work, I have to be behind him all the time telling him what to do!

Fernand looked around at my plants: roses, bushes of sage and rosemary. He said: I really like gardening, I'm the one who grows things at home, all the vegetables. Courgettes I like, when they're small. He sketched with his hands in the air what looked to me more like a biggish marrow. Showing off my knowledge of Italian cooking, I said: I love eating the flowers. Fernand trumped me: oh yes, you can buy those in the supermarket.

I offered him some of the aquilegia seeds I've been collecting. Would Isabelle like them? France shook his head: she doesn't care about flowers. Unlike her mother Paulette, who is passionate about them. Once she said to me: flowers are half my life. Hardly surprising if Isabelle chooses that way of being different from her matriarchal, omniscient mother. As he left, I gave Fernand a pot of mint. He laughed at me. There's a great clump of it growing just down the lane! But he accepted the mint and drove away on his tractor.

I dug up another three barrowloads of *terreau*, to mulch the last of the rose bushes, then slumped back onto the step. What to do now? I could have swept up dead flies from behind the fridge, I could have cleaned the kitchen windows, I could have made sure I'd extracted the last of the pine marten poo from the boiler cupboard upstairs, I could have cleaned the gas stove. I just went on slumping.

Bertrand turned up to mow the orchard grass. A baseball cap shaded his sunburnt face. He didn't look anything like as overheated and sweaty as I knew I must do. We kissed each other on both cheeks. In the olden days here, I mean twenty years ago, everyone kissed each other four times. Perhaps that was to reassure each other that they hadn't got a sword tucked away somewhere on their person. Your entry into a house was necessarily stately, slow. By the time you'd circled a room kissing everybody in it four times you'd feel less desperate to stab one of them much as you might loathe him or her for stealing the fields you were after. Grégoire instructed me: all that's over and done with, two kisses is quite enough.

It was Grégoire who recommended me to get Bertrand to come and cut the grass. I was having lunch with him and his wife Lucie, a rounded, merry woman who really enjoyed food and just ignored Grégoire when he became patriarchal. She had prepared foie gras from a neighbour's geese, beetroot salad with thyme-scented vinaigrette, blanquette *de veau*, green salad, cheese, *crème au chocolat*. How did Grégoire remain so skinny?

He and Lucie used to work the farm just over the hill from Jim and me, and we got to know them when Jim was flying his kite in the top field one day and Grégoire appeared and introduced himself and soon afterwards invited us to supper. Lucie showed us round the house, very proud of how they'd modernised it. On either side of their big double bed Grégoire had fixed up a closed-circuit TV screen, so that in the night they could both keep an eye on the distant stables should a cow be ill and need supervision, they each took care of one lot of cows, and over the bed hung a tapestry picture stitched by Lucie of a pouting bare-breasted *sultry temptress* as Jim named her.

Now their son has taken over the farm and they have retired to a modern house on the outskirts of the nearby little town. They take care of their grandchildren, whose parents work in Paris. On that occasion of my lunchtime visit one of the little boys kept reaching his foot under the table, lifting the hem of my long silk skirt, brushing my calf with his foot and grinning at me. I grinned back. The game involved Grégoire not seeing. Now, thank goodness, the little boys can dodge him when he threatens to hit them for a breach in manners, they just race off. I used to interfere, to tell Grégoire it was wrong, and he would look cross and baffled.

As Bertrand and I stood outside the house and chatted, Fernand reappeared, on a different machine, one with a huge scooper in front. Bertrand and he greeted each other, as neighbours whose parents and in-laws are friends. While Bertrand strimmed the grass, Fernand drove to the apple tree in the meadow, scooped up the logs, brought them up past the house, halted at the woodshed door, dumped the logs, slung them in. Next he drove to the top of the lane and pushed back the *terreau* into the dip at the barbed wire fence, where the land fell towards the meadow. Perfectly cleared and flattened brown surface. *Magnifique!*

Bertrand came up to take a look. He and Fernand began a conversation about their work, clearly not involving me, so I left them to it and went to put a jug of white wine in the fridge. I set three chairs in the shade of the bushes I had been pruning, got out three glasses. I summoned the two men for a celebratory drink. We chatted in a desultory way, then Fernand went off. Bertrand said, he's nice, a friendly type, isn't he! He hasn't got a wooden tongue, as they say.

After Bertrand had gone in his turn, I went to the woodshed, expecting to have to sort and stack the logs. Fernand had done that, built a long steep pile. How fast he'd worked, and how kind of him to spare me so much labour. I'd make that bottle of whisky a really large one.

I sat on the step again, with another glass of wine, and ate supper, two slices of grilled bread spread with fried tomatoes, the tomatoes nicely blackened at the edges, the way Dad used to do them. I listened to dogs barking, cattle lowing, tractors revving, birds chitter-chattering. Nonetheless the landscape felt empty, hollowed out: something should be happening for the evening to feel complete, but wasn't.

I realised I was waiting for Ambroise to drive past on his huge, high tractor, en route to check on his cattle. Over the past five years or so, ever since he'd taken over Monsieur Nouard's fields at the top of the lane and begun grinding past my house each evening with great bales of hay, we had developed a ritual of greeting each other. I'd hear him coming from far off, chugging up the hill from the bottom of the lane, and would open the front door. He would slow down and wave, a graceful, majestic salute, then chug on and disappear round the corner to his fields that stretched up to the forest. Returning, he would wave again. Sometimes he would halt and I'd go out and stand to the side of the enormous side wheel as tall as I was, keeping a wary eye on it, and we would chat, he leaning back in the high cab, the engine running. If I was in the middle of reading or writing, or if it was raining, I didn't always want to be interrupted, or to go out and get wet, but the chat was always worth it. Gradually out of these quarter-hours we built a friendship. He offered me anecdotes and jokes and bits of wisdom, and in return I offered him bunches of flowers to take home to Bénédicte.

He was a tall, big man, with thick grey-brown hair, a noble countenance, blue-green eyes, a formidable nose, a wide mouth curling up in a smile. He wore ancient-looking handknitted blue or green pullovers or jumpers, big loose stitches unravelling here and there, brown wellington boots. Usually he had his small dog, Petula (named after the pop singer Petula Clark) riding with him, at his feet or on his knee, and his much larger dog, a St Bernard, perched behind. We would discuss the crops and the weather. *Mi-figue, mi-raisin*, he would say of days mixing sunshine and cloud. Like jam!

Ambroise read the French version of *Hello!* magazine, with its pictures of the British royals and gossip about raunchy Prince William casting a fancying eye on his sister-in-law Pippa of the celebrated *cul*. He would enquire after the Queen's health. And *le petit prince*? How's he getting on? Ambroise worked harder than anyone I knew, never taking a holiday, never coming to the annual village dinners, concentrating on making money. He and Bénédicte lived a kilometre away from me in a four-storeyed sixteenth-century farmhouse with a steeply pitched roof. On my first visit to them, he showed me their sitting room, complete with large TV and glittery, mirrored, Formica dresser set with ornaments. 1970s, at a guess; perhaps from the early days of his marriage; perhaps what Joe would snap up as a retro bargain if he found it in Emmaus. Well-off people like old things, Ambroise explained: but poor people like new things.

I'd be summoned to visit at 2pm, just after Sunday lunch, when Ambroise and Bénédicte enjoyed a moment's repose. In their kitchen, with its 1980s heavy, brown, faux-rustic fitted cupboards and built-in cooker, we'd have a cup of coffee and a slice of fruit tart, or a glass of wine and a piece of cake, and Ambroise would discourse on modern life or on philosophy, while Bénédicte gazed at him affectionately, and then he'd halt the flow and break into a joke. Once he thundered about *la libération des femmes*, which was no joke: OK, Michèle, men shouldn't beat their wives, but there is too much divorce! He was very proud of Bénédicte, who came from a higher-status farming family than he did, and who had been cut off by them for marrying a peasant. She was a sweet-faced woman in her late fifties, who loved a laugh. She walked with a rocking gait, several hip operations not having really helped her disability, and like all the women here worked both inside and outside all day long. In summer she wore brief shorts; I admired her long, strong brown legs. When I arrived with a bunch of flowers she'd pick me some of her big, cracked, juicy tomatoes, or a fat marrow. After our coffee or wine, she and Ambroise would take me to see their great barns full of hundreds of poultry that they raised for a firm that supplied the local supermarkets. By day the poultry roamed free-range in the meadows, where Ambroise had planted trees so they could enjoy some shade, and by night they were shut up in their smelly dormitory. Bénédicte would pick up a downy chick and caress it, then hand it to me to stroke, while Ambroise watched us indulgently. The tour over, the visit completed, they'd wave me off in my little car.

9pm. On this still evening, I could hear the village church bells chime the hour three kilometres away. Still light. Streaks of chilly rose, wisps of grey cloud, low in the sky over the far blue hills. I stayed sitting on the doorstep, realising that yes, I was waiting for Ambroise to drive past in his tractor, waiting for him to wave as he always did.

Two months previously, on the Thursday after Easter, a very hot day, I was gardening out front when Pierre, Ambroise's son, whizzed past in his van, going up to check Ambroise's cows I supposed, and so we waved, and then when he returned he slowed down and halted and said out of the side window: have you heard about my father?

I was diddling about in the flowerbed. I dropped my trowel and ran across the flowerbed to the van. I said, what's happened? Pierre said, my father has died.

The shock was a blow to my heart. To my brain too. Stunned, stupid, I couldn't grasp this news: Ambroise had been diagnosed with cancer just before Christmas, had gone into hospital just before Easter, had died on Good Friday and been buried on Easter Monday. Pierre said: I'm sorry that no one told you, we were in too much of a state to let you know.

I began crying but tried not to because Pierre was being so brave and dignified. He stayed in the car, talked to me out of the window for about fifteen minutes, staring ahead, not looking at me, telling me what had happened: at the end he was just *drogué*, put into a coma, then they gave him more morphine and he had a heart attack and died. Pierre kept repeating that he would cope, he had to. He was taking on the farm. He said: I still need him, I still need his advice.

We clasped hands. After he'd gone I streamed with tears. I wished I had known of Ambroise's death at the time, I wished I had been able to attend the funeral. I'd been here on Easter Monday, holding a merry lunch party for friends, I could have cancelled it, gone down to the village church.

I still missed Ambroise. He was irreplaceable. There was an Ambroise-shaped gap in the landscape.

I stayed sitting on the step until it grew dark, well after ten o'clock. I like to wait for night, watch everything outdoors grow dim and blue and shadowy. Alain, the local plumber, when I stopped to greet him and his wife in the market one day, asked, aren't you frightened all on your own in that remote place? I said no. I wasn't frightened of the darkness, either. Only when I was feeling very upset about something, as for example when my mother died, did the darkness begin to feel uncanny, the loneliness peopled with presences, the house to creak and sob in the early hours, and I knew that I was producing the hauntings, not yet able to comprehend how my mother was leaving me and returning, leaving and returning on waves of my grief. So with Ambroise. I sat on the step, thinking about him, then went indoors and climbed up the ladder to my bedroom.

I couldn't sleep. I put the light on and decided to read for a bit. A single book lay on the dusty top of the little chest of drawers next to the bed: Keats's letters, newly edited by John Barnard, a friend of mine. John had kindly sent me a copy on publication. I picked it up, opened it at random, and began to read about Negative Capability.

In a footnote John pointed out that Keats began defining this term in his letter of 22nd November 1817 to his friend Benjamin Bailey: 'I wish you knew all that I think about Genius and the Heart... In passing however I must say of one thing that has pressed upon me lately and encreased my Humility and capability of submission and that is this truth – Men of Genius are great as certain ethereal Chemicals operating on the Mass of neutral intellect... but they have not any individuality, and determined Character.'

Keats went on to assert: 'I am certain of nothing but of the holiness of the Heart's affections and the truth of Imagination.'

Keats pursued this thought in his letter in late December 1817 to his brothers George and Tom. He was walking back from the Christmas pantomime with two male friends when 'several things dovetailed in my mind, & at once it struck me, what quality went to form a Man of Achievement especially in Literature & which Shakespeare posessed [sic] so enormously – I mean Negative Capability, that is when a man is capable of being in uncertainties, Mysteries, doubts, without any irritable reaching after fact & reason.'

When I first read this passage in my mid-twenties, I couldn't appreciate it. In those days I longed to be invulnerable, in complete control of myself. I was going through a difficult time that I could not handle at all, which involved conflicts – 'uncertainties, Mysteries' – that I could not tolerate. I just wanted to get rid of them. In the end I found a way to use them: I let them fire my first two novels.

Much later, I used to quote the passage from Keats's letter to my UEA writing students when they got stuck, and were either thrashing about determined to Solve Problems Immediately or else were sunk in gloom convinced they couldn't write and should give up now and for ever, and indeed I quoted it to myself when I got stuck in my own writing difficulties, or when I'd been commissioned to write a short story but felt blank.

I'd learned that when confronting a block, or what seemed an unsurmountable structural problem, I just had to wait, for as long as it took, resting gently in not-knowing and not-being-able and not-being-in-control, not so much ignoring the problem as just holding it and not fretting, it was the very gentleness and calming down and ceasing to struggle and even to think that did the trick: eventually, after days or weeks of waiting, up out of the still waters would jump the silvery fish of inspiration. The solution having presented itself, I could indeed feel powerful, not invulnerable but simply able to work, get on with making something.

However, it often seemed hard to remember Keats's bit of wisdom at the time I actually needed it. Why was that? Something in me kept on wanting to feel in control, that any difficulties were safely in the past, that I'd mastered my writing problems, could painlessly invent a new form, finish a book, do well. Part of me wanted to avoid the uncertainties involved in beginning to write a new piece of fiction even as another part wanted to go forward and plunge in. It always felt frightening, starting a new novel, because it required going beyond conscious ego into the unknown, tearing myself open, tearing myself apart, letting destruction happen, destruction of old grammars old fictional shapes old ways of seeing, in order to let new ones happen, and that felt very close to going mad, with no guarantee that you'd ever come out the other side.

Routine helped: you went 'mad' for four or five hours every morning then you came out into the kitchen and made lunch, took a walk, rang a friend, that's to say re-entered a composed and composing narrative rather than whirling non-stop in the timeless chaos of the unconscious imagination. Then next day you redrafted and rewrote, plunged on again, went 'mad' again.

Now, rereading Keats's letter, suddenly I felt able to see that perhaps I'd written that early version (the nineteenth century one) of my novel too quickly, too eager not to have to go 'mad' at all. So the Publisher had been right to reject it, even if she hadn't been able to help me see what was wrong. She had indeed tried, saying 'too heavy... too intense', but I hadn't at that point been able to understand what she meant. I had failed in understanding. However, at least I had gone back to spending every day rewriting, rewriting.

Perfection of the life or of the art? Recently I'd perfected neither. But why did Yeats think you have to choose? Was the choice inevitable? Perhaps I valued writing fiction so highly not simply because I wanted to serve language, my beloved mistress, but because my life often felt such a mess as I lurched from crisis to crisis. Sometimes, I reminded myself, the mess did feel creative, the formation of a different pattern of living, my life could feel cheerfully unconventional, and that was fine and dandy, but sometimes, as recently, the mess felt like failure, and that hurt.

Some people suggested that writing novels had a compensatory function, like daydreaming, enabled you to reshape the world, to live in one you preferred and controlled; to 'perfect' it indeed; to live inside your head rather than in the 'real' world. I could worry, in black pram moments, that I sometimes did that. At calmer moments I knew those people were not accurate, because writing a novel meant living in a world that made serious demands, that had its own real existence, the world of psyche and imagination and language, definitely part of the 'real' world, the inside world and the outside world co-existed, sometimes overlapped, sometimes just touched, but you did live in both at once while writing, I mean that while in the thick of writing a novel I could still read the paper and cook and talk to friends and go to meetings and look at art. You entered that expanded world when writing, but also of course when reading a good novel. A fine, delicate, golden vision both outside you and inside you.

Lying in bed at La Lièvrerie, rereading Keats's beautiful, wise assertions in his letter, musing over them, I began to redefine Negative Capability, to expand its conceptual relevance beyond the field of literature. That was what he must have meant anyway, surely, that it could be a way of living as well as of solving writerly problems. For him the two were not separate, indeed, but connected, integrated.

Perhaps Negative Capability could not only mean dwelling peacefully within contradictions without striving for rapidly arriving rational solutions, but could also more broadly refer to all situations in which a person felt out of control, helpless, powerless. Perhaps all you could do in such cases, to begin with anyway, was simply admit how inept you felt. How failing.

This helped me see that that starving baby (myself) stuck in the deep black pram down the bottom of the garden had survived, though she certainly didn't know at the time that waiting to be fed, supposedly (according to the childcare experts) learning patience, supposedly learning trust in the eventual arrival of comfort, could be called Negative Capability, no she certainly did not, she had screamed and screamed in despair and anguish but nobody came, but nonetheless thanks to help along the way she had survived, she had fantasised and dreamed, she had grown up, earned a living, followed her desires, loved people, had adventures, made homes, written books.

Freud seemed to think that what mattered wasn't so much what happened to you as what you made of it through fantasy and thought; Winnicott seemed to allow for actual experience having an actual effect on the infant or child; but they did seem to agree that our creative inventing minds were part of our survival instinct. Imagination helps us survive. So Negative Capability could refer both to the experience of a happy-enough infancy, the child surviving the repeated, temporary loss of the mother by eventually learning that she regularly returns, and also it might refer to the experience of a difficult infancy whose wounds could nonetheless be mediated by imagination.

So perhaps Negative Capability wasn't so much a temporary state of mind, a strategy, as a country in which I had to live all the time. Well, much of the time. At the moment, certainly.

I could become an immigrant in that country rather than a tourist. That's what had happened to me with France, after all. In my thirties I'd been able to acknowledge to myself that since it was my mother's country I longed to spend time in it. In my twenties I'd felt turned away from that mother-country, the bad daughter both self-exiled and banished, unable to return and unwilling to try. For years I'd visited France as a tourist, and then, aged forty (with that sudden acquisition of prize money), had bought my house here in the Mayenne. It was as though all those years previously I'd had half my self cut off, the French half, or had cut it off, and now that I was in France it could grow back, and I felt completed, psychologically bigger, psychologically the right size.

Here at La Lièvrerie I didn't have a room of my own at first: my priority was restoring the barn at the side of the garden to make Jim a studio. In winter I worked happily in our bedroom, and, in summer, in the pigsty Jim restored for me. He reroofed it, put in a window, furnished it with table and chair. I wrote two novels in that peaceful, tree-shaded pigsty. Then, when thanks to a generous advance I had enough money to pay for restoring the broken-down side of the house, I did acquire a workroom.

In my own space I wasn't half of anyone (as a child I'd fantasised that Margi and I were each half of a single whole); I wasn't half of 'the twins'; I was just myself. Spending months in the Mayenne each year I got to know France in a completely fresh way, no longer as someone remembering childhood in Normandy but as an adult discovering a new place. Paulette had certainly been clear about that: the Normans were not the same as the Mayennais!

They ate completely different food, for a start! Living here first with Jim and then on my own, I had gradually got to know neighbours and local people, had made friends, had learned local ways, customs, turns of phrase. Living in both England and France made me happy, felt true and right, and the more I criss-crossed between them the more previously split parts of myself got linked back together again and that made me feel happy too.

I had spent my childhood summers travelling to and fro across the Channel. This being ferried back and forth had become a symbol of translation (being carried across – yes, like Vic Sage's Greek removal vans) between languages, that I'd written about years back in *Daughters of the House*. Nowadays I travelled to France on the Eurostar. In the middle of the tunnel I'd feel my soul start to expand (as Jane Eyre put it about hers), and bliss would fill me: being in the middle, in between, neither English nor French but a mixture of both. At that point, ten minutes into the tunnel, I'd usually start a new notebook, write something. Part of the ritual of the crossover.

Perhaps that pleasure in hovering between identities, languages, places, was itself a form of Negative Capability. I could carry it with me, stay inside it. I would have to learn its ways and speak its halting, doubting language.

All right. I didn't have any clear answers to the problems currently besetting me. I'd just have to live with them. Perhaps I should take that word *failure* and redefine it? How would I do that? I didn't know. I'd just have to wait and see.

How interesting and lovely that I'd learned such helpful lessons from an English poet while in France. Thanks, Mr Keats.

I clicked off the light and went to sleep.

CHAPTER 4
JULY

One Day In Paris

Yesterday I woke up soon after dawn, when light streamed through the transparent scarlet curtain at the window. I got up carefully, because the thin mattress balanced on an unsteady low base and was liable to tip over if you put your full weight too suddenly on one side, as had happened last night when I flumped heedlessly into bed. The flat in the 10*ieme* had been advertised on Airbnb as sleeping four people. Two very thin couples, perhaps, who in addition to tolerating narrow beds didn't mind that one bedroom led out of the other. I'd slept in the far, tiny room, which had a marble fireplace set across one corner and a nice old door, wide, with thin panels and an egg-shaped china handle.

The unpolished parquet floor slid warmly under my bare feet. I crept through the bedroom next door, past Val, curled face down fast asleep in her 'double', her dark hair spread out on her pillow, and along the corridor.

The cramped lavatory had a high-up iron cistern, painted white. The tiny bathroom held a shower, a couple of open shelves filled with Laure's tubes of make-up, Veet cream to remove underarm hair, body moisturiser, foot moisturiser, face moisturiser, eau de toilette, perfume. On arrival, peeking at these, I'd felt all the guilty enjoyment I did as a child, going through the bathroom cabinets in strange houses I happened to be visiting. Now, surveying them again, I wished I'd not brought my pots of Nivea Creme (Day and Night but not Noon) but just helped myself to Laure's much posher ones.

I opened the double window in the small sitting-room-cum-kitchenette, furnished with ugly freestanding IKEA shelving in raw pine, looked out at rooftops opposite, up at our L-shaped building sheering two floors higher, down at a tiny courtyard garden laid with artificial turf. A red square caught my eye. On arrival, the flat's window rail had featured two cleaning cloths, one red and one blue, hung out to dry. Overnight the red one had fallen off onto a glass roof a couple of floors below. No chance of rescuing it. We should have brought them in the night before, when we shut the window, but we'd been too tired to think about such things. Would Laure, the flat-owner, mourn her lost cloth? Alan Bennett's mother would have. He once recounted in a charming essay how his mother turned old clothes first into dusters, then into sink cloths, finally floor cloths. He loved his mother and watched her doings and so could grade her cleaning cloths' hierarchical status exactly. Laure wasn't that kind of housekeeper. Her flat held the basics: one milk saucepan, one cooking pot, one plug-in wok standing ceremonially on a box draped in a piece of batik. A few dirty ashtrays but no matches for lighting the gas. We had to trek out and buy them.

Val had had the idea of coming to Paris to visit the big

Bonnard show, due to close quite soon, at the Musée d'Orsay. She had gone online and organised the Airbnb flat and the exhibition entry tickets. My contribution had been to write emails in French to Laure, checking and confirming details and announcing our arrival time. We were officially allowed by the Airbnb site to arrive at 2pm but Laure began dithering, saying she'd have to let us know, it might have to be a little later.

The last time I'd seen a collection of Bonnard's paintings was a couple of years back, when Nell and I travelled by train to Cannes and took a local bus up the green, flowery hill to Le Cannet, to visit the newly opened Bonnard museum. Nell's idea that time. Her kitchen in Fulham looks like a Bonnard interior, with a tiled floor, one pink wall and one yellow one, blue cooking-pots hanging up above the stove, and French windows opening onto a small courtyard with pots of flowers and an old wash-house painted apple-green. In Le Cannet, which still felt like a village, Nell and I spent a joyful morning looking at pictures in the museum based in an ornate fin-de-siècle villa near Bonnard's home, Le Bosquet, which remained in private hands. Before coming, I'd reread my copy of *Bonnard In Le Cannet*, written by his nephew, which offered an affectionate portrait of a reserved, gentle man, getting older, still obsessed by painting. The text and its accompanying photographs discussed Bonnard's work process, above all evoked his commitment, simplicity. He took a morning walk round the garden (a practice I began to copy), noting the plants and the weather, and drew rabbits' ears and dogs' ears in the corner of a page of his diary. Yes, he'd had family money to live on, and women to cook and clean for him.

Nell and I wandered to and fro in the near-empty, air-conditioned rooms, luxuriating in the lack of crowds, looking separately at the pictures then coming back together for quick discussions. We had lunch on the little terrace of the bistro across the road, in hot sunshine, gazing down over red roofs and green hillsides. A woman regular arrived with her small dog, which curled at her feet. The waiter set out her chair with a special thick cushion (we sat on hard wicker), and she worked her way through the *menu du jour* while we munched robust salads scattered with lardons and croutons. Then we returned to the villa to look at Bonnard's paintings again.

Afterwards we visited the little local park and studied its black granite memorial to the local Jews who'd been taken away to concentration camps in WW2. Nell lingered here, as she is very open to all kinds of new information, and I felt ashamed, because it was difficult to hold in my mind both the joy engendered by the paintings and the sorrow engendered by the memorial and I wanted to solve this conflict by denying it, running away from the gold letters spelling out what had gone on and listing the names of the murdered.

Later, Nell and I caught the packed bus back down the hill. We stood near the door. A middle-aged man said to me, do you want a seat? I replied: no thank you, please give it to Madame. Gesturing at Nell. He got up, and Nell sat down. The bus slowed, stopped. The man approached the door, came close to me. The bus door opened. The man grabbed my breast and squeezed it hard, hurting me, then jumped off the bus and was gone. Speechless with shock, I didn't manage to yell after him.

Next day we took the local train along the coast to Nice and visited the Matisse and Chagall museums. Chagall's work has seemed to me too folkloric and whimsical, almost sentimental, though the odd fiery angel whizzing above village rooftops pleasingly stirs up the dark sky, but when I watched him on film passionately talking about making art I began to understand him and his work better. That was another good lunchtime outside, in a shacklike café-restaurant in the green and flowery Chagall garden, eating *oeufs mayonnaise* and watching Niçois be sweet to their children.

That trip with Nell reminded me how much fun it was to go abroad on jaunts for two or three days, which I rarely did, because I was always writing and also usually too broke. If I went to La Lièvrerie, I stayed there and just worked. Lovely, but not jaunty. But now I did have some money, thanks to the evening class I was teaching, so leaped at the chance to go to Paris when Val suggested it and thought to hell with worrying about the future and my likely penniless state, try living in the present, keep channelling Keats and Negative Capability and just accept I don't know how I'll be earning my living this time next year, I might be dead anyway, enjoy myself now.

Laure's latest email, sent just before our departure, had declared that we couldn't turn up before 6pm, since she and her flatmate Jérémie were both out at work until then. We'd already booked ourselves onto an early train. *Tant pis, alors.* I dressed in my black cotton Dutch trousers, ballooning and wide-legged then curving into the ankle, bought in Carmen's company in Amsterdam (she bought a pair in grey), and my blue and white striped *matelot* T-shirt, and left home at 6.15am, in cool air and pale sunlight, hardly anyone about, picked Val up at her house round the corner. She looked cheerful and sparkling-eyed, all ready for holidays: freshly washed hair, a grey linen dress, blue sandals.

We caught the 45 bus. At the Elephant and Castle a flow of people boarded, including a blonde white woman with two children, one fair and the other darker-skinned. She frowned at this child, scolding him, and made him sit by himself on a seat near Val and me. She took herself off to a distant seat with the other child, put her arm around him, spoke to him kindly. The child abandoned and scolded kicked at the opposite seat, his face clenched and tight. I longed to console him but couldn't think how to do it. I smiled at him but he did not respond. Probably he knew I'd witnessed his humiliation; why would he want to acknowledge me? When the three of them got off just past Borough, the mother speaking as before crossly to one and kindly to the other, a dark-skinned man stepped out of the crowd waiting at the bus stop. The dark child's face broke into beams of happiness, he hurled himself into the man's arms hugging him and the man caught him and hugged him back. I made up a story about the parents being divorced, and the boy very unhappy, and the mother favouring her younger child by her new lover, and this kept me going until we reached King's Cross and entered the Eurostar terminal at St Pancras.

We'd decided to travel light, with small rucksacks, but walking around Paris for an entire day in blistering heat nearly finished me off, my rucksack (no Kindle, too many books, a large old-fashioned alarm clock, those pots of Nivea, etc) growing heavier by the hour, sweat pouring down me. From Gare du Nord we took the metro south, made for the *1er arrondissement*, turned into the cool of the Palais Royal arcades, idled past shop windows displaying super-expensive modern jewellery, wispy chiffon frocks held by gold beads, antiquarian books and prints. I saluted the ghost of Colette, who lived here twice, once in a regal apartment on the first floor, then in her final Parisian pied-à-terre, a *pied-en-ciel* up in the attics (or was it the other way round?), where tended by her faithful maid Pauline she lay on a daybed and contemplated her collection of glass paperweights and wrote enchanting letters to her many friends by the light of her lamp in its blue shade. In her last years she suffered from excruciating arthritis, and so wore sandals everywhere, unusual in those days, much more comfortable of course than the high heels most Parisiennes felt obliged to endure in order to remain *dans le vent*. The sturdy sandals I was wearing for Parisian walking looked oddly like Colette's, I realised. I wasn't yet quite as plump as she became in her final years, but just give me time.

Killing time before lunch, we strolled in the Tuileries Gardens. Crunching along the sandy avenue leading to the fountain, past the stone nymphs, past Diana with her slender hound, I remembered all the times I'd crunched there before, from my early twenties onwards. I remembered for example the intense misery of one weekend visit in the 70s with a rejecting lover who talked in the Jeu de Paume, vis-à-vis Monet's water lilies, about Monet anticipating Jackson Pollock and I shamed him by not knowing who Jackson Pollock was, and who spent more time choosing juniper-scented aftershave in a *parfumerie* on the Boul' Mich than kissing me and who I discovered afterwards was working out his sexuality and quite soon came out as gay. On the other hand I remembered the bliss of another visit, staying with Roy and Pascale in their flat on Rue St-Honoré when they would go off to work each morning and I explored all day long by myself, going into the Marais' Jewish shops, which in those days still existed, before the shabby, charming district became restored, fashionable, expensive. (Returning to the Marais three years ago, to visit the newly opened Jewish Museum, I was struck by how artificial and over-clean the district seemed, so very carefully preserved as picturesque.)

Later, business visits courtesy of the British Council or the BBC let me meet cigarette-puffing French writers, mostly charming and intriguing. The dead ones equally so. As a presenter for *Night Waves* I pursued the ghost of Camus, entered the flat that was formerly Manet's studio, explored Mallarmé's little house at Fontainebleau. Sometimes we broadcast live from Radio France. The philosopher Bernard-Henri Lévy made me giggle, turning up for an interview in a billowing white shirt unbuttoned to reveal chest hair and a medallion.

Some Parisian intellectuals were daunting. When I explained to her about living part-time in the Mayenne and loving it, novelist Sylvie Germain exclaimed scornfully: the English think all French people are peasants. I could have replied: and the mayennais peasants think that all Parisians are snobs. They weren't, of course. Briefly, in the 1990s, I had a French publisher, Calmann-Lévy (Flaubert's publisher), for three of my novels, and the foreign-rights editor there was full of kindness and joie de vivre, consulting me on translation, inviting me to parties in the historic office, introducing me to coffee-cream macaroons, whisking me out to little lunches, taking me to stroll in, yes, the Tuileries Gardens. On one particular walk we discussed the publicity for *Flesh and Blood*, published in the UK in 1994, which was just about to come out in French. The editor warned me that some readers might find it too experimental, that I was teasing them too much with my Orlando-like narrator who changed from a girl into a boy and back again, with my form of stories enclosing each other, with my narrative that went backwards then forwards, the broken-apart stories getting zipped back together by the reader. The novel did OK but was not widely popular. It got put in for the Booker; I heard later from one of the judges it had been tossed aside. Pouf! I did mind bitterly years later when certain younger, British writers were inspired (it seemed to me) by *Flesh and Blood* to write similarly constructed kinds of novel and received enormous acclaim. Marina Warner comforted me: that's what always happens to pioneers. Pioneers had to grin and bear it whereas I wanted to pioneer new ways of shouting: it isn't fair! When Calmann-Lévy was taken over by a conglomerate, the new owners decided I was not enough of a bestseller, and dropped me. I wasn't the right kind of English writer, someone explained: I wrote as though I were French. I thought, fuck it! I *am* French, well, half-French. My lovely editor retired and went to live in the Lot with his lady-love, his Eve he called her, and I got on with writing my next book.

Perhaps I remembered those times of envy and paranoia, resenting the younger writers for seeming to copy me, because I was still worrying about my current novel's fate. Just before I left for Paris the Publisher had emailed with the good news that her reader (a different one from before) had liked and praised my novel, really got what I was trying to do, but thought nonetheless the text still needed some more work, so now I would have to wait another three weeks for a final decision while she, the Publisher, read it herself. This was an advance on having to wait until September when she returned from her summer holidays, which had been her previous stipulation. I'd said OK, trying to sound as gracious as possible. But I still felt anxious and insecure and powerless and often could not achieve Keatsian calm and instead longed to drink sufficient glasses of wine to calm me down and dull these unpleasant feelings and sometimes did. I'd been living with them for too long. I'd emailed the reader, thanking her for her comments, and had asked the Publisher to forward it to her. I hung on to knowing that I had one reader who recognised my novel's value. Three, when I added in Jenny and Sarah, who'd read early drafts of some chapters. That was far far far better than none.

Val and I left the Tuileries Garden, passed the funfair, the pool in which children bobbed about in huge plastic bubbles, regained the street. On the pavement we weaved through the throngs of passers-by, the troops of tourists following guides with flags who reminded me of Jesus, in Italian paintings, waving a triangular flag marked with a red cross and leading the holy souls out of purgatory. I was a tourist too, of course, but tried to be an inconspicuous one. Walking in a foreign city I like to merge with other pedestrians if at all possible, to be the one who sees not the one who is seen. Plodding around Paris with my rucksack, albeit a discreet one, and my normcore sandals, my armpits and face damp with sweat, made me feel not only visibly a tourist, but also deeply, uncomfortably English. Completely unreasonably, I didn't want Val to address me cheerily in English. I didn't want her to get out her camera and take photographs. I didn't want to be a pink-faced, perspiring foreigner. I wanted to be a chic, cool, thin local and if I couldn't be that I wanted to be invisible. Also I wanted to sit down in the shade.

I tried to hide my grumpiness under enthusing over stationers' windows, bits of street furniture, the design of lettering on signs, the faded lavender-blue paint on the high wooden doors of apartment courtyards. My eyes searched for something I used to enjoy noticing in Paris: the little hessian bags, weighted with sand, which lived in the gutters, checking and directing the flow of water towards drain-holes. Someone washing the pavement outside his shop would adjust this tiny sandbag so that the soapy suds flowed off in the right direction. Sometimes simply small rolls of old carpet sufficed. They seemed to organise the flow of rainwater too. They'd all vanished and I couldn't work out what had replaced them.

After a quick café lunch we prowled through the Musée des Arts Décoratifs, full of exquisite gilded porcelain and engraved glass and embroidered-satin armchairs, fascinating if you were in the mood to appreciate such finely wrought items, but disappointing (to me) as alongside these testimonies to high-class money and taste the museum contained no mocked-up kitchen or array of cooking utensils. The servants were invisible, like those in the palace of Eros. In Amsterdam with Carmen, I'd visited Rembrandt's many-storeyed house (Sarah's tip), and admired the layers of rooms of making, from painting studios at the top to well-stocked kitchen at the bottom. Sufficiently inappreciative of rococo and baroque and neo-classical furniture

Val and I nodded at each other, that's enough, and lugged our rucksacks back outside. We sat on a bench in the cool shade of pleached limes and clipped hedges, facing a large naked stone nymph with well-rounded haunches and belly. Nobody had ever told her she was too fat. Feeling very hot always makes me feel fat. Because of having to wear clothes I suppose. Whereas the nymph perched nude and free on her plinth under the green branches one leg cocked over the other quite at ease and not red but pale. She reminded me of Posy Simmonds's drawings of the cheerful art student Jocasta, uncaringly plump, very pretty. Fat young women can still look beautiful. Fat older women not necessarily, though I hate thinking so, hate myself for objectifying other women, judging them, even though I keep these perceptions private, since I loathe women policing each other, discussing diets, assuming that *you've lost so much weight!* is the best possible compliment. Women I hardly know have sometimes told me that I am too fat, or that I am good to have *lost so much weight*, and either way I want to hit them. It comes down to: sensual women who like themselves, who enjoy their bodies, whatever their age, whether fat or thin, look beautiful, whereas anxious women who don't, don't. Jim always said that all women are beautiful with their clothes off. Thanks, Jim! I hugged my rucksack as pillow, dozed for ten minutes.

There followed a hot and bothered journey by metro towards our Airbnb, on the far side of the Canal St Martin. This should have been straightforward, but a crucial interlink station having closed a roundabout route had to be devised. In the end we decided to get off and walk. The journey took longer than the map suggested. We got lost. We were pointed by Parisians who should have known better the wrong way down endless long hot boulevards with little shade. We got lost again.

I did not feel at all like a *flâneuse* happily idling along in *Capabilité Négatif*. I felt like the tired, pissed-off tourist I was. I began to feel so hot I could not cope, almost sun-struck, wanted to collapse, my rucksack growing heavier and more cumbersome with every step. We crossed the Canal St Martin. Nearly there. We passed a grocery, a wine shop, a boulangerie, but Val, still managing to look calm and cool, thought we should do our small bit of necessary shopping in the 'nearby' Lidl, which would be much cheaper. I agreed grumpily and tersely. Yes, OK!

Along another hot boulevard we plodded. Lidl was full to bursting with people but less so with produce. We ploughed back and forth along the aisles packed with determined shoppers wielding pushchairs as battering rams. I wanted to snarl with frustration, tried not to show my bad temper but probably failed. We bought supplies for breakfast, tracked back to the flat and sat down outside the nearby café, which was closed, where we had agreed to meet Laure's flatmate Jérémie, who'd let us in and show us around.

At least we'd arrived. We relaxed, cracked jokes. Jérémie, however, did not turn up. Laure had changed her mobile number without telling us, so we could not contact her, nor did she respond to emails sent on Val's phone, nor did Jérémie respond to the texts I sent him on my ancient but sturdy Nokia. I've never met anyone else with a mobile well over ten years old: my first mobile phone, which I bought solely because I'd begun the love affair with my dear mayennais farmer and needed to be able to contact him on his tractor to arrange assignations. We texted each other: short sexy prose-poems. The affair broke up but the phone did not and all these years later I have not yet replaced it because it still goes on working and still contains a couple of messages from the dear farmer. I've not even had to replace the battery.

Val and I went on waiting at our table on the pavement. Val worried because it had been her choice to book flaky Laure's flat; she thought I'd hate her for this debacle. I was relieved just to be sitting back, rucksack at my feet, drinking in the sights and smells of the neighbourhood busy with people returning from work, traffic tearing by, and I was busy inventing Plan B, which involved finding a nearby hotel, checking in however much a room cost, having a bath, sipping an aperitif and deciding where to go for dinner.

The owner of the café, burly and bearded, arrived and opened up. He cast us questioning looks, shrugged, went inside. Clearly if we were taking up space outside his café we should buy a drink. Accordingly I entered and asked for two glasses of white wine. The café owner looked astonished. He shook his head: impossible. I realised he'd have to open a bottle and feared wasting it. Perhaps most women round here were Muslim and teetotal. Or perhaps, being Parisians, they didn't drink wine in cafés. Only tourists did that. Apparently, someone had told me, that was how you recognised tourists: not just by their sportswear and rucksacks but by their glasses of wine; Parisians simply drank coffee. The café owner went off to confer with the colleague who was sweeping out the back. He returned, offered me a half bottle of Muscadet for thirteen euros. Outrageously expensive. Never mind.

Back outside on the hot, dusty street loud with hooting and sirens, we filled and clinked our glasses. I suggested playing a game to while away the time. I'd done this many years before, when arriving at Berlin airport with a group of other writers on a British Council visit, the four of us forced to wait a long time at the carousel for our cases; I got us to guess or spot each other's luggage once the carousel began to turn and the bags to circle. Julian Barnes sternly put in place a system of fines, in an ascending scale, for each suitcase wrongly identified. I hoped I impressed him by getting his bag right almost immediately. Simple: it was very chic; dark blue canvas with toffee-coloured leather corners and leather straps; clean, new-looking, obviously expensive. When I got back to London I bought myself one just like it in a sale. It did not last long. Arriving in France the following year, Jim and I were in a car crash when a young man driving too fast round a bend skidded and hit us and Jim's cans of paint in the boot tipped and opened and flooded my smart new bag.

Now Val and I played Spot the Flatmate. Spot the Jérémie. Would he sport a goatee? A hipster beard? Ride a bicycle? Every young man who loped up got our full welcome: eager gaze, warm, propositioning smiles. They averted their eyes and hurried past.

Eventually, well over an hour late, young, dark-haired Laure arrived, apologising light-heartedly and rattling keys. I felt so angry with her I could not even mutter *bonsoir*. She hustled us into a dark, narrow, panelled foyer, through a heavy door then up four oval flights of wooden stairs. She pointed out the computer, pulled out some tourist brochures and slapped them down, then raced away again.

The night's sleep followed by several cups of coffee, and of course the prospect of the Bonnard show, made me feel better. The plastic-wrapped croissants we had bought in Lidl were disgusting, solid with lard, so we threw them away and ate cherries instead. We decided to walk to the Gare de l'Est and take the metro from there. We took a backstreet route.

We went over the canal, its steep banks lined with green trees, their heavy, bent-over boughs giving pleasant shade. A young woman with long brown hair sat on the ironwork steps of the bridge, rucksack and bottle of water close by, writing in a notebook; her diary, perhaps. Like a young Anaïs Nin.

Six months back I'd reread Anaïs Nin's novels and diaries in order to be interviewed for a TV film about her, shot in a Notting Hill flat on Talbot Road, very near where I illegally and briefly lived in a sublet damp, cold-water-only housing-association flat in the early 1980s. Walking past the corner of Powys Terrace, looking up at the second-floor window of my former flat, I saw that the building had been restored, as indeed the entire district had been newly smartened up, now featuring a café-restaurant called Raoul's, with orange plastic-leather banquettes. I dropped in as I was too early for the film appointment. I was the only customer. The waiter, busy chatting to his pal, obviously hadn't yet got into role and served me a cappuccino that was cold. The film interview was shot against a screen featuring a glowing image of the interior of a retro-style Parisian café. I talked about Nin's erotica, written to help support Henry Miller, about porn's necessary lack of history and emotion, about femininity and fakery, about Nin trying to repair the wounds inflicted by her sexually abusive father, about why women lie. I was passionate and serious and probably waved my hands in the air too much, but afterwards the friendly cameraman, a veteran of the 70s like myself, exclaimed: well done! That wraps it up beautifully! And of course I was delighted, a delight that did not last since in April, just before the programme was screened, I was informed that my interview had been pulled, the Sky TV executives apparently having decided I'd been over-complicated and talked too much about Nin's ideas and not enough about her life story. I didn't get paid, either.

Perhaps the Sky TV rejection would feed into the sense of Negative Capability I was trying to practise that wasn't always exactly the one Keats described but which suited me. Why not? A writing exercise I had recently given my students was to write very fast as though they were doing automatic writing a list beginning with *I don't know*, they had to complete the sentence, then to repeat *I don't know* and complete another sentence, and so on and on. Once you got going you could continue for page after page and rather exhilarating these negatives turned out to be too, suggestive and powerful and beguiling. I can't, I don't know how to, I'm not able to – these negative formulations became paradoxically charged with positive force and presence, took the students' imaginations far out beyond their usual writing boundaries. I often invented writing exercises for my writing students that touched on my own preoccupations. I didn't tell the students about my difficulties with Lily-the-agent and with the Publisher, which would have been self-indulgent and inappropriate, though I did try to show them that writer-teachers were human, not know-alls, that writing went on being a struggle. Some of them appreciated this honesty; others clearly considered me a poor creature.

Stretching out her long brown legs, her glossy dark head bent over her notebook, the young Nin-like woman lounging on the canal bridge's ironwork step existed both in a public space, where she could be seen and admired, also in a private one, her world of writing. She hadn't necessarily set out to be seen let alone admired. I remembered an article I read in *Honey* magazine in May 1967. Student revolution, feminist revolution, was beginning to ferment but *Honey* was instructing its female readers: this month, be seen eating a green apple. The article jolted me because it clarified something I'd not been able to articulate before: women existed to be looked at and judged by the male voyeur though they were supposed to pretend that wasn't so. Your looks were supposed to make you flatteringly fanciable and other women were supposed to help by suggesting suitable diets and hairstyles and so on. Simone de Beauvoir put it as: either a woman is feminine or she is unfeminine. That's more true in France, where either women are highly groomed and expensively dressed and made up, however subtly and apparently casually, or they go *au naturel*, whereas in Britain there's a great range of female style and women dress far more inventively and creatively than do their French counterparts, who operate within strict restrictive rules. De Beauvoir in middle age opted for the feminine look: little turbans, stylish suits.

I used to argue with Jack about women as objects of the male gaze. He had a beautiful woman friend, in her late forties perhaps, who stepped proudly along, tall and slim and sexy, always exquisitely if simply dressed, shaking out her mane of long dark curly hair. She had a sculpted, thoughtful face, almost haughty in repose, and she'd drift by apparently unheeding of men gaping at her and going weak at the knees and Jack would exclaim to me that she really ought to be aware of the male attention she attracted, how men could not possibly ignore her and would fancy her and she ought to know how she'd made them feel, which she declined to do, and I'd argue back that beautiful women were not to blame for men's longings and frustrations, why couldn't they walk along the street thinking their own thoughts, being *flâneuses*, being subjects not objects, and not having to be aware of men's reactions all the time? I seemed to surprise Jack with these observations. You always stick up for women, don't you? In any case, I liked his friend and she liked me, we'd embrace when we met, we appreciated each other. I'd wonder if Jack assumed that a less beautiful woman could not admire and like a more beautiful one.

Once across the canal Val and I progressed through the boho-chic end of the district, full of young tourists and hipster locals, narrow streets full of chi-chi dress shops, Internet cafés, walls with stencilled Banksy-style images, expensive flower shops. We dived into the metro at Gare de l'Est, going south, then got off at St Michel and walked along the Left Bank quays to the Musée d'Orsay under the scorching sun. Quite a trot in this heat. I dripped with sweat once more. We'd made a mistake; we should have taken a bus. I longed as usual to look cool and elegant but knew yet again I must be purple in the face. Heat has never suited me, makes me feel weak and faint and want to lie down in the gutter. On I plodded. Val, with her long legs, walked faster than I did. She would race ahead then wait for me to catch up at street corners.

Crowds thronged the entrance to the *Musée*. Inside the exhibition the atmosphere was suddenly, blissfully calm: soft green carpets to walk on; coolness; subtle lighting. Not so many people that you couldn't see the paintings at all, but enough that you did a fair bit of dodging back and forth, barging in, sidling past, to the accompaniment of buzzing and droning earphones. In Amsterdam, in the vast, lofty barnlike hall of the Rijksmuseum, I couldn't concentrate on the Rembrandts and Vermeers I'd come especially to see, that time with Carmen, for the hordes of people massing in front of every painting and taking pictures with their mobile phones. You couldn't relate to the paintings. They were obscured by the hordes and of course I was part of the horde. In the end I escaped to the smaller side galleries, almost empty of people, where I could look in peace at works by 'lesser' masters and not feel distracted. The same thing happened at the Van Gogh Museum, noisy with sound installations. There were too many explicatory panels of text, too many reproductions and photographs, too many lectures being given, too many maps and family trees. We were getting the Van Gogh Experience. Dodging to and fro you occasionally glimpsed actual paintings. Actual paint. Not until we went into the Matisse exhibition next door at the museum of modern art was there quietness and the chance to stand in front of a picture and just concentrate on it.

In front of me, here in the first room of the Bonnard show at the Musée d'Orsay, a young man was darting along not looking at a single picture except to focus his camera on it, snap it.

Afterwards he'd be able to prove he'd seen it. He couldn't trust his own eyes. Perhaps he felt nervous at the prospect of having to look at a picture, that there was a correct way to do it that he didn't know. Taking a photo let him stay in control. Looking at a picture takes time. You have to abandon yourself to it, let it work on you. That can be very unsettling, scary perhaps, even overwhelming. You can't make that happen. You have to let go, let it happen. Rather like sex. Perhaps that's the attraction of S&M sex, you can feel in control whether you're the top or the bottom, you're contained by a mutually agreed set-up, you don't have to hazard spontaneity, be taken by surprise. You don't have to practise Negative Capability! And yet I know the best sex I've ever had came out of a sense of freedom, a give and take equality between partners playing together and within that a relaxation, a not worrying or straining, moments of change, moments of comedy, liking the other person a lot, who always was someone who could talk and joke in bed as well as touch. The one time someone tried to get me to whip him I half-heartedly had a go, was useless at it, couldn't bear it, ended up hating him for being masochistically controlling.

So painting isn't simply about controlling the brush and the paint, it's about embodying, letting be embodied, a relationship with the paint, the canvas. Same with looking at pictures. Jim used to stress looking at paintings as paint, you didn't need to read labels, you concentrated on the non-linguistic language of paint, let it speak to you as itself. He believed that good painting revealed itself to anyone who opened up to it. You didn't need an art history academic education, he insisted. But perhaps you needed a Jim to remind you of that, to give you the confidence to trust your own eyes, your own self, taking in the picture, letting it talk to you in its own way on its own terms. Certainly that had been one of his gifts to me. Look at the paint! Look at the paint! Thanks, Jim.

Bonnard's paint shimmered and gleamed, bringing alive Marthe's flesh in the water in her bath in the room irradiated by golden light, transfigured by it. One room was hung with nothing but paintings of Marthe in her bath. You spun round seeing one Marthe mirror another, and another, a whirl of pink yellow purple gold. And there was the cherry tree, the last picture Bonnard painted before he died, in full blossom. A film near the entrance to the show featured Bonnard as a young man boating with friends, picnicking with friends. He wore the same big round glasses he wore as an older man, that I remembered from the photographs of him at Le Cannet. Here he was, smiling, at the beginning of his life as a painter, reaching out to the world.

We found a side-street café in the *7ième* for lunch, sitting outdoors at a pavement table tucked beneath the shallow awning, nudging our chairs in under it, towards the nearby counter, to avoid the scorch of the sun. Whiteness dazzled just beyond us. The entire front of the café was open, waiters dashed in and out, passers-by knocked against our table, Val had thin golden chips with her salad, I had a glass of wine with mine.

We walked back along a street parallel to the quays, keeping close in to the shopfronts, the running strip of shade they offered. I was idly looking for a birthday present for Carmen, the red and white checked tablecloth she'd mentioned she wanted, which was my excuse to dive into exclusive fabrics and furnishings shops and flick over piles of antique tea towels at thirty euros each, antique cushion covers and antimacassars and bedspreads. No red-checked tablecloths: no longer in fashion. Or perhaps not high-class enough. One haughty, well-corseted shopkeeper with sculpted hair and too much rouge, stroking a piece of antique damask (an aristocratic floor cloth?) addressed us with such disdain we turned and fled.

We gazed at the windows of toyshops, print shops, engravings shops. I spotted a letter by Colette for sale, some sort of reference written for a friend, signed with her married name de Jouvenel, that's to say the name of her second husband – she had three. (Nana once said, possibly quoting someone else: every woman owes it to herself to get married, but once is enough, you don't have to overdo it.) A square of nice thick white writing paper; black ink; strong loops of her handwriting. Val whipped out her phone and photographed it for me.

We debouched eventually into St Germain and walked along the Rue de Seine, first to pay homage to George Sand, who briefly lived here when she first came up from the Berry to chance her luck in Paris as a writer, and then to salute Simone de Beauvoir, who used to stay at the Hotel Louisiane and relish not having to do her own cooking. I'd stayed here a couple of times, once with Jim and once when making a *Night Waves* programme. Both times I slept badly, since at 5am the refuse lorry came round, causing a crashing of bins. I remembered peeping down at the street from the window, spotting a man with a white pet rat on his shoulder. I remembered the market setting up below, and buying mini spinach quiches and raspberries for a lunchtime picnic.

Val took photographs for me again. As an aide-memoire I always used a notebook, snatching it out when necessary and scribbling down images, bits of found language. Now I wanted to record the images directly. A tiny phone-camera, that was what I wanted, matchbox-sized, to be held in the palm of my hand, invisible to onlookers. As invisible as I myself longed to be on this trip.

We made our way back towards the Odéon metro stop, discussing the plan for tomorrow. A visit to the *puces* (flea market) at Clignancourt, lunch out somewhere, more wandering, and then the train home. And now – showers, an aperitif, dinner, bed.

CHAPTER 5
AUGUST

One Day In Evron

Yesterday morning I woke up at seven to the cheep-cheep of the alarm. The rain had at last stopped drumming on the Velux windows, after a night of violent storms that had begun the evening before. A hot, humid wind had blown in my face as I sat on the front step at nightfall, and the owl flapped out of her owl-hole just above the kitchen and flew off across the field opposite, and cows bellowed in the distance, and then *claque!* A thunderclap banged immediately overhead, lightning flashed repeatedly, the rain fell in torrents, and I dashed about unplugging the phone and the laptop. Then I fetched a chair and sat at the open front door, watching the light-show.

I would have welcomed more sleep but I wanted to get some writing done before going off mid-morning to market, also a man from the bank was due to ring me at 9.30am about insuring the new (second-hand) car now sitting in the open-faced shed I call a garage. I had spent much time on the phone to the bank in previous days, pinging my way through the robots before being shuttled from one human being to another, each saying different and often contradictory things about how to tackle the various steps in the insurance procedure, which I'd forgotten about having purchased my previous car so many years before, each adviser in turn being stumped by my not having the Internet. It hasn't seemed worth paying the extra for broadband here, since I visit so erratically, for such fluctuating lengths of time, but people in offices do get annoyed if you do not reply to their emails sharpish, and then to their emails enquiring whether you got their emails, so I suppose I should buy that smartphone and receive my emails that way, though in fact it's hard to get a mobile signal here, because of the high hill and forest behind the house. I have to stand on the top front step and hold my ancient Nokia high in the air and hope for the best, which makes texting awkward, especially when it is night-time and raining. In fact most of the time I do not want to receive emails while I'm in France. I love being out of reach of them. I love being a part-time hermit: I feel free. I can call friends on my landline, after all.

If the landline is working, that is. For well over a year my landline didn't work, after winter storms, and France Orange just could not be bothered to send engineers to fix the blown-down cables. I had to keep walking to Béatrice's house, because the car wasn't working either, and phoning the helpline from there. Eventually they roused themselves. So now I had been able to telephone the bank, negotiate with its robots and eventually find a human being to talk to.

The meaning of Negative Capability certainly stretched to dealing with computerised switchboards and French bureaucracy. 'Irritable grasping after facts' would certainly not have helped. First of all, I was informed by the final adviser I spoke to, I had to send a registered letter to them, cancelling the old insurance and enclosing the *certificat de vente* (certificate of sale). Ah. I had not yet been paid for the car but had let the new owner, a New Zealander newly arrived two villages distant, take it away in Larry's trailer, since he wanted to get to work on it immediately, being an able mechanic, a welder by trade, and I being ignorant of the bureaucracy involved in selling a car in France had assumed that since I could trust the welder to cough up the cash sooner or later he might as well have the car now. I certainly had no certificate of sale. I'd have to fake one. I asked the adviser: can't I bring it in with me, can't I come and do the insurance in person? A kindly neighbour (Jim) will run me in. *Ah non, madame*, the letter must arrive via the post, it must be registered, and you will need to make an appointment with the insurance specialist, who, however, has no slots free until the 21st of August.

Zut alors! That was the week before I was due to go back to London, and the day on which I was having this conversation was only the 10th. So after some teeth-clicking on his part and some Keatsian deep breathing on mine we settled on a phone appointment to begin with.

I went outside, walked up past the house to survey the garden, the practice I'd learned from Bonnard, see what it had got up to overnight. Fresher and greener, thanks to the rain, after weeks of drought. The heat and dryness had ultimately been good for the harvest, safely got in. Various neighbours, dropping by, had all boasted how they'd finished well ahead of each other. Presumably they assumed I wouldn't compare their stories. Back indoors, I made a cup of coffee and began writing.

I propped the front door wide open with a rubber clog so that I could see out into the garden, the lane, gaze at the cherry tree.

At 9am Pierre whizzed past in his van, going on up the lane to check on his horses. He doesn't keep heifers in that top field, as Ambroise did. I don't know why. Perhaps horses are less trouble. He waved to me, exactly as Ambroise used to do. On his way back, ten minutes later, he halted the van, so I went out. He rolled down the window and handed me three large marrows: my mother thought you'd like these, she knows you like marrows. I thanked him. I put the monsters in the *garde-manger* (meat-safe) in the storeroom, and went back to writing.

9.30am. Monsieur Jarré rang, bang on time. In a polite tone laced I thought with awful irony I thanked him for calling. He brushed this off: *pas de soucis*. (The French for *no worries*.) We had just got down to the business of confirming that, yes, it was exactly the same type of car as before needing insurance and certainly not at a higher cost, when we got cut off. I waited ten minutes, then rang the bank back, fought through the robots to a colleague of M. Jarré, who could not reach him, but who helpfully went off in search for him but could not find him, and who took my message asking him to ring me back later. Pouf!

I always relish Thursdays – market day in Evron – and I always go, if at all possible. However, without insurance I could not drive the new/second-hand car, and Jim, knowing this, had kindly offered to give me a lift and turned up on the dot of ten, as arranged. He consented to my bringing my bag of recycling in with me, for dumping in the big bins at the supermarket. There used to be rubbish bins and recycling bins at most cross-roads locally, which was handy, because you could walk there, and build dumping the rubbish into your evening stroll, but no more. Too expensive for the lorries to collect and empty the bins I suppose. Now we have to drive our stuff into the village and put it into the new mega-bins in the little housing estate next to the school. The first time I tried to do this I landed up in a cul-de-sac and just as I was executing my three point turn the mayor stepped out from behind a group of men watching some other men dig a hole, halted me, thrust his face in at the open car window close to mine. He is lean and rangy, with a big nose and black hair, my age or thereabouts, quite handsome until he opens his mouth revealing his brown teeth. Were you looking for me? he enquired with a tender tawny smile. No! I said, and zipped off.

A few years back, the mayor, once he heard I was newly divorced and presumably lonely, had begun turning up in the evenings, sometimes as late as 9pm, to check I was all right. One of the seven cardinal mayoral virtues: kindness to divorcées. Four kisses on the cheeks, deep searching looks, an insistent: can I help you with anything? What can I do for you? Actually I wanted him to ring France Orange on my behalf, tell them my landline was down, would they please send an engineer to put the cable back up. There it was dangling low in the trees, we could both see it swinging in the breeze. He promised to ring them, and left me his mobile number on a piece of paper: ring me any time. At first I didn't twig the mayor's intentions, I even invited him in for a glass of wine one night and chatted to him as I would to any neighbour. He began dropping round more often so I stopped offering him Kirs, took to talking to him first on the step and then down in the lane.

I'd reported these pastoral visits to Ambroise and Bénédicte one Sunday afternoon a year ago, when they'd invited me over for post-lunch coffee. Hmmm, said Ambroise: he fucks like a rabbit, that one, you be careful. As I left, Bénédicte dashed out into her vegetable patch, returned bearing three club-shaped marrows, which she handed to me with a smile. There you are! That'll keep you going for a bit! I thanked her, and she said: I'll keep you supplied, I've got a glut. How to tell her I didn't actually like marrows? Watery and tasteless I considered them. Why not pick them young and small as courgettes? Ambroise gazed at the marrows. You know what they remind me of? Bénédicte and I dutifully roared with laughter.

I got rid of the creepy mayor for ever one hot afternoon later that summer when he arrived to visit and I was piling the fallen branches of the apple tree down the hill in the meadow into the barrow. It is, or was, a large, beautifully shaped tree, a dome of green above a straight trunk. I remember looking at it one September, seeing how the apples still on it, among the curving green boughs, made a three-dimensional picture; and how, simultaneously, the apples fallen on the ground underneath it made a flat circular pattern of dots, in two dimensions. By falling, the apples transformed the image from three dimensions to two, you saw the vertical drop of the apples, falling, caught exactly in the shape of their horizontal pattern spread on the grass; like a strange shadow; the apples below simplified the perspective of the apples above. Two years back, as I've already mentioned, the apple tree had produced so much fruit that several big branches had cracked and broken under the weight, and then later Jean-Luc had pruned the tree for me and dumped the branches just anyhow, and I'd got as far as piling them near the trunk, out of the way of Fernand's cows, but disposing of them was yet another job I had neglected. I was red-faced and sweating and exhausted. I cried to the mayor: you want to help me? Help me haul these! He recoiled, got back into his car and sped away and did not return. It was Fernand who helped me, as I have said.

Although the recycling bag of plastic wrappings and empty bottles is always clean I don't like leaving it too long in the storeroom next to the kitchen, in case it attracts mice. The local mice are keen on plastic and will chomp through bottles of UHT milk if they feel really deprived of snacks. I put down mouse poison every time I go away, then sometimes the mice die in concealed places and I don't discover the corpses for months, and the room where they have died smells fusty and foul. The pine marten poo I had swept out of the former boiler cupboard, which opens off the guest room, had also left its traces, vaguely stinky. I had cleaned up using a powerful disinfectant, recommended by Tom and Caroline who had also had pine marten trouble, specially designed for rabbit hutches and poultry houses. The guest room now smelled like a very clean rabbit hutch, and although the label on the packet had mentioned that the disinfectant came with an overlay of lavender this was difficult to detect.

Jim arrived in his swish new car, easily four times the size of mine, and, luckily, fitted with air-conditioning; the day had heated up and become humid. As we cruised townwards Jim told me tales of his recent holiday in La Rochelle with his girlfriend Sue, their expeditions and adventures. Sue had subsequently travelled off to Albania, to her ex-husband's sixtieth birthday celebrations. She and I get on. Why wouldn't we? We both appreciate Jim. I get on well with Linda, his first wife, too.

In Evron we parked short of the market, near the bar where my neighbour Marie-Barbe and I go for an aperitif if we've been to the market together, a friendly bar patronised by locals from the nearby housing estate, where everyone shakes hands on entry and makes strangers like myself feel welcome. Before getting out of the car I suddenly needed to tell Jim about the Publisher's phone call the afternoon before. She had promised, back in early July, to read my novel in three weeks and then phone to talk, but had failed to do so, accordingly after three and a half weeks of anxious waiting I had rung her and left a message with her assistant. Perhaps the Publisher had mislaid my French phone number? Here it was again. Thank you so, so much.

The Publisher, prodded, did ring the following day. She apologised, she'd only read about half the novel so far and she didn't know when she'd have time to finish it, she was so busy, but, in any case, she'd begun finding the novel 'heavy' again, it was 'dreamy', the two intertwined narratives weren't exciting enough, the ghost story was perhaps too obvious, the market for novels was really bad, she was thinking of my career, what was I writing at the moment, oh, a memoir, and I was planning my next novel, about an artist, now she could see how she could sell those yes she could.

I thought, unfairly and childishly: she wants me to write two more books for her and then she'll reject those too. I had a memory-flash of my mother rejecting my novels one by one as

I published them, and yet for years I'd gone on hoping to please her, hoping one day I'd write a novel she'd like, and then finally thinking sod it, all that's over, it'll never happen so why bloody bother, I'd stopped caring what she thought of my work and just got on with doing it, but now here I was suddenly plunged back into those feelings of anguish at her disdain. But come on, I was no longer that abject daughter, I was a grown woman. I regained my courage and spoke firmly to the Publisher. I insisted she give me a specific date by which she'd have finished reading my novel and she said September 1st.

Underneath my bravado the old anxiety went on jumping up and down, the sneering voice whispering tee hee! We told you so! Sitting in Jim's car, telling him about the Publisher's call, I felt the pain revive. He listened as I blurted out a few words, trying hard not to cry. He was comforting, strengthening. You will survive this. You will get through this. You will.

As we walked towards the market the church bells began to ring, summoning people to the eleven o'clock Mass with a deep clanging and tumbling, a sound I have loved since my childhood holidays in that Norman cottage backing onto fields across which came every quarter of an hour the sound of the church bells. Evron is celebrated in tourist guides (*vaut le détour* – worth the detour) for its magnificent basilica, a palimpsest of Romanesque and Gothic, built to mark a staging post in the pilgrimage from Mont St Michel to Compostela. To the right of the massive, nail-studded wooden door marking the main entrance, a crescent of old houses adjoins a tiny square, where an archway frames a side door to the church. One day I saw two small, stocky ladies carting a huge basket full of vegetables towards one of these houses, so I stopped to help them. Sisters, surely, perhaps even twins: both had thickly curling grey hair and black eyebrows, and both wore blue-flowered overalls and tiny gold earrings. I carried their basket in. They pointed out the brightly painted Our Lady of Lourdes adorning the niche over their front door. There used to be an old statue of St James of Compostela there, one of them explained, but the landlord took it away, because it was so valuable, and so the nuns had a rummage in the convent attic and found us this replacement. I imagined rows of identical plaster Virgins under dusty eaves; the solid ghosts of ethereal nuns; the image haunted me, and finally found its way into my novel *Ignorance*.

The convent, a three-storeyed neo-classical eighteenth century building to the left of the basilica, fronts the main square. Hilary (she who gives me eau-de-vie made from her cider apples) and I used to joke: ah, this is where we'll spend our twilight years. Double wooden doors in the high wall, when open, reveal a large rectangular formal garden, flowerbeds, vegetable plots and walks laid out under fruit trees. The convent gatehouse used to display an oil painting of the Foundress, a stern lady in a frilled white cap and dark gown. For a while the portrait went missing, then it returned, restored, brightened up, as one of the nuns explained to Jim and me with a proud wave of the hand: look, we had a smile put on her face.

The numbers of nuns dwindled over the years. A few grey-haired figures in blue crimplene dresses and grey cardigans and clumpy shoes still scurried to and fro, eyes modestly cast down. Suzanne of the newsagent's in the row of nineteenth-century shops facing the basilica furiously described their limited lives:

they have to get permission just to come in and buy a biro!

Eventually the nuns were put out to grass and a phalanx of male Dominicans arrived, some of them simply monks, others monk-priests striding importantly about in flapping soutanes. One summer they conducted a mission to the outlying villages, including mine. People here may be *croyants* (believers), but most are too busy to go to church except on major feast-days or for weddings, funerals and baptisms, so I suppose that looked a bit slack to these eager chaps who, following modern modernising charismatic Catholic fashion, longed to reconvert lazy believers and make of them keen *pratiquants* of an austere and purified sort, henceforth non-reliant on wayside shrines to the Virgin, miraculous statues of saints, sacred wells and holy relics and other folkloric paraphernalia.

Until recently, many people here, not just the older generation either, used to consult witches and wizards. At village level there continued a subculture of esoteric practices, the Mayenne having remained a little pocket of old beliefs, for example a pregnant woman might ask the advice not only of her gynaecologist but also her local soothsayer or shaman, phoning both from her home quite matter-of-factly one after the other, as I was once told by my neighbour Patrice's wife Clémence who worked as a rural midwife; and people routinely queued up outside the house of the local witch/wise woman to ask for her help. It's quite normal to possess these gifts. For example Marie-Barbe, who lives near me at the top of the hill beyond the forest, has clairvoyant capacities for finding things, she explained to me one day over an aperitif: she swings her watch over a paper sketch of your house and garden, which you have given her, and discovers in which abandoned corner you dropped your purse or locket or whatever it may be. Marie-Barbe would certainly have been had up by St Dominic as a heretic and hauled before the Inquisition, though mostly as we know that belligerent stamper-out of disobedience stayed down in the south of France investigating the Albigensian heresy and having Cathars cast into the flames. The heretics here lay lower than did their unfortunate *confrères* around Carcassonne, perhaps hiding when necessary in the tiny fields and narrow lanes of the *bocage* (hedged fields) whenever a crucifix-flourishing bishop or Dominican hove into view, and seem mainly to have escaped torture and early death and to have been able to pass on their beliefs to their descendants.

So I was sitting reading in my garden one afternoon when a red-faced, white-robed monk panted up the hill to the house. I offered him a chair, gave him a glass of water and told him I recognised him as a Dominican immediately because of his habit. He exclaimed: you're the only person I've met round here who knows what Dominican robes look like! I longed for him to try to reconvert me, so that I could expound the feminist heresy espoused by my friend Patricia, her concept of the Virgin not only as God-bearer, as conventional Catholicism named her, but also, crucially, as an aspect of God, but he was too hot and tired for theological discussion and so I let him off. I was very impressed he had walked so far. He confessed that in fact he had come by car, but left it down on the side road. Off he went. Perhaps he popped in chez Béatrice and reconverted her. At any rate it was not long after his appearance in the district that she began neglecting her husband and housework in order to train as a *compagnon de deuil* (lay funeral helper), taking funerals and accompanying the mourners to the cemetery.

Shortly after the nuns were booted out of their fine convent in Evron and the Dominicans swept in, the local *mairie* (town hall) decided to smarten the place up. The basilica square has been pedestrianised, with nasty pinkish-grey paving stones glittering in the sunlight, and a nasty municipal water feature, huge slabs of tilted concrete, whose water is rarely turned on. A few dull shrubs sprout from black boxes. Tubs of skinny oleanders surround the outdoor tables and chairs of the café to one side, whose owner offers free Wi-Fi, so can pull in a larger clientele than the proprietors of the other café further along, which has just gone bust. This latter café, set back from the street, half-veiled on Thursdays by the flower and plant stall, had blue paint and nautical décor, ropes and seashells and photographs of bulging-muscled sailors in leather vests and thongs all up the stairs. The middle-aged male locals used to gather on the *terrasse* here, drinking elevenses of white wine and gossiping, enjoying what Jim and I called their men's group. The café-owner's ancient Labrador padded about, a red-spotted kerchief tied around his neck. In front of the café shoppers meandered to and fro, choosing lettuce seedlings and bunches of young leeks for planting out, and here too, much to the absorbed interest of passing children, the bearded, moustachioed, ringleted, beret-sporting knife-grinder manned his machine, next to the stall of the pork butcher, whose paper bags bore a design of happy, smiling piglets rearing on their hind legs next to their happy, smiling mother, clearly none of them having a clue that they would shortly be entering the abattoir to be turned into sausages.

Acknowledging the piglets' fate did not stop me from buying the pork-butcher's *saucisson* and rillettes. Paulette and my other women neighbours would have scorned to buy rillettes. They made their own. I used to go and do Paulette's ironing for her on Thursday afternoons, in the days when she still farmed locally and lived near me in a rented fifteenth-century house. It was formerly a small convent, the chapel turned into a storeroom and a tunnel leading from a vaulted opening in the farmyard all the way to the church of St Martin in the next village, used, said Paulette, by local priests fleeing persecution during the Terror in 1792. One winter day, the pig having been killed the week before, an operation I had witnessed just as I drove in to the farmyard, slung up by its heels on a forklift truck and its throat cut, spouting a fountain of blood, Paulette put me in charge of stirring the rillettes, simmering in a cauldron in her high-ceilinged kitchen, with a wooden spoon long and thick as an oar, while she got on with some work outside. After several hours, the pork having melted off the bones, the rillettes were poured into earthenware pots, the pork fat cooling to seal the tops. Tasting rillettes for the first time I remembered how as children in Edgware we loved scraping up the dripping from the pan, after a Sunday roast of pork, with crusts of bread, sprinkling the dark jellied grease with salt.

Gaps in the rows of market stalls showed where people had gone on holiday. The egg and chicken seller, for example. I have known her for the twenty-three years I've been here, watched her hair turn from black to grey, her two daughters turn from toddlers into teenagers. Her birds, properly fed, are lean and muscular from having been allowed to run about in a field, good and tasty when pot-roasted. I'd cooked one the previous week, when I invited Paulette and her husband Roger and Marie-Barbe to lunch. I made *poulet à l'estragon*, with extra tarragon added to the sauce of stock and cream thickened with an egg yolk and flecked with grated lemon peel that was poured also over the boiled potatoes, the latter cut into barrel shapes exactly as my Norman aunt Brigitte instructed me many years ago. To begin with we had a dish of long scarlet white-tipped radishes, trimmed of their whiskers but with a tuft of green stalk left on the ends, since that looks pretty and also makes it easier to pick up each radish and dip it into the butter, in Paulette's case, and into the salt, in mine. (The cut-off radish leaves I had eaten a day back as salad.) Alongside the radishes we had a slab of pâté I didn't let on I hadn't made myself but had bought from the piglet-butcher in the market. Then we ate halved hardboiled eggs, the yolks mashed up with home-made green mayonnaise (parsley, chervil, tarragon, sorrel) then stuffed back into the whites and topped with anchovies, on a bed of grated carrots with vinaigrette (these eggs a retro recipe from M. Pellaprat's 1950s cookery book I'd inherited from my mother), then the chicken, then green salad, then cheese, then a compote of cherries and plums from the garden. As she kissed me goodbye Paulette said: well, I think we can say now that you do actually know how to cook. Roger protested: she knew how to cook before coming here! Marie-Barbe merely lifted an eyebrow. She never dared criticise Paulette to her face, though in private she'd say to me, the girls in our village rather looked down on the girls from Paulette's hamlet. Paulette said: no, but you have learned well everything I taught you. Roger said: but has she got another *petit copain* (boyfriend) to cook for? That's what I want to know! Paulette shouted at him to be quiet. I said *non*.

Paulette had not given me cookery lessons as such, the closest I ever came to being her sous-chef my stirring of her rillettes and my attempting to catch snails for her and my accompanying her on *cèpes*-foraging expeditions in the forest. When visiting her I picked up her *trucs et astuces*, her thrifty tips, for example making vegetable stock from bean pods and parsley stalks, putting the coarse outer leaves of lettuces into soup, picking young dandelion leaves for salad (never after the plants had flowered, when the leaves grew bitter), and at her house I had feasted on treats such as sweetbreads, or rabbit roasted under a coat of mustard, or stuffed trotters. I'd stopped accepting invitations to lunch chez Béatrice after she served calf's head brawn, horribly gristly and chewy, preceded by her sister-in-law's gift of a glut of artichokes, ditto.

Paulette is of that older generation that still bottles fruit and vegetables for winter consumption, makes terrines and pâtés, crème de cassis, Pineau, conserves and jams. The hard-pressed younger women have much less time for such labour. They usually work as book-keepers for the farms, and since EU regulations now demand ever more form filling, they spend their days hunched over computers when not cleaning, gardening, taking care of children and of course shopping and cooking. No wonder they turn increasingly to convenience foods. The supermarkets, obliged by French law to stock a certain amount of locally produced fresh food, now display more and more shelves of plastic-sealed ready meals and salads, industrially produced chicken breasts, fizzy drinks, etc. Super U also has a shelf of Foreign Food for the expats, featuring Marmite, Branston pickle, Bird's custard powder and English Breakfast tea.

The supermarkets on the Evron ring road circle the town like hungry wolves, gobbling up the smaller shops. The town's bookshop has closed, along with Suzanne's newsagent's shop, the children's clothes shop, the gift shops. Super U now has a bookshop section: a rack of magazines, a few paperbacks. You can't buy a postcard anywhere. The shops reopen on brief leases, selling electrical goods, then close again. The two good *boulangeries* remain, plus one butcher's, one delicatessen, the shoe-mender's, and the dress shop selling 1980s-style feminine fashions in strange colour combos and shapes.

On Thursdays in spring and summer troops of English schoolchildren, on educational visits, patrol the market, doing their shopping in groups, looking both excited and baffled, I imagine because back home they are probably not asked to help with the shopping, which is very likely ordered online and delivered by lorry and now they have got to budget, decide on menus, choose one type of peach over another. The stallholders are wonderfully patient with them as they dither and shuffle and check their palms full of loose change and elbow each other to be the ones to do the talking. In particular, one small black-haired man, with a neat black moustache, dances to and fro behind his ranked trays of avocado pears, snow-white closely packed mushrooms and neat clusters of cherry tomatoes and always smiles and sings out please and thank you and makes you feel how utterly delighted he is to be serving you. The schoolchildren buy from him because he is so non-threatening, so friendly, and the townspeople tolerate queuing behind these gangling foreigners with shy mumbled French because the black-haired man dispatches their business with such rapidity as well as charm, and so he does good business and keeps everybody happy. Next to him the red-cheeked cheese man is equally friendly, but at greater length, chatting slowly, helping you make up your mind, discussing the merits of this well-matured Comté over that, so that you must not feel impatient when approaching his stall nor indeed during the long wait to be served. To while away the time you can study the droll labels, adorned with comic poems, on certain cheeses. Vierge Folle (Mad Virgin), for example, comes with a rhymed warning: don't leave me too long, take me now, don't let me turn sour and curdled with waiting, etc etc.

Arriving in the market, Jim and I, as usual, followed our own separate rituals. He went off to the Wi-Fi café, iPad under his arm, and I shopped for vegetables.

The small-scale vegetable merchants, selling their own locally grown produce, have all been pushed into the little square in front of the new cinema, which has a huge beaked prow, useful I suppose as shelter on rainy days if you are waiting to be let in to one of the American blockbusters that are mainly the only films that get shown, similarly on TV, Paulette's afternoon soaps being always American ones from the 1980s, strangely dubbed, featuring agonised blondes with tempestuous hairstyles and well-groomed men in blue suits. If I visit her too soon after lunch I have to sit in silence and watch, Paulette explaining the plot to me as it goes along, until finally the episode finishes and Paulette lets out a sigh of pleasure.

My favourite stall in this bit of the market is run by a blue-aproned daughter and her majestic, overalled mother, who is referred to by her daughter never as Maman but always as La Patronne. La Patronne never used to appear on market days. It was her husband who did, he of the handsome brown face, the big belly bulging over his blue workman's trousers, the quick chat and jokes, whom I put into my novel *The Mistressclass*, wishing to celebrate and cherish him. However, he has vanished, and presumably has died, though I can't ask whether that's so, since that would seem intrusive and rude, also just in case he has not died at all but has run off with some fetching divorcée sporting the lingerie featured in the windows of Gougeon Modes, all pointy bras in black and purple rayon with matching briefs. On the dot of twelve, as the bells rang out, this merry man would stop work and make for the café and a pastis, leaving his daughter to serve tardy customers on her own. Most stalls began packing up at midday, when people drifted home to lunch, and the rubbish-sucking machine, called Le Glutton, complete with rustic birch broom tucked to one side, made its appearance on the street.

La Patronne exclaimed irritably *eh b'en toi!* (Really! You!) when I asked for two lettuces, round green silky ones, proper lettuces, no not dark red oak-leaf, which she was obviously trying to get rid of, but then she mellowed, recognising me as a faithful client, and put in an extra lettuce free. The black-haired, rosy-cheeked, sturdy daughter, slinging green beans onto the scale, chats to me if she has time. One day she told me how much she loved driving the lorry to market. The bigger the lorry the better!

From other stalls here I bought a couple of sheep's milk yoghurts, a pot of cream and a pat of butter, a walnut-studded sourdough loaf, a dozen eggs. Nearby, the *bio* (organic) stall, run by two pretty women, with grey hair, dark eyebrows and youthful, fresh-skinned faces, had attracted a cheerful queue. They sold both vegetables and salad plants. Local people growing their own greenstuffs have always been able to eat produce free from insecticides and dodgy fertilisers. Now organic food is being sold in markets too, and even in supermarkets such as Super U, sections of its shelves catering for the most precious of food faddists, which I fear the (bourgeois) French have always been, with their devotion to liver-cleansing sessions at spas, disgusting tisanes drunk after supper, and *régimes maigres* (light, meat-free diets) such as those detailed in my mother's old cookery books. In fact the examples given by Madame Saint-Ange in *La Bonne Cuisine* of four-course *maigre* lunch menus (such as *moules à la marinière, quartiers d'artichauts au riz, carottes à la crème, tarte aux fraises*) made you understand why if you regularly ate the *gras*, non-*maigre* ones twice a day (different only in that they included meat dishes) you might indeed need after a while to visit a spa and be put on a strict regime. Here at Evron market the faddism was not much in evidence, if you ignored the single stall selling esoteric salts and teas and supplements and soaps like pumice stones for getting rid of spots.

The *bio* stall simply offered seasonal veg such as spuds and carrots not coated in poisons. It signalled its status with a big bunch of red, purple and pink gladioli in a pottery jug. As well as wooden trays of seedlings ready for putting into your own potager, the two fresh-faced women sold parsley, also basil, the purple and the green, laid out in open baskets, with a red and orange still life of peppers and gourds nearby, but I couldn't face the wait required, as they talked everyone through their purchases of shallots and onions, recommended particular growing plans to suit particular gardens, enquired after the health of great-aunts and grandchildren, and generally acted like two lay saints.

Instead I approached the nearby equally *bio* but much smaller stall of the melancholy blonde next to them. She never has a queue because she always looks so sad, though beautiful, and people must imagine her vegetables infected by her gloom and so steer clear of them and her. For years I have paused at her stall, have bought bunches of garlic and handfuls of gherkins, have cracked jokes trying to cheer her up, which is egotistical and arrogant of me I daresay, since why should she necessarily be cheery to customers, we haven't bought her along with the uneven tomatoes and black-eyed potatoes, have we, so why should I expect that as well as being given some small, brown-flecked pods of peas I also qualify to receive a dazzling beam of delight? Still I persevere. She wins every time, listlessly putting a couple of small cucumbers into a brown paper bag, glancing indifferently at the coins I proffer, looking past my shoulder as I say *merci, au revoir*.

The poet John Burnside, during that British Council trip to Germany years back when I invented the luggage-spotting game at the airport carousel, explained to me late one night over drinks in the bar of our hotel in Berlin the allure of *la belle dame sans merci*, who by coldly withholding her favours challenges men and makes them run after her. I'd never managed this. When I fancied men I let them know, I courted them, I wrote them poems, I asked them out to lunch, and quite soon afterwards, if they accepted the invitation to a date, I suggested they come to bed with me. Whether or not rejection ensued, or disaster, or pleasure, I was clear that female desire might pre-date that of the male or at least meet it halfway. Heavens above, French literature indicated this, being full of female would-be seducers, whether or not they came to sticky ends as unfortunately they often do in opera, nineteenth-century opera at least, as Catherine Clément brilliantly pointed out in her book on the subject.

Sarah was telling me recently about a young female literature academic she knows who has just discovered Doris Lessing's novels, in particular *The Golden Notebook*, and was intrigued by her heroine's view that the male gaze alone creates female desire. Sarah and I both said: no no no! Lessing was writing in pre-second wave feminist times, spouting smooth 1950s ideology not difficult female truth. Quite rightly she disliked being seen as a feminist since she wasn't one, even though she wrote about female sexuality, which was indeed daring for the times. Her heroine Ella is introduced to the clitoral orgasm by her male lover, and dislikes it, since she feels he is less committed touching her with his hand than plunging his cock deep inside her and thereby, accorded to the male wisdom of the time, giving her the only true orgasm, the 'purely emotional', vaginal one, and I remember feeling worried by this when I first read it as a young woman since though I could come easily on my own I couldn't come with a male lover from penetration alone and thought there must be something deeply wrong with me.

I wasn't a Real Woman. Then aged twenty-three I met lovely Freddy, who matter-of-factly touched my clitoris while we fucked, and I was amazed how easy coming with him was. One night he explained that while waiting for me to come he held off his own orgasm by thinking about school sport or the football results; anything erotic wouldn't have done the trick. His openness first disconcerted then charmed me.

Later, by which time I sometimes had 'vaginal' orgasms if lovemaking went on long enough, reading *Our Bodies Ourselves*, I learned that all orgasms were clitoral, since the vagina has no nerve endings. Perhaps, like other women in those pre-feminist times, Lessing believed the male Freudian pundits on feminine psychology who ruled that the penis was everything for both sexes, the magical totem that swept you romantically away, and that the clitoral orgasm was childish and inferior, though nowadays the new orthodoxy instructs us that an orgasm is an orgasm is an orgasm, and we should come in whatever way we fancy, a wank or a spank, sex is all about technique far more than emotion, you just tell your lover what to do and get on with it.

Today the *bio* ice queen fingered two heads of garlic towards me, received my money, shrugged, sighed, returned to looking like an anchorite on a very high-up pillar. She refused to smile. Would she have smiled for John Burnside? Perhaps a twitch of the lip and then he'd write her a poem. I found I was holding a conversation with him in my head. Perhaps fancying ice queens is all about mothers who were too stern; some men love being reminded of their childhood adoration of the mother who pushed them away and told them to grow up and turn into

Real Men, problematic as that status has become in recent years thanks to the poking and probing of feminists at gender categorisation. Freud can be accused not only of getting it wrong about women's pleasure but also of having reductive attitudes to our psychic lives, since not everybody wants to be too often reminded of their mothers and their childhood fantasies, as for example my ex-lover Jack certainly did not. Yet when I seek to understand why some men like women being nasty to them rather than nice, it is to thoughts of unconscious desire, as expounded by Freud, that I turn.

I continued my tour of the little square. A new vegetable seller, a slender young man with dark curly hair and dark eyes fringed by dark lashes, had appeared. On his plywood table the size of a butler's tray he had laid out a dish containing three cucumbers and some tiny new potatoes, two bowls of blackberries, and a few tomatoes. Impossible not to smile at him. He smiled back, told me about permaculture, mixing vegetables with flowers, discussed mulching with grass cuttings, and happily sold me one large tomato.

Madame Trôo, the dark-haired, aquiline, bright-eyed seller of pelargoniums and petunias, hydrangeas in pots, and plugs of culinary herbs, had spread out her shallow boxes of plants on the ground, leaving tiny paths between them, so that you could walk through the marigolds and salvias as though you were a giant in a fairy's garden. Her husband, who runs a gardening business, had come to La Lièvrerie one rainy springtime twenty years back to give Jim and me an estimate for helping us hack our way through the ten-foot high wilderness of brambles behind Jim's studio barn. Monsieur Trôo's lorry got stuck in the mud, as he tried to turn at the top of the lane, and it took us a long time to push him out, while he swore mightily *putain bordel!* and revved and pulled at the wheel and eventually lurched free and then decided he didn't want the job after all and roared away back down the hill. Madame Trôo's tall, slender daughter, with wavy dark hair and big dark eyes, who now helps on the stall, looks very like her mother. Their beauty has nothing to do with make-up. Both have faces and arms burned brown by working outdoors in the sun. They wear blue cloth money bags tied round their slender waists and dart nimbly between the pots of flowers, deftly selecting blooms and giving change and always knowing who's next in the milling queue.

Nearby, the beekeeper, another pretty woman, with blue eyes, her greying blonde hair knotted up behind her head, and a flowered scarf tucked into the neck of her blue jersey, was selling her various honeys, beeswax candles and bars of soap, jars of royal jelly, beeswax ornamental hearts stamped with patterns of arabesques. At her stall I ran into Marie-Barbe, my neighbour gifted in clairvoyance. A small, sprightly woman, with bobbed hair dyed rich auburn, she has weathered two husbands. Her first, Maurice, was a humorous, solidly built, square-faced man who always wore blues. He taught me some gardening, some digging and forking techniques, and he used to come down to my garden in early spring to pick dandelion leaves for his rabbits if I wasn't around to pick them for my own salads, also to feed the cat when we were away. A wild little creature Jim tamed who stayed around for several years, she'd bound out to greet us when we arrived from England, accompany us on winter walks through the snow up to the forest then at night leap onto Jim's lap to be absentmindedly stroked as he sat by the fire playing *Tomb Raider*. Thus one night he discovered that she was in fact a male: such was the bliss of Jim's caresses that a little pink penis stuck right out.

In our absence, kind Maurice would fill up the cat's food bowl from the store of biscuits we'd left in a shed. His trouble was drink. When we visited him and Marie-Barbe he'd disappear into his own shed to take nips from his stash. I found it hard at first to understand his mix of patois and French, his broad accent, then got used to it. He said of Paulette: *c'est une bonne fille, mais il faut être sur sa branche* (She's a great girl, but you need to be on her side). He died of liver disease. A while later, Marie-Barbe began going out to tea dances in the afternoons, or to lotto, much to Paulette's disapproval.

I always stuck up for Marie-Barbe. What was she supposed to do with her free time once she'd finished her housework and gardening and cleaned out the rabbit cages and fed her hens, just twiddle at crochet and watch daytime TV? Heavens above she'd laboured all her life as a cleaner, including doing some of Paulette's housework, which was how I first met her one day in mid-December when I turned up chez Paulette to do the ironing but was asked to help instead with hanging up paper chains ready for Christmas and spotted near the Christmas tree a small thin fairy high up on a ladder in the barn-sized living room swiping with a mop at cobwebs far above our heads. As far as I was concerned she had a perfect right to go out and enjoy herself. That day she fought back with her mop a flock of geese advancing on me hissing and writhing their necks, as I crossed the farmyard to reach my car, and she laughed and danced to and fro, relishing her battle with the great gander, and made me see how she seized every chance for a spot of fun. At one of the tea dances she met her second husband, who turned out also to have a drink problem. She nursed him through successive bouts of illness, as she'd nursed Maurice, then when he in turn died she went on going out dancing but decided not to marry again. As Jim used to say in his mock-awful French: *assez est assez!*

After Jim and I split up I continued to visit Marie-Barbe, and during these tête-à-têtes got to know her better, so that after a while we began discussing our love lives, or the lack of them, over aperitifs in her kitchen, while her lunch bubbled in the pressure cooker on the stove. All my farmer neighbours ate beef or pork every day, which was far more often, they conceded, than their parents would have done, but now everybody raised cattle for meat as well as milk, and also raised pigs for the supermarkets, that was the way of things, so they had a grilled chop or some stew most days for lunch, with vegetables and salad, and at night soup made from leftover veg plus perhaps rillettes and saucisson. My friend Michel, Bertrand's father, ate rillettes or saucisson for breakfast too. Christian, Béatrice's husband, never ate vegetables at all.

Marie-Barbe could safely confide in me because I was an outsider, with an unconventional life, though I lacked witch skills, and I didn't gossip, and certainly relished a drink. During the recent months when I hadn't had a car she kindly gave me a lift to market a couple of times, as I've mentioned. While I dawdled, admiring hand-carved wooden hinged butter pats or Laguiole penknives or coral-pink flounced muslin skirts, or women's blue-flowered and blue-striped overalls all in slightly different patterns, looking like something Matisse might have liked to paint, as well as doing my usual vegetable shopping, she costed two-kilo bags of apples at the fruit stall, good for preserves, never ever buying something just on impulse as I so often did, presents to take back to friends in England, whether beeswax candles and pots of acacia honey from the bee-woman or packs of traditional blue-checked handkerchiefs from the drapery stall. After the market we'd go and have aperitifs at her favourite bar, that one I have already mentioned where all the customers knew each other and shook hands with everyone when they came in, and then she would drop me home, gracefully accepting, after a short argument, some money for petrol, pleased I think to know I didn't want to exploit her neighbourliness. Now, she and I agreed we would have an *apéro* together soon. Ring first, she warned me: don't just turn up, you know I'm always out.

The seafood stall was selling whelks, sea snails, heaps of mussels and prawns, the latter piled up on ice. Live crabs lay on wet seaweed slowly waving their claws partially constrained by string. I wondered about buying mussels and cooking *moules à la marinière*. Brigitte, my Norman aunt, taught me how to make that fishwife's dish. You put the mussels in a colander and scrubbed and rinsed them under running water, discarding any open or cracked ones, never leaving them in to soak or else they'd open and release their lovely juice, and at the same time pulling off their beards with a sharp knife. You steamed them in a large heavy closed pot with some finely chopped onion and a little garlic, a glass of Muscadet, and a handful of minced parsley. After a few minutes you seized the pot in both hands and shook it well. You did not add cream, as some British restaurants do, as that spoiled the clean fresh taste, and nor did you add butter, as Mme Saint-Ange recommends when she gives her *methode Charentaise*. You served the opened mussels in soup plates and ate them with your fingers, tearing apart the hinged blue shells and using one shell to scoop out the bright yellow morsel nestling in the other, and then spooned up your sea-water broth. Exquisite. The used shells were exquisite too, gleaming blue-black. I used to wash them and keep them, since I always meant to make a mosaic with them, but never did. This often happened: brilliant-seeming ideas for artworks I was too lazy or feeble to implement. I strewed the mussel shells on the path through the woodland behind Jim's studio, as a weed suppressant. Then a year ago I'd been writer-in-residence for a few days at the five-star Le Royal Monceau in Paris, newly refurbished and interiorly designed by Philippe Starck, and there at the entrance to the terrace restaurant was a fine mural made of mussel shells, a baroque-inspired abstract featuring the shells' insides and outsides both. *Chapeau, maître!* However, the food was dire. The chef, when he showed me round his kitchen, where the only woman present was stamping full stop-sized pieces out of mint leaves and looking depressed, explained to me that the super-rich super-thin clientele liked super-minimalism, the gloop favoured by certain American film stars, which meant that plates arrived artfully decorated with a few drops of this paste or a few drops of that paste, a few dots of mint, with possibly a seared non-gluten crumb parked alongside, and that was dinner. They certainly weren't serving any item as large as an entire mussel.

Jim and I met up, as arranged, at the Wi-Fi café, and decided to pay a visit to the basilica, as we always did if we came to market together, to admire the stained-glass Gothic windows of the nave, the fourteenth- and fifteenth-century polychrome statues of Mother and Child posed on plinths, the glass-cased wax effigies of martyrs with slit throats. We entered the little Romanesque side chapel, stone below and brick above, some of its decorative brick zigzags picked out in lines of red paint, the fresco on the inside of the dome high above the altar depicting a huge Christ in majesty surrounded by emblems of the four Evangelists, also done in red. To the left of the altar sits a thirteenth-century Virgin, coated in silver from the neck down. She used to have a dark face, and I believed she was one of the Black Virgins who some scholars suggest evoke ancient goddesses such as Aphrodite, but the resident priests disbelieved this heretical notion and declared she was simply dirty and needed the soot removing from her cheeks, and banished her for cleaning. She returned pink as a cooked prawn. Her official title is Madonna of the Hawthorn, and the story goes that a pilgrim, returning from Jerusalem with a sacred relic, a leather bag full of the Virgin's breast milk, took a nap under a hawthorn bush, hanging the precious bag on one of its branches. When he awoke the bush had grown into a tree so that the bag was out of reach, so in despair he prayed to the Virgin and she, being the opposite of an ice queen, kindly leaned out of heaven and bent down the branch. So he got his bag back and in gratitude donated money to good causes. I put the silver-coated Madonna and the legend of the hawthorn into *The Mistressclass*, and also recorded the book, set on a table in front of the wrought-iron screen separating benches from sanctuary, in which people could write down their supplications to the heavenly mother, and very touching many of these were. Jim and I bought candles, costing one euro each, tall thin tapers we lit then drove onto spikes on the black iron stand, and then sat in the pews for a little while.

A candle, its flame darting upwards, symbolises the prayer you make rising towards heaven. You leave the still-burning candle behind you when you depart, to continue representing, despite your absence, what Catholics call your intentions. Catholics say to one another, or used to in pre-Renewal days: I'll pray for your intentions. Over the years, despite being an ex-believer, I've burned many candles for many intentions. My sister Margi, a practising Catholic, told me once she always prayed for Jim and me to get back together again, and when this failed, she prayed for me to meet another truly lovely man, and in fact, or perhaps as a result, I'd met several, because there were quite a few truly lovely men around, as Susan had tartly pointed out, and you simply had to understand how to show them you liked them, even if they could not always reciprocate, some of them married, some of them gay, some of them preferring you to pretend you didn't care, and some, of course, just not interested.

Lighting my candle I wondered, however, whether I did really want another lover. Love affairs with men, however truly lovely the men in question, did take up a lot of time and energy, especially if you had not perfected the *belle dame sans merci* method and especially if you had not obtained references beforehand but just plunged romantically in and certainly especially if the men were married, as my dear farmer had been, and as Jack had been, at least part-time, when he was not being separated. I didn't notice for a long time how married Jack was, since he talked often and at length about the anguish of his marriage problems leading to his wife's exit, which led me to assume the marriage was over, when of course it wasn't, not in his mind anyway, it flourished greenly there, and when his wife reappeared, after his heart operation, shouldering me out of the way, my status as mistress became all too clear. I retreated. Jack retreated. We were equals in leaving each other, at least.

I'd heard that each time I began a new love affair a couple of my friends joked about me: there she goes again! They were both in longstanding marriages, leading very different lives to mine. Did fulltime live-in marriage suit everybody? No. Certainly, I thought, sitting on the shallow bench of the basilica chapel pew and looking at my candle's flame, Nell's model of love had worked well. She and Dan had not lived together but across the road from each other. They met in the evenings, after the working day, cooked supper, spent the night together, then next morning jumped up and went back to writing or whatever and also were free to go out on their own at night with their separate friends, which indeed was how Jim and I had operated while married. He could go off to the Chelsea Arts Club or the pub with his chums and I'd meet up with mine, and if I went out while he stayed at home he never complained, as he never complained about my travelling abroad on writerly work trips however lengthy. The problems that led to our divorce were other and I shall not rehearse them here, I'd only add that love evolves, and that the anger necessary for divorce – a violent pushing away by me for reasons right at the time – eventually after some years transformed itself back into deep affection, agape rather than eros, which I was now realising, as though for the very first time, felt like a blessing, a true blessing given by the universe not by a priest.

You don't have to believe in God, or in the intercessionary power of the Virgin, in order to light a candle and pray. A prayer is a message sent out into the unknown, a cry erupting from a human place, an acknowledgment of feeling joyful or sad or powerless or grateful or praising. Sometimes those feelings just have to burst out in words. Currently I prayed that my novel might do all right in the end and that the Publisher might not be an archetype of the punishing Virgin with her stern face, she who threatened to chastise the unfortunate sinner with her flail, but she who leaned down and poured the milk of human kindness onto a poor suffering pilgrim, etc etc.

Artists, apart from the starry exceptions who prove the rule, have always had a tough time; they are underpaid and exploited just like other workers who do not own the means of production. (Hence the current appeal of Internet self-publishing.) I looked at the painstakingly stitched newly cleaned Gobelin tapestries, featuring Old Testament stories, which hung on the chapel walls to either side of the pews. How much had those nameless women workers been paid for their intricate, time-consuming labour? I looked at Jacob, and at the angels going up and down the ladder to heaven, and the sheep with tightly curled coats. One day you're an angel for your publisher, and the next you're a wrestling Jacob, and the next you're a sheep sent out to graze and just get on with growing your coat of wool before you're shorn then slaughtered then popped into the pot.

The summoning bell had been tolling as we came in, and

now people began filing into the chapel for Mass, so we left, and went back out into the church. Here, the door to the vestry stood open and we peeped in, glimpsing several Dominicans robing up in their vestments. One stood near us in the side aisle, wearing a gold-fringed green stole over his white habit, nodding and smiling smugly as he addressed two parishioners speechlessly soaking up his every word, doubtless giving them good advice about avoiding heresy, whether Albigensian or feminist, although in fact the two overlap since as is made clear in *Montaillou* female Albigensians having sex with their heretic priest believed it wasn't a sin so long as you had an orgasm (the Inquisition scribe didn't record whether these were thought to be clitoral or vaginal).

I felt abashed to realise I loathed priests as much as ever, for surely I should have got over my adolescent rage against them by now, since doubtless some of them were well-meaning kindly men who really cared about their flocks, even if others secretly considered women unclean, polluted because of menstruation and childbirth (which led eventually to death – oh dear we don't want death – it's women's fault we have to die – quick – suppress the women and thereby suppress death), hence not allowed to officiate at Mass and turn bread and wine into flesh and blood. Although women could do that for the child they carried while pregnant it was hugely inferior to a non-pregnant man magically doing it, this being an ancient prejudice of the Fathers of the Church papally whitewashed in modern times and re-presented as the idea of women's special vocation, serving their families and occupying a separate sphere to men's. It was no good: I scorned this preening whippersnapper, his complacent face, his easy fingering of his cord girdle encircling his narrow waist, as he dismissed his two interlocutors with a gracious nod and turned to join the group of fellow monk-priests behind him settling their vestments and fussing at the surpliced altar boys. They were all prancing about showing off their fancy costumes just as much as any group of actors standing in the front stalls before curtain up and unwilling to sit down until the very last minute, chatting to each other as though oblivious of anyone watching but obviously desperately needing to be noticed by the poor brutes up in the gallery. Pouf! I swept past. Jim said: nice frocks, are they Dominicans?

We got back in the car. We went to Super U of necessity, to buy staples such as rice, olive oil and wine. Super U caters for its clients from birth to death, babygros and adorable bootees at one end and funeral services at the other, special dignified and sober flowers such as chrysanthemums, plastic or not, and gilt-lettered headstones included, and in between, holding the two well apart, school stationery and home-office furniture as well as barbecue equipment and garden chairs.

A printed notice informed us that taking into account the recent demonstrations by French farmers against falling food prices, hence the impossibility of farmers making a decent living, the store had decided not to stock foreign processed meats but only French ones. Paulette had told me, soon after my arrival twelve days back, when she dropped by, that things were as bad as they'd been in the thirties. She'd been a child then, but she remembered her parents' struggles. Some days later, driving past me on the road, when I was out for an evening stroll, she stopped her van and told me that her daughter Isabelle, Fernand's wife, had become so depressed by their debts that she'd run away from home a few days back, and the entire family had turned out to look for her. I'd known something was badly wrong, because that morning Roger had driven up *chez moi*, not willing to say for whom he searched, just looking very grim and asking: have you seen anyone, have you seen *une personne*? I worried that it was Joseph feeling troubled and despairing again, but it was his aunt. They eventually found her sitting in her car deep in the forest. She went home in time to see to her cows and do the milking.

Jim drove us back via Lidl on the ring road, since we had heard about local farmers dumping a load of old car tyres there in protest at Lidl's cheap prices and imports of foreign food and we wanted to take a look. Not just car tyres but a great heap of earth, dung and rubbish filled the car park. Nobody seemed to be doing anything about it. Nobody had set the tyres alight, unlike the striking ferry workers currently set to lose their jobs because of a takeover and blocking the Channel Tunnel entrance with burning tyres and successfully disrupting traffic for days. In June, after my half-term break in France, travelling back to London I'd got as far as the Gare du Nord, then been forced to wait for hours in a very long queue, until at last the trains started running again, and while part of me felt solidarity with the strikers another part of me felt anxious and cross about getting stuck in Paris and missing my teaching session next day. Various Brits in the queue, when not keeping an eagle eye on anyone trying to queue-jump, commented irritably on how all the police and SNCF workers were just Standing About Doing Nothing. Well, I expect they were all good trade unionists.

Jim came in for lunch, the only way he would let me thank him for the lift, as he wouldn't take money for petrol. We had a slice each of melon with *jambon de Bayonne*, some tomato salad with anchovies, then a lettuce salad with hardboiled eggs and potato. Too much food, but it consoled me to cook. If I couldn't write a novel acceptable to the modern market, then at least I could produce something good to eat. The leftovers would feed me for the next couple of days. Jim had one glass of wine and I had two. We talked about painting and writing. I gave Jim the note I'd saved from his studio at the side of the garden here, which he'd pinned to the wall years back, which said in capital letters: Go Too Far. One of his favourite slogans. He tucked it away in his wallet.

Normally, in London anyway, I don't have lunch with friends because I often write through lunchtimes and don't stop much before 2pm, and anyway most of my friends, being writers too, remain hidden away until early evening, when they emerge as I do ready to play. Journos mock *ladies who lunch* as idle bour- geoises resting between bouts of shopping, and indeed gone are the days when one had lunch with one's publisher or agent in order to discuss business in pleasant surroundings. However, in rural France lunch is still taken seriously, proper food needed by hardworking people who'd think you were mad if you suggested *grabbing a quick sandwich*, and so, as I have said, I have lunch occasionally with Paulette and with other neighbours, and now with Jim, and sitting chatting to him I realised that it is indeed one of my favourite ways to be with friends. Recently I had lunch with my friend Pete Ayrton at the Dulwich Picture Gallery, before visiting the Ravilious show together, and over delicate salads artistically arranged on big plates we talked about books and writing and the Spanish Civil War anthology he has just finished compiling and editing, and just before that, again in London, I gave my friend James Le Fanu (Sarah's brother) lunch at my flat. James rang up asking for an omelette, since his wife Juliet, a superb cook, does not like eggs so rarely uses them, and so I made him *omelette aux fines herbes* with herbs from the garden, the ones the fox had not crushed while sunbathing, and he brought strawberries, and we talked about religion and about the Tablet conference on the religious imagination, back in June, which James had also attended.

How lovely to have lunch with men one is not in love with but of whom one is very fond. The deep, deep peace of the dining-room chair after the hurly-burly of the chaise longue.

After Jim had left I felt cheerful for a while because of our good conversation, then upset about the Publisher's response all over again, so thought sod it, I need more comfort, so had a third glass of wine. I was drinking too much. I would have to cut down drastically. Easier for someone of my all-or-nothing temperament to give up completely. But not today.

To stop myself drinking a fourth glass of wine I went out to pick some flowers for the vase in the kitchen. Idly I checked the postbox, which is placed on a tall, flat rock in front of one of the sheds, close to the lane that runs past the house. I'd told my neighbour Béatrice the post-snatcher that while I was in residence I preferred that she didn't take in my mail but instead let the postman bring it up to me. This was of course a reasonable request with which perforce she complied, though I was guiltily sure she knew that my real reason was wishing to avoid her as well as looking forward to the brief chats I enjoyed with the pipe-smoking postman when I'd heard his van in the distance and gone out to meet him to take the day's delivery of *pub*. (publicity flyers for frozen meals etc) from Super U et al. before he raced off back down the hill.

The former postman, a *croyant* and *pratiquant*, discovering that I'd been raised Catholic, sometimes discussed his faith and other matters with me. He described his pauses in the forest, to eat his mid-morning *casse-croûte* (snack) of tartines (small round slices of bread and butter), and he clearly enjoyed his pauses *chez moi, l'hérétique*. He approved, when I told him, of my possessing a statue of our local mayennaise Virgin, Notre Dame de Pontmain, who'd appeared in an unusual costume of a yellow crown and a dark blue gown flecked with stars, no veil, a red cross in her hand: he considered her correctly fierce, one of those Virgins armed with a whip for chastising sinners. Early on, soon after buying the house, I'd put in the empty niche of the ancient wooden cross at the turning up to my lane a *brocante*-bought antique porcelain Virgin. She'd got nicked. The postman said: don't worry, the thief will burn in hell.

One morning, grey-faced, he told me his twenty-year-old son had killed himself. On subsequent mornings I listened to his grief-stricken words, his terror that his son, having committed the sin against the Holy Ghost, that of despair, was now burning in hell and would burn there for ever more with no hope of rescue. Perhaps six months or so later, I can't remember exactly, the postman turned up radiant: he had dreamed of his son, smiling and saying: Papa, it's all right, I am not in hell.

The metal postbox no longer locks, why I don't know, rain-warped perhaps, but flaps open, and of course I should replace it, but haven't yet: it remains way down on the list of jobs, or as Lenin termed it What Is To Be Done. The postman must have come by while I was out at market: I found a letter addressed to me and took it back indoors to read.

I'd been contacted by a saintly internationally renowned clairvoyant named Angelina, graced with a gift of secret powers passed down from her great-great-grandmother through the female line, desperate to help me cope with the disasters threatening to overwhelm me, if only I'd let her. In six photocopied typed pages of reiterated warnings alternating with words of comfort, my name repeatedly inserted in bold at strategic intervals, which seemed an interesting attempt at hypnosis by remote control, Angelina condoled with me on my miserable life so full of problems to do with failures in love, work and money, she seemed to know exactly how things stood with the Publisher's low opinion of my novel, my worries about making a living, yet nonetheless she consoled me energetically: things could get better if only I would read her words attentively. She warned me against that terrible sin of despair and finally she promised to transform my existence once I had wafted the enclosed *Talisman de Chance*, an A5 slip of yellow paper inscribed with mystical symbols in red, around the four corners of my living room then sent it back to her in the enclosed envelope (a poste restante address in the Netherlands) so that she could proceed to her *Grand Rituel de Dégagement Psychique*, that's to say commence an in-depth analytic séance probing my soul's wounds, then make a diagnosis, and subsequently effect her magic, and oh yes, if I would also include a cheque for thirty euros that would speed things up otherwise forget it.

In her photo helpful holy Angelina sported soft white hair, an intense smile, a facelift, gleaming white teeth, and an amulet. Angelina or Mme Saint-Ange? I preferred my kitchen saint for miracles.

I took an hour's siesta. I usually do. The days sag and drag if you don't insert some kind of semicolon, and indeed possibly my sentences do too. I even used to sleep at UEA in my office. I needed to take a break from consciousness, from admin pressures, from my sense of being a fake academic, no longer my true self the writer the poet. I'd just close the door, lie down on the carpet for a bit of shut-eye and hope the Dean didn't decide to pay me a visit to discuss my inadequate performance at measuring outputs.

When I got up I sat on the front step, watching a tiny wren hop back and forth, obviously looking for water, perching on the edge of the watering can and peeping in, then flying in but finding it empty and flying out, finally discovering the overflowing saucers under a couple of pelargoniums in pots, so balancing there to sip. Sometimes when I'm writing the wren hops over the step and into the room, explores a little way, while I sit as still as I can in order not to startle her, then flies out again.

The humidity turned to rain. Good excuse not to continue weeding the garden. Tiny frogs, who must have hatched out somewhere close by, began to hop past the door, in twos and threes, all heading to the right, towards the patch of grass and the rockery. For a while I just sat and watched them, then picked up *Solitude*, by Anthony Storr, which I'd begun a few afternoons earlier. I reread this book every five years or so, cherishing the author's tolerance of artists' and writers' eccentricities. He has helped me distinguish between my need for solitude, in order to write, which feels Good, and my desire to escape the loneliness that feels Bad, that can strike for example when I'm here in the winter on my own, and it gets dark at five o'clock and I suddenly want company and haven't got it. I have discussed these matters with Patricia, who regularly goes off to her own house in France to write, without her husband. The loneliness is unavoidable, she says: we have to learn to live with it if we want the solitude too. So Good and Bad get fruitfully mixed up. Well, sometimes. Not always.

Every time I looked up from my book the tiny frogs were still coming, utterly determined, driven by need, jumping past in their twos and threes. Pierre raced by in his van, went up the lane, obviously to check his horses before evening, came back, stopped in front of the door where I sat, beckoned me. He tossed me another three big marrows. Here! My mother's sure you'll be having guests for 15th August, so she's sending you these extras. She's sure you'll be needing them. She knows how much you really like them.

Right. Now I had six large marrows. How could they be incorporated into my menu for the 15th? For the vegetarians I had planned *panzanella*, that Italian salad of tomatoes, basil and bread with olive oil, followed by stuffed mushrooms. They could also eat the green beans and the potatoes in cream I planned to serve the meat-eaters. We'd have that cold poached chicken dish again, now it had the Paulette seal of approval. We could also have marrow soup, stuffed marrow, grilled marrow, marrow *frites*, slices of marrow baked in béchamel sauce. If I had remembered to bring a spiraliser out with me we could have had marrow spirals cooked like fusilli, with a pesto sauce.

I peeled and de-seeded the marrows, tried cutting them into long pencil-narrow lengths, wondering whether they'd turn into spaghetti once dropped into boiling water, then realised they wouldn't so chopped them into shorter lengths and decided to mix them with sage-scented batter and make crisp golden marrow fritters. I put the marrow lengths into the fridge and poured myself a glass of white wine and sat on the step again. The frogs were still hopping past.

At 7pm Monsieur Jarré from the bank rang to apologise for having cut me off earlier. The computers had suddenly crashed, because of the overnight storms we had had. He was very sorry. I thanked him for calling. *Pas de soucis*, he replied. He would do his best to hurry the insurance, and with luck I could pick it up when the bank reopened after the 15th August. I thanked him again.

Perhaps I could offer him some marrows, to show my appreciation. Or perhaps I should pack them into an envelope and send them off to Angelina in the Pays-Bas.

Back on the front step, doing nothing, lolling dreamily, I became aware of a movement to my right at the curve of the lane. Carefully, not wanting to disturb whatever it was, I turned my head.

A large hare was loping along. I stayed as still as possible, so that it wouldn't be frightened away, watched it come towards me, pass in front of me, continue on down the hill. I hadn't seen one near the house for a couple of years and feared that Grégoire must have shot them all. Hares are elegant, shy, wild, graceful. They bound through myths. I can easily believe that the hare is a sacred animal, I can easily believe in stories of metamorphosis, women transformed into hares and leaping through fields in order to escape brutal suitors, and perhaps hares transformed into women in order to escape eager hunters, as well as agents and publishers turned into hares to escape importunate annoying complaining writers.

Seeing the hare made me feel very happy. Blessed, even. The second time that day I had felt blessed. The first time was lunching with Jim and remembering lunching with James and with Pete, and the second time was seeing the hare.

The happiness rose up easily and buoyantly as the memories, as the hare, a feeling of inner warmth and lightness I hadn't experienced for a very long time. The past two years had been sad and painful, seasoned by bitter failure and loss, and I had been depressed. Part of learning to dwell in Negative Capability had been tolerating dwelling in depression as well as in 'doubts, Mysteries'. Now here was this flooding sense of happiness.

It was telling me something about love and friendship. There were quite a few women in my life whom I loved dearly, to whom I felt very close, soul sisters as my niece Helen puts it, some of whom I'd known for over forty years, and yes, there were also one or two from whom I'd become estranged. Loving women (which included sometimes fighting them) was the core of my life. I had fewer men friends but those I had I loved. Now I realised that after splitting up with Jack I'd assumed I'd never have another lover, and that therefore I wouldn't be able to love men any more, I'd have to repress and hold back my love for men. I'd got that wrong. The opposite was true. Letting go of the yearning for a lover freed me to acknowledge how much I loved the men who were my friends, freed me to acknowledge those friendships more than ever, I could love my men friends without fear of being misunderstood, I could just get on with it and express love.

I went on sitting on the step in the deepening dusk. A loud huffing and puffing above me to the left indicated the owl getting ready to go out. Hawked-up pellets flew down. A wide white wing flared and dragged, like the skirt of a white feather dressing gown.

The frogs had ceased their progress to the right. Now they turned round and began hopping past the other way. Why? I hadn't a clue. No point grasping after facts, explanations. Negative Capability would do. I watched them until it grew completely dark and then I went to bed.

CHAPTER 6

SEPTEMBER

One Day In La Ciotat

Yesterday morning the change in the light fidgeted me awake. I was sprawling on a single sofa bed, the top sheet thrown off in the night because of the heat. The fringed woven bedcover, no heavier than a shawl, grey with a dark blue stripe, I'd left folded over the back of a chair. The sheet under me felt faintly gritty: I realised that although I'd had a shower after swimming the previous afternoon, I hadn't washed my feet carefully enough and so overnight sand had leaked out from between my toes. Sand can cling doggedly. I remembered Tommaso, one day in the mid-1980s in Vicenza, when I lived there, pointing out a row of cars, each with the angle between bonnet and windscreen lined with red silt, and telling me that that was sand blown in overnight all the way from the Sahara.

I got up, pulled aside the long grey curtain swishing on a grey metal track, veiling the enormous porthole-like window, and looked out, just as a round red sun swam up on the horizon, beyond the two large, rusty skeletons of warehouse sheds once used for engineering projects and storage by Monsieur Eiffel (of the tower in Paris). Since these are listed buildings of cultural interest, part of the *patrimoine* (cultural heritage), they still stand, and the sandy, muddy wasteland around them remains deserted, no high-rise hotels blocking the view of the sea from Pete and Sousou's flat on the fourth floor.

Looking out from one of the bedrooms or from the balcony you can see past the shells of the warehouses and the enormous gantry used in the shipbuilding yard straight to the dark blue waters beyond. La Ciotat in its day was as famous for ship-building as La Rochelle. The local shipbuilders, formerly all good Communists, these days have to build luxury yachts for the super-rich. The local fishermen still operate as a collective and share what they make rather than competing over prices and profits. Fish gets sold on the quayside in the early morning, next to the bread stall with its big loaves of *pain au levain* (sourdough). Matisse lived here briefly, Sousou told me, before he moved further along the coast to Nice. Did he come to the quayside to buy fish or did he send his wife Amélie? Did he paint the silver and scarlet scales of red mullet? We had those tasty fish for supper the night after I arrived. Grilled. Two each. Washed down with *vin rosé*.

I went back to bed for a couple of hours then got up again at 8am, when it felt OK to go in search of coffee. I put on a white T-shirt and my ankle-length black and white striped cotton skirt, with slanted patch pockets with a pleated, turned-down edge, that I bought in Rome twenty years ago. I'd taken Mum there for the weekend, and we'd been wandering through Piazza Navona, spotted a samples stall at one side, had a rummage and found bargains. The skirt is full, tightly gathered into the waist fastened with white cord, so that it swishes and floats, and I love it so much that even though the worn cotton keeps ripping in places, to the extent that Alan Bennett's mother would have consigned it to the floor-cloth bucket under the sink, I keep mending it so that I can go on wearing it. I bought a couple of metres of striped black and white cotton from the haberdashery stall in East Street and slowly I am building a new skirt on top of the old one.

The flat's floors are tiled. Hard and cool, pleasurable to walk on barefoot. I entered the living room, a large open space brilliant with light pouring in through the glass wall-like doors opening onto the balcony, fitted with a kitchen at one side, everything minimal and modern and elegant, nothing merely decorative, no mess, no ornaments, just clean, simple lines.

Pete, seated on the balcony studying his I-Pad, had his back to me, the debris of his breakfast, crusts and honey and fruit stones, on a plate on the table in front of him, a coffee cup at his elbow, so I didn't call good morning, not wanting to disturb him, but made fresh coffee. The grey ceramic coffee cups were small, espresso sized, so I drank my café au lait from a matching grey ceramic cereal bowl. We had bought peaches, *reine-claudes* (greengages), mirabelles and Muscat grapes in the market the day before, and they sat gleaming, piled in clear glass dishes, on the countertop, but all I wanted was coffee, and my book. I was on volume 2 of Elena Ferrante's Neapolitan quartet, determined to finish volume 3 before I left. I'd been reading it at every possible moment during my stay. I was immersed in it, so that while reading it I forgot where I actually was and all the time believed I was in Italy, soaked in the Italian language (no I couldn't speak Neapolitan), and when I looked up, because I was summoned to go to the beach, or for a walk, I came to with a shock, realising I was living in parallel universes, one in the south of Italy, one in the south of France; not, this week at any rate, in the south of London.

What joy to read for my own pleasure all day long, to swim and splash in a novel as long as I liked as long as I wanted, to read a novel so emotionally truthful about its female protagonists' lives. This past year I've spent a lot of time reading my students' writing, reading books for the two literary prizes I helped judge, reading books I was reviewing, and interesting and thought-provoking as such texts may be reading them out of professional duty is very different from reading driven by my own desire.

Sarah had recommended Elena Ferrante's work months back, and had brought vols one and two on holiday to lend to me, affording me that deep pleasure of discovering a new writer for the first time realising with delight how greatly one admires her. Yes I'll dive in, yes I'll stay in this writing as long as I possibly can yes I don't want to leave I don't want this quartet to end. Such was the pleasure I had in childhood, reading every day for hours, lost to all else, impervious to my family, escaped from the rules and confinement of home life into a vast universe I explored without constraint or fear, where I felt so free that I could dissolve, rapturous, until my mother began to worry, especially when I cried at the end of a book, and then she would drive me outside for fresh air.

This similar sense of freedom and liberty was made possible by Pete and Sousou, who had invited me, along with Sarah and Chris, to come and stay for an entire week, and who proved the most easy-going, permissive and tolerant of hosts, urging us to do whatever we wanted, for example read novels at breakfast time and not speak, letting us take turns to cook supper, letting us drink wine at lunchtime which we suspected they did not normally do, letting us feel, yes, completely at home. We had set up a food kitty, so that we contributed equally, and that seemed in particular Sousou's generosity, not remaining in control of meals but letting us help choose menus and shop for them.

The five of us were all old lefties of one sort or another, we'd all lived in communal houses in our youth, some of us had endured what a celebrated pamphlet circulating at the time described eponymously as 'The Tyranny of Structurelessness': the unconscious re-creation of old family structures of authority hidden beneath the freewheelingness. I didn't regret at all having lived in communal houses, far from it, but I did appreciate that here in the big flat in la Ciotat there existed a visible structure, Pete and Sousou were obviously, clearly, the flat's owners, they were our kind and tolerant hosts, and we gratefully and happily found our places as their guests and then felt very free and unconstrained. If we did ever overstep the mark and misbehave in any way they certainly didn't point it out. I wasn't sure I was always that laid-back when friends came to stay with me at La Lièvrerie: I enjoyed being the hostess too much.

Outside, the sun glittered on the balcony's red-tiled floor and waist-high pink concrete walls, beyond which to the right loomed three 'mountains' sculpted by alluvial mud deposits from the former river. Already the air felt loaded with heat. To escape the brilliance and scorch I drank my coffee inside, sitting feet up on the sofa covered in smart black cotton, and went on reading. Once I'd dipped in I didn't want to come out again, but when Chris and Sarah decided to go for a swim I joined them.

Pete and Sousou preferred to swim in a local *calanque*, one of the tiny coves on this part of the coast, just ten minutes' walk away. We three visitors had tried it on our first afternoon, by which time it was in shadow. The water was cloudy, floating with a skim of weeds, and the waves choppy. To get down the strip of shingle and stones to the water I'd kept my sandals on, and had swum in them, but they had acted as lifebelts, tipping me off-balance when I swam breaststroke, my feet kept wanting to stick straight up in the air, so I had to turn over and swim on my back.

On the second day we had investigated one of the small sandy beaches beyond the port, twenty minutes in the opposite direction, and had preferred it, the sand easy for walking on barefoot and the sun shining brightly overhead and no drifts of seaweed. So to return to this beach we walked around the edge of the horseshoe-shaped *vieux port*, following a paved path close to the boats. To our right, the water jostling with masts; to our left the line of tall houses, Italianate blocks of pale yellow, pale blue, cream, pale salmon pink, with shutters in lavender blue and pale green. White umbrellas shaded the tables outside one quayside café, pale rose pink ones guarded another.

We met few other tourists. Early September, the end of the holiday season for French people: children back at school and parents back at work. Unclogged, peaceful streets. Past the pink church at the top of a flight of wide steps we went, past the harbour full of yachts, past the little headland with the green-draped gilded carousel, until we reached the beach, where a line strung with bright yellow plastic buoys kept us within the stone-walled arms of the *calanque*.

Light glittered and sparkled and danced on the tips of the tiny waves. Swimming blissfully back and forth, not thinking about anything, just letting go into the rhythm of movement, after a while I drifted out of consciousness into somewhere vast and nebulous, I became porous, flooded with memories of dreams, memories of thoughts, of scraps of speech, couldn't distinguish one from the other, began to realise I'd lost myself, dissolved into a timeless space, back into the unconscious, swimming in it, I'd come loose, no edges or boundaries, I was composed of sparkles of light sparkles of seawater blue-green-silvery leaping points I was a fish with silvery scales I was nowhere just lolloping along in a sea of language a sea of dreams.

Held by the real sea, caressed by the sun's warmth and light, I felt less frightened than during the similar (night-time) experience back in March. I was able to remember that I'd gone into these fugue states before. Twenty-five years ago, when I was still living with Jim in Holloway, I'd lain one evening in a bubble bath by candlelight, in the tiny dark bathroom, idly staring at the flame's reflection glittering on the silver-white bubbles rising up all round me, crystalline foam, and had entered a similar trance state. Afterwards I'd hurled on my dressing gown, seized a sheet of paper and tried to record the experience, scribbling down a jumble of images and broken sentences, a turbulent flow of thoughts, fantasies, imaginings, metaphors. Once, more recently, while walking around Dublin, at a time of great personal and emotional pressure, in the throes of a tricky love affair, I'd lost myself, couldn't remember the date or what I was supposed to be doing. I recovered, went to the IMPAC Award judging meeting, carried on talking with the other judges. These were different kinds of experiences from those I'd had when younger, taking LSD or magic mushrooms or simply hillwalking, when 'I' dissolved completely and just became part of the physical universe; these were more linguistic, somehow. Perhaps I was simply discovering yet again that words, 'personal' thoughts, were just as much part of the universe as rocks and trees. The drug/mystical experiences brought intense happiness. The hypnotic trance states felt weird. Perhaps both related in some way to Negative Capability?

I made a connection between the fugue as *the flight of the mind* (Virginia Woolf's phrase) and the fugue as the movement of the *flâneuse*, each a metaphor for the other. The wandering woman, the wandering mind, the wandering sentences. The woman in flight from something, also towards something; willing to get lost in between a starting point and a finishing place and trusting that she'd eventually find her way out of the labyrinth. At the time I couldn't call that trust in wandering a capacity for Negative Capability but now I did.

The writer was Ariadne, marking her course into the labyrinth of the unconscious, the chaos of language, with unreeled narrative a string to guide her on the way back. Writing; going in; then rewriting; coming back out. The Minotaur of writerly difficulty you met at the heart of the labyrinth and wrestled with. You'd slay her, but she'd come back to life for the next bout. Like my mother! Both of us pawing and snorting and trampling. One of Jack's names for me was based on my family nickname Mimi; he called me the Mimitaure. He played Theseus, I suppose, but he didn't finish me off.

Emotional conflict hadn't sparked off my present state in La Ciotat: just the sun sparkling on the brilliant dancing surface of the water. Perhaps I was experiencing a particularly benevolent version of Negative Capability. There was just this flowingness of water, of mind, of language and dreams and memories.

From time to time, as I have said, I recommended Negative Capability to my writing students, told them not to strive too hard for results, not to need to know always exactly what they were up to, to trust the unconscious, the deep writing mind-self. How difficult it had sometimes been to take my own advice! These past two years had been painful and grim, full of insecurity and despair. Now that I was so much happier because I'd let go of wanting a lover, so perhaps I could let go also of wanting a quick resolution to the problems with my novel and just accept that there were difficulties, I was swimming in dark water and just had to float there for some time.

In my changed, more relaxed state I could let myself realise that certain difficulties cropped up with every novel I wrote, and regularly caused me to wrestle with editors. They always won. If I wanted them to publish my novels I had to do as they wanted and simplify, simplify. Often I wanted to put too many flowering free-associating thoughts on the page, had to prune my material back to a much clearer shape, let go of a lot. If an editor, suggesting cuts, spoke too briskly or negatively I fell into childish resentment, even if days later I was able to see that she might well be right.

Novels were always fuelled by powerful emotion, usually

desire: desire for a person, for a lost place, aspects of a lost child-hood. The easiest ones to write had a clear objective correlative, for example *The Looking-Glass*, which was inspired by seeing Mallarmé's little house at Fontainebleau and meditating on his story, combining that with my current fascination with Flaubert, also my memories of my grandparents' cottage in Normandy.

The image of *the house*, a material container, on one level functioned as a version of my own mind full of shifting, leaping images, helped me marshal, compose, connect them into a coherent shape eventually recognisable as a novel. As I began writing, those images inside were like a picture of the eternal moment, everything happening at once, as in an abstract painting. I had to translate that inner mandala-world into a narrative existing in time, unreel it, put one thing after another. That is one version of the Fall: falling from the eternal now of the inner world, everything existing at once, into time, the outer world of the page, one word arriving after another.

Sometimes novels had no such clear inspiration as *The Looking-Glass* had had, began simply from scraps of language, scraps of images that obsessed and haunted me, and inventing the story involved working out why that was so. The novel ventured into what seemed completely blank terrain. There was no *donnée*. I blundered forwards in the dark.

The interesting technical problem was how to twist the strings of images and streams of thought into a narrative coherent and compelling enough to keep the reader swimming along through it wanting to get to the end. I thought I'd done that with my current novel, had thought it sufficiently story-driven, particularly the sections narrated from the man's point of view. However, my agent and the Publisher did not agree.

I knew that these days story was everything in the commercial world. Language as such did not seem to matter. Pouf. Lily-the-agent had told me I was 'a brilliant writer', but that didn't save my poor male narrator from being unlikeable. Off with his head! OK, I thought snootily, I wasn't writing the sort of nice or nasty feminine novels that went down well in the wide commercial world.

I knew perfectly well that the literature-loving Publisher did not require me to write such a novel, but I also knew that she did need me to produce something she thought she could sell. Once, she'd said to me (when? I couldn't remember): beautiful language isn't enough! Of course she was right. Sarah had once said to me: you care so much about language because you're a poet. I'd thought: all novelists should be poets.

OK, I now thought, I would have to go on dwelling in not-knowing, in not-being-able. Perhaps in not-being-published, in not-being-read. Perhaps Negative Capability could mean, this morning, here in La Ciotat, just treading water, swimming, just lying on my back, floating in the present, the buoyant present holding me up and rocking me and I could turn over and swim energetically again and just love doing that and not mind about anything.

So the streams of memories drifted away like water weeds and I swam over to Sarah, who was stroking along nearby, and chatted to her. I mentioned that I felt I'd been hypnotised by the sun sparkling on the water and she just nodded matter-of-factly, which was reassuring. She was having a nice swim; she didn't require a description of my inner state!

After our swim we sat on the rocks at the side of the beach, reading. Often when I'm with Chris and Sarah this is what we do. Forty years back I stayed with them a couple of times in the Lake District, over New Year, with other friends, and we'd build up the fire in the freezing cold cottage and huddle round it, all reading, embraced by a companionable group silence which could last hours, until it was time to go out to the pub for beer and darts. Similarly when I go and stay with Chris and Sarah in Somerset we'll often sit by the fire reading, joined by our silence; a peaceful way of being together. Books line the walls of every room in their house. As their guest, you live in their library, you go to sleep in it, you wake up in it, you wake up under bedcovers and between the covers of books.

We began to stroll back along the boulevard lined with palm trees and pink-flowered oleanders. We passed the casino, its 1950s façade decorated with a border of patterned tiles, and we passed the villa-style frontage of the Eden Theatre, formerly the cinema where the pioneering Lumière brothers showed their films and in front of which, to honour their memory indelible on celluloid, the road tarmac has been laid in white with black edges and stripes exactly resembling strips of film.

At the church of the Blue Penitents, who Pete had assured us went in for flogging, we detoured inland in order to buy fresh bread, also a litre of rosé for two euros from the little wine shop in the Rue des Combattants, where, petrol-pump style, the wine was hosed by Madame from the big vat into recharge-able plastic bottles. The dark narrow streets cut slits through the *vieux centre*, between the tall buildings and shops beginning to close their shutters, you could stay in coolness and shadow scented by the melons and thyme in the greengrocer's opposite the wine shop, then the moment you emerged back into the dazzle of the open boulevard you streamed with sweat again.

Back in the flat we all joined forces to make lunch. Sousou, a vegetarian, nonetheless pressed us to eat any meat we wanted, she knew Pete would like that and she wanted her beloved Pete to have his wishes fulfilled, so we included prosciutto and *saucisson* in our array of dishes. We'd bought the vegetables in the market the day before. Proper tomatoes, each one with a different, irregular shape, with their seductive earthy smell, their flesh warm, sweet and juicy when you bit into it. We sliced them and interleaved them with basil, we ground black pepper over them, sprinkled olive oil onto them. We ate them along-side green salad, goat's cheese, sheep's cheese, and then fruit. A classic holiday meal. Nothing fancy needed because everything was so fresh. Glasses of rosé of course. We ate inside, in the cool, then while the others drank coffee I went off for a siesta.

First of all I checked my phone messages. The Publisher had rung, only a day later than she'd said she would. She apologised for this. Where are you? Are you in France? Her message was indistinct and faint but she seemed to be saying that she wanted to speak to me. That was a good sign, wasn't it? Or perhaps she meant that she wanted to tell me she was definitely rejecting my novel now that she had finished reading it. I listened to her message three times. On the whole I concluded it seemed positive rather than negative but I couldn't be sure.

Right. Stay in Negative Capability. Right. Respond. I pressed 'ring back' but couldn't get through. The line beeped then broke. My antique mobile just wasn't up to it. I went into the salon and asked for help. Chris got out his iPad and googled the publishing house and found the phone number. Back in my grey-curtained bedroom I rang the office switchboard and was put through to the Publisher's assistant, who told me that the Publisher was working at home today, and so I left a message: I was on holiday in the south of France and would ring her next Tuesday on my return.

I was putting off the possibility of hearing bad news. I lay on my bed, reading Keats's sonnets, then lulled by my *beaker of the warm south* I slept for an hour.

In mid-afternoon we set out, all five of us, to play pétanque. The pitch was an oblong sandy space, set with low-branched plane trees, near the beach where we'd swum. We divided into two teams of two, Sousou deciding to sit on a nearby bench under a tree and read while Pete and I played Chris and Sarah. Trying to re-find the knack of throwing the balls efficiently I kept getting distracted by the picture Sousou made, slender and composed, sitting very still on her green-painted iron bench with curled-over arms. She wore a turquoise long-sleeved ribbed shirt, a knee-length cotton skirt patterned in blue, navy and grey whorls, apple-green sandals. The golden-green branches of the plane trees waved over her, light dappled over her, the sandy grit underfoot was yellow-grey. While she read we took turns to throw the heavy silver balls scuffing towards the red *cochonnet* (jack) and cursed our own bad shots and praised others' good ones and laughed and teased each other. Pete at one moment would look very serious, planning a throw, his lips pursed, then at the next, in response to a joke, or amused by an odd or unexpected remark by one of us, would break into a shout of laughter, and then look serious again.

Pete and I won, small thanks to me, and so as victors duly offered the others a pastis. Sousou shut up her book and we wandered back along the boulevard, then turned in to the small square behind the pink church at the top of the wide steps. In fact only Chris and Pete drank pastis. Sousou had a Kir, I had a glass of *vin rosé* and Sarah had a beer.

We decided to go out for dinner, back to the *calanque* where Pete and Sousou liked to swim, because tonight the owner of the café there was offering a *sardinade* (sardine feast). Accordingly, after returning to the flat for showers and change of clothes, we walked there, up the little hill leading to the park at the foot of the brown mud mountains, past plastered walls covered with bright tags and graffiti, descending a zigzag concrete path and so arriving at the shacklike restaurant-café, its tables set along a narrow *terrasse*, that's to say a wooden deck hugging the cliff and overhanging the narrow strip of shingled beach. The warm air smelled of seawater, of salt. The small gleaming waves rolled in and out just underneath us.

A large platter of fried sardines arrived, another of chips, a bowl of green salad. The light began to fade, darkness to cover us. We drank *vin rosé* and talked idly and happily. We wondered what we might do tomorrow. Nobody could decide. Nobody knew. Nobody minded not-knowing.

CHAPTER 7

OCTOBER

One Day Back In Orchard Terrace

Yesterday morning, Saturday, I woke up before the alarm went off. I went into the frosty back garden with my cup of coffee and walked around. Pink roses, pink cyclamen. The pink and the purple clematis had rebloomed. Pink Japanese anemones, very tall, leaned over. The apricot-coloured nasturtiums looped up the trellis in long swags.

The garden was full of light. The council had sent in some workmen a couple of weeks back to cut down my neighbour Mike's leylandii, as they had promised earlier in the year they would do, thereby opening up the view, letting in the sun. No more sombre dark green canopy keeping the beds in starved dry shadow and forbidding plants to flourish.

The sky seemed huge. The world felt empty and clear. I was reminded of Christmas morning in childhood, normal routines disrupted and abandoned, the day opening up spacious and free.

Everything felt changed and different, inside me as well as outside. On my recent return from France, I'd found a postcard from my old friend and former lover Stephen, who was travelling in Andalusia. He sounded merry and happy, just as he'd been two weeks back when he came to Sunday lunch with other old friends. He sent a characteristically affectionate and self-mocking message in his hallmark turns of phrase: '*muchisimas gracias* for a most splendid lunch! ... Tucker worthy of the Festa dell'Unita. Onwards to *l'educazione, cultura e digusta! Saluti communisti* – Stephen xx'. Stephen was a brilliant cook, so a culinary compliment from him really meant something. He ran an independent publishing house, Serif, and his cookery list (which I've mentioned before) featured not only Alice B. Toklas and Edouard de Pomiane but classics of Moroccan, Caribbean, Bengali and ancient Roman cuisines. I propped the card, with its image of sardines grilling on a driftwood fire on a beach, on my worktable.

Two days ago, Thursday, the phone had rung: Stephen's mother Gay telling me that Stephen had died suddenly, while still in southern Spain. He'd been found dead on a bench near a café in Almeria. He looked peaceful, apparently, with his hands by his sides, an open book in his lap, his head fallen back. The police doctors had discovered in his pocket the card declaring him a heart patient, presumably had seen the scar from his heart operation ten years previously, had concluded there was no need for an autopsy. He would be cremated the following day and his ashes brought home by his sister Vicky, who lives in Madrid. Gay sounded calm: still in shock. I can't believe it, Mimi, I keep expecting him to walk in, with all his jokes. We talked for a bit. She told me she'd had a premonition of a death: she'd felt an angel's wings brush past. One day, ten years back, when Stephen and I were having lunch with her, she told us how as a child she'd seen two angels sitting on the windowsill of her father's study, and later that day he had died. She also once saw a leprechaun in the woodshed. Stephen laughed at her, but she insisted. Now she said sadly: well, at least I had a son.

On Friday Aamer Hussein had emailed me to say that another old and dear friend, Irving Weinman, had suddenly died of a heart attack in hospital in Sussex. He'd gone in, following one heart attack, then had another.

Two friends dead. Dropped out of sight. I'd never see them again. I couldn't understand it. From time to time the grief would erupt, roll over my head like waves. I cried in the swimming pool as I swam up and down, I cried talking about Stephen and Irving on the phone to mutual friends, I cried when I saw something that reminded me of them, which was just about everything. The dry sparkle of late afternoon light with a low golden sun; the view of the Thames at Blackfriars viewed from the top of the bus. Oh, they'd have liked that.

After Gay's call I'd talked to my friend Georgie Hammick on the phone and she told me that she and other friends had tried to track me down to tell me about Stephen's death, which they'd read about on Facebook; they were worried about my receiving the news while I was alone in France. I felt their care and concern, the net of friendship holding us all together. Feeling loved: a heat penetrating one's skin.

How very kind of Gay to ring me herself. How does a mother cope with losing a child? She can't. It is against nature. My mother lost three children before she died. My brother Andy died just two months before Mum. Margi and I were caring for her at home. We sat on her bed and Margi took Mum's hand and told her of his death. Mum said: I can't cry.

At other times the tides of grief receded and I felt muffled, as though tied up inside a rolled grey mattress that stifled my mouth. Waking up yesterday I thought I was lying face down on an ice floe, broken off from other ice floes. I got up because you have to; you must go on living. I came back inside from the garden, drank more coffee, while trying and failing to read. Then decided it was time to go out. I put on the dress, not dirty but just creased, that I'd been wearing for the last two days. I remembered to wash my face and comb my hair. I'd seen newspaper pictures of Palestinian women grieving, enacting public rituals of grief: tearing their hair and rending their clothes and stretching out their arms and wailing. In Britain you have to keep quiet and tidy and clean so that you don't upset others. Jewish-American Irving had sided with the Palestine cause. He'd driven a lorryload of supplies to try and beat the blockade of Gaza. With his local pro-Palestine group he used to stand in Tesco with a banner protesting about imports of Israeli products. Because I'm so tall, he explained to me, I stand very still and calm, so that people can see I'm not threatening them.

I had promised Sandy, a neighbour who comes to the local book group, to lend her a copy of Elena Ferrante's *My Brilliant Friend*, which we were due to discuss in two weeks' time, at my post-holiday suggestion, so I walked to her block of flats through the back streets, lined with early nineteenth-century houses behind railings, a route which bent past small public gardens filling in the gaps (former bombsites) between stretches of terrace. Trees burned russet, red, bright brown. Ash leaves painted the pavements yellow-grey. Bigger plane leaves, greenish-yellow, swept along in drifts. The air smelled of earth, rotting leaves, chrysanthemums.

I got lost, as parts of streets under the railway line soaring overhead had been pulled down and new blocks of flats put up and alleys renamed that were not in the *A-Z*. A friendly man and woman trying to be helpful, locals who had never heard of Sandy's street, pointed me in what they thought might be the right direction but wasn't. Grief made me careless, lose my bearings. I blundered along, feeling less like a *flâneuse* than a nincompoop. Eventually I chanced upon the street.

Sandy had workmen redoing her kitchen so couldn't invite me in. She took me into the flats' communal back garden, a courtyard surrounded by walls of old London brick, grey-mauve, formerly the site of an old laundry and wash-house. A strawberry tree grew against one wall, laden with small red fruits. A vine hung over another, and Sandy picked me a small bunch of black grapes. Turning out her kitchen cupboards she had come across a stash of white plastic forks, an orange plastic beaker, a white china mug. These she handed to me to take to the local community house in case they'd come in useful. They're a bit grubby, she said, and indeed they were. I knew she was trying to be generous and helpful but nonetheless child-ishly resented being given this errand. I stayed hiding behind a glass wall of politeness and hypocrisy. I wanted kindness but couldn't ask for it.

Grief made me very angry and I was afraid of it erupting like red lava and scorching people. I'd felt angry with groups of tourists blocking the pavements on Southampton Row, near the British Museum, when I went into Holborn to have my daily swim; I felt angry with young men riding their bikes fast along the local pavements making me jump out of the way; I felt angry with the many pedestrians risking their lives darting across the roads through hurtling traffic. I wanted to yell at them you could be killed! How terrifying, and enraging, for the poor drivers, so easy to run someone down.

I didn't like this egotistical angry self, I disapproved of it. I wanted just to think about my two dead friends, life's promises broken, lives cut short, all the publishing projects Stephen was planning, the writing Irving was involved in, I wanted to feel pure sorrow for their deaths, but, shamefully, I kept thinking about myself. Wound raw like being burnt, your skin torn off, you can't bear to be touched. It hurts too much. The world scrapes at you and you have to go to the supermarket and you want to howl and can't. If only you could hide inside somewhere safe and private where you could weep and indeed weep at length if you needed to, talk about the dead friends as much as you wanted, feel heard, listened to, held. In Jewish culture, in Pakistani culture, and I'm sure in others of which I'm ignorant, they allow for this, which is very wise because then afterwards you can cope with normal life a bit better, social occasions for example, or just having to be amongst people who have no idea someone you loved has died. You'd have on an invisible protective coat. Your insides wouldn't threaten to spill out and embarrass others. Last night I'd been due at supper at Pete and Sousou's and I'd gone, thinking I'd like to be among friends. Miriam, whom I'd last met in La Ciotat in September, when we all had dinner together, was one of the other guests. She'd recently come through severe illness, talked candidly about it over supper, mentioned the invention of grief cafés for modern urban people. Could be a good idea.

Walking back from Sandy's I picked up a big plane leaf and put the grapes on it. I gave them to my neighbours Keri and Hal, whom I dropped in on for a short meeting about our proposed community supper club. Keri, an interior designer, had taken down internal walls inside his ground-floor flat and created an open-plan living space. A huge flatscreen TV dominated one wall: flashing colours of a reality show, sound turned down. While Hal served caramel biscuits, apologising for their not being home-made, Keri's glossy brown spaniel tore about, barking, jumped up, out of control. I felt angry again: why not train the dog to sit down and shut up? That's what I had to do! The dog should do the same! We agreed on a date for our first neighbourhood supper. Keri and Hal would design and make the posters, organise the emailing. I listened, praised their ideas, agreed with everything they proposed.

This being a Saturday, next came our monthly gardening club. We were due to tidy up our little local park at the end of my street. I worked my way through the mixed beds of shrubs and flowers, weeding them. My neighbour Dave appeared, seized a broom and began sweeping up fallen leaves. Various other male neighbours wandered in, started sweeping and weeding, then spotted other men arriving, towing small children, and went over to greet them. They downed tools and stood about chatting in twos and threes. I felt enraged all over again. Why didn't they help? Why didn't they do some work?

Keri appeared. He sat on a bench, smoking, checking his phone. After a while he shouted, who needs refreshments? I'm putting in an order! This meant, it turned out, that he was calling Hal, back at their flat, just round the corner, and asking him to make us coffee. Colin went to fetch it and brought it back on a tray. He handed me a mug: here, this will you do you good, your eyes look as though you need it.

I'm fond of Colin and his wife Kath, both professional gardeners, who together founded the gardening club. Young enough to be my son, Colin is friendly and affectionate, always gives me a kiss when we meet. I knew my eyes were red with crying. I wished I could tell Colin I was sad about my friends dying but decided it was inappropriate on such an occasion, with everyone chatting gaily. I hunched over the earth, pulling up sycamore saplings, pruning leggy lavenders. A young blonde woman, posh-hippyish, wearing a vest and jeans, beads in her hair and a stud in her nose, appeared with her three small daughters. While they played on the swings she wandered about, watching Dave and me work. Spotting the drifts of chopped lavender sprigs she asked for some, for making sweet-scented sachets. I gave her a big handful. Then she asked whether there were any jobs her children could help with. Colin got them to trample down the garden debris in the bins: he lifted them up in turn and held them while they danced on the packed leaves and shouted with joy.

After the usual two hours were up, everyone began packing up. Colin came to inspect my work: you've done a really good job. He likes to feel we are a happy team, he was trying to be nice. I tried to be nice back, felt tongue-tied. I found myself near Dave. We wheeled the brown bins, full of leaves and weeds, through the gate in the railings, back to their stations on the pavement. I made a bitchy remark about all the other chaps having enjoyed their gossip. Dave smiled. Yes, they did!

I wanted to tell someone about the two friends I'd lost: handsome, tall Irving, who loved jazz and cooking and partying, who wrote thrillers, who looked after his chronically ill wife devotedly; witty, darting, eccentric Stephen, passionate about left-wing politics, who could crack jokes in three languages. I wanted to wail oh poor me I am so full of sorrow, I wanted my grief recognised I guess, I wanted sympathy.

I said goodbye. At the gate, another young neighbour, George, caught me: would it be OK if the children came round for trick or treat tonight? I said yes! He and Anny have two boys: serious Ned, bouncing Jem. Once when I'd dropped by to deliver a card to Anny, Jem, opening the front door, seized my hand and dragged me across the threshold. It's my birthday tomorrow! This is the last day I'll be three! You've absolutely got to come in and see my cake! George turned, spatula in hand dripping chocolate icing, smiling.

I returned home, gave my earthy hands a quick scrub, then went to the newsagent at the end of the road, to buy the Saturday *Guardian*. The young man there whom I especially like, the one with whom I exchange smiles and greetings, told me he is leaving soon, to go back to Mumbai. He has got married, and wants to live with his wife, not in this city where it is cold and rainy and he has to get up at 4am for work and people come in to the shop and steal things and they beg, too, but they want the money just for drugs, oh life here is very hard. A little while back I'd given some money to a young man who'd been hanging about near the newspaper racks, he accosted me just as I was leaving the shop, he followed me out and asked me for cash, which I gave him, he talked rapidly and excitedly about his difficulties, long-term unemployed, no educational qualifications, living in a hostel, feeling desperate. His talk flew past me glancingly like bright spears. I tried to make a helpful suggestion or two but that wasn't what he wanted, I think he just wanted to be heard. As I did. A day later I saw him in the supermarket, racing up to another shabbily dressed man and shouting, I'm not hyper, I'm not on an up, I swear I'm not.

I walked back home down my street. I saw Dave going back into his flat so called hello. He paused, waited for me to come up with him, began telling me about pulling the ivy off his cherry tree, how he had taken on doing several local front gardens for old people who couldn't cope with them. Good, kind Dave. He waved away my praise: I like things to be tidy, and I've got so much energy!

Other neighbours approached, carrying shopping, wheeling pushchairs. They waved hello, continued past us along the street.

This sense of life going on all around, somehow inexplicably, often unbearably, while you're suffering: Auden wrote about it; I had it every time someone close to me died. Somewhat different was the intensification of ordinary experience when you were afraid that someone you loved *might* die. Back in 2005 Stephen was diagnosed with heart trouble, told he needed an operation, a new valve. I accompanied him to visit the consultant, and then the surgeon. The surgeon, brisk and brutal, told Stephen there was a chance he would die under the anaesthetic. We came out, walked for a while by the canal. Terror heightened perception:

the grass glowed luridly green and the flowers' colours radiated light and Mile End was full of glory, all the beauty of the world that Stephen would not see again if he died. Then the vision faded, the world became ordinary again, and we walked back to Stephen's house to make lunch.

He survived the operation. His mother Gay, his sister Vicky and I tiptoed in to visit him in intensive care. The nurse assigned to him sat on a high stool by his bed, keeping under surveillance all the blinking, whirring machines that sustained his life. Now she began summoning him back from the underworld, calling him very gently: Stephen, Stephen, you must wake up now. Hovering over him she seemed like his winged guardian, his own personal angel, she brought him back from that deep darkness, out into the sunlight. Next day Stephen gave us a more down-to-earth version of his awakening. Apparently I grabbed her tit!

Back at home I tried to read the *Guardian*. Accounts of the suffering of Syrian people fleeing war seemed meaningless. I felt ashamed. I couldn't take in properly anything I read. I felt very hungry, didn't want to cook so ate a fig. I drank a glass of white wine, which I should not have done since I'd sworn to myself I would not drink at lunchtimes any more, but now I broke that rule. Wine my version of a tranquilliser. So what the hell.

I tried to do some work. I remembered my university tutor, Rosemary Woolf, her bracing advice for how to cope with pre-exam nerves, any kind of emotional upset. Just get on with your work, Miss Roberts. She had taught me you just had to keep going, keep at it. The Publisher had spoken to me after I'd got back from France in early September, to say that she still had doubts about the novel but was giving it another chance. Her reader Arabella T., whose opinion she trusted, was willing to become my editor and work on the novel with me.

I'd met Arabella years back at a literary party, remembered her as witty, distinguished-looking, formidable. I went to meet her at her house in Canonbury. Elegant and slender in a black polo neck and grey pencil skirt, she welcomed me with a kiss: I *love* your novel! She was the first professional reader who did. I almost burst into tears. We sat at her long table in her dining room, opening to the kitchen, on the ground floor. She produced coffee and a plate of madeleines. We went through her list of comments. Mainly to do with clarifying the motives of the two male characters: I'd been over-subtle, apparently. I hate spelling things out too clearly; I expect readers to do some of the work, but some get cross and impatient. Am I simply arrogant? After I've spent a long time writing and rewriting and rewriting a novel, once I deliver it I don't want to change it. I want my novels to embody my vision, not an editor's. From the publisher's point of view I may be self-indulgent and narcissistic as well as arrogant, completely childish; a novel has to survive in the commercial world, after all. My conflict perhaps derives from childhood: familial codes of silence and repression pitted against the child's need to speak herself. It's a power battle and I want to win it. Parents have power over children and publishers do over authors. Arabella reassured me: I know I'm a good midwife. Then she opened a bottle of Prosecco and swept me upstairs to her drawing room, made me sit next to her on the sofa, lit a cigarette and talked charmingly and entertainingly.

Arabella had given me fresh heart and hope. So I had

embarked on my final, final version. Another month's work, I thought, and I'd be done.

My ex-neighbour Dorothy dropped in at tea-time. She and her husband Matt have moved up to Leeds, in order to take care of their baby grandson while his parents earn their livings. The government wants women to go out to work, but how do they expect them to pay the prohibitive costs of childcare? In the 1970s, state-funded childcare was a feminist demand. Unthinkable in today's privatised world. So the heroic grandparents step in, do a second shift. Matt and Dorothy come back to London occasionally, to see their friends at St James's church in Piccadilly. This time Dorothy was down for a memorial service for one of these friends, a Methodist clergyman well-known for his charitable works, which had taken him away from home for most of his life. Dorothy talked cheerfully about how well his wife was coping with his death. A merciful release for both of them?

After Dorothy had left, Sonia, the sister of Sousou and sister-in-law of Pete, came for tea. She lives fulltime in France, three villages away from me, and has become the friend there with whom I discuss French novels, gardening and cooking, also Life and Love when necessary. She regularly visits Sousou in north London, but this was the first time she'd visited my flat. I felt her affection, her willingness to trek south (my flat is close to the river but I always worry north Londoners fear it's far, far off). She arrived an hour late, having got lost, I don't think she realised how late she was, I'd been worrying she'd been mugged, but here she was, *insouciante* and smiling, bringing me a feathery-leaved plant from Sousou's garden as a present. Her sister pulled them up as weeds but she thought I'd like the yellow flowers. In fact I disliked that pale yellow (except when embodied in wild primroses in the countryside) but of course didn't say so. She inspected the back garden, made encouraging comments. Back inside, instead of a second cup of tea we had a glass of wine. We talked, but I felt weird and knew I probably sounded *distraite*. I wanted to be fully present for Sonia but felt weighed down by grief. It was like a spiky sack in my lap. I couldn't pretend it wasn't there. She knew my friends had died. She knew I felt sad. She obviously wasn't expecting me to play perfect hostess. Why couldn't I just accept that that was the situation rather than feeling social guilt? Sonia was wearing a delicate, striking pair of antique earrings. When I complimented her on them, she told me how originally she'd bought them for her daughter in Brazil, posted them off, but they'd been returned to her months later, undelivered, so she'd kept them for herself. Listening, concentrating on her rather than on myself, I calmed down. The friendship current flowed easily again.

I told Sonia that Anny and George's two children were due to arrive soon, doing trick or treat, and urged her to stay until they did. I described the grave, clever five-year-old and his extrovert younger brother with his mop of blond hair. A week back I'd dropped in on Anny, taking her some sweet pea seeds, and the two boys, perhaps wanting to put off bedtime, had decided to stage a play and I absolutely had to stay and see it. We'll do Goldilocks and the Three Bears! Little Jem shook his blond curls. Who'll be Goldilocks? It'll absolutely have to be me!

A bang on the front door: Anny, handing me a tin of Quality Street. Just in case you haven't got any sweeties for the children when they arrive.

Good idea, Anny. I certainly hadn't. Anny retired. I closed the door. Sonia and I waited. She wanted to start on her journey back north but I begged her to hang on. Just wait another minute, just say hello.

A second bang on the front door. I stood close to it, shouted theatrically back at Sonia: oh my goodness, who can this possibly be?!

I opened the door and jumped: a large, shrieking crowd of toddlers costumed in Hallowe'en hooded cloaks surged forwards waving their arms. Trick or treat! Trick or treat! More baby witches, wizards and ghouls flowed down the area steps. They all clutched small brown-paper carrier bags for their spoils. Here were Anny's two, and here were Pat's, the wonderful sturdy Mick shouldering his way to the front, and his equally wonderful sister Fenella shouldering him aside. I scooped sweets into the children's bags, waved at Anny, who was hovering in the street, threw her the half-empty tin: you may need this for the next place you visit!

After Sonia left, to catch her bus back north, I realised how hungry I was. Scoured out with hunger. Just as I was wondering what to have to eat, Stephen's sister Vicky rang. She talked about her plans for the memorial celebration, for the continuation of Stephen's publishing firm, for clearing out his house. Under the urgent flow of details ran her unspoken distress. She and I had lost touch (my fault) a couple of years after Stephen and I split up as lovers. Now she was talking to me as though we'd continued a friendship. Certainly there was great goodwill expressed by both of us.

Too late to make a proper supper. I ate a bit of salad, went to bed, lay sleepless, remembering how as a child I'd imagined the souls of the dead flitting about like bats in the dark garden outside. The nuns taught us that we had to pray for the Holy Souls especially on this day, the eve of All Saints', to get them out of purgatory, where they were being fierily purged of their sins, and into heaven. Then tomorrow, All Saints' Day, newly winged, gold-winged, like angels, they'd form part of that happy throng surrounding God's throne.

Jim, who loved flying and for a time had a microlite plane when we were together in France, used to joke about future projects, art for him and books for me, as aeroplanes circling above us in the air, waiting to land. He'd imitate Air Traffic Control, speaking into an imaginary walkie-talkie: come in Blue Leader, come in Red Leader. In my childish imagination St Peter, who traditionally held the keys to the gates of heaven, acted like that: you can come in to heaven, and you, and you, but not you. I didn't believe in heaven or hell any more, I did believe in a strange dimension as described in quantum physics where narrative time did not exist and different states of being danced alongside each other, I did believe in the unconscious imagination peopled with the beloved dead. Tonight I simply wanted to pull wandering souls home somehow. Come in, Stephen, come in, Irving. Were the dead *flâneurs*? You had to leave them in peace. Mourning meant letting go of them, acknowledging our broken attachment. I was just at the very beginning of the process.

CHAPTER 8

NOVEMBER

One Day In Avignon

Yesterday I woke up at 6am. At 8am I made tea and carried up one mug at a time to Margi and Richard, who were sleeping in the doorless room next to the bathroom at the top of the flimsy wooden corkscrew staircase. I'd slept on the sofa bed in the open-plan space below, a combined sitting room, dining room and kitchenette. A sink, a microwave, an electric kettle; no cooking pots or implements or tea towels. Another Airbnb owner who disdained cooking. Mica obviously didn't live here: nowhere to store clothes, no personal possessions visible. I'd thought Airbnb meant renting out your spare room, but Mica was simply a professional buy-to-let landlord. We met the over-nighter of his other flat, across the landing, when she rang our doorbell, asking how the hot water system worked.

We had arrived in Provence to visit Luc, Mum's younger brother, and his wife Marie-Yvonne, who lived an hour's drive from Avignon, in the Lubéron. Marie-Yvonne had recently been hospitalised with a heart attack, had then had a stent inserted, and was still weak, so could not have us to stay. Luc would come to pick us up in the morning and then drive us back in the evening. He scorned our offer to rent a car or book taxis instead. I may be eighty-seven years old but I can still drive!

When they moved to Provence years back, they had bought a run-down *mas* (farmhouse) and gradually converted it. The décor was a mixture of old cupboards, chairs and pictures inherited from their parents on both sides, some of which I'd grown up with in my grandparents' cottage in Normandy and which still gave me a shock every time I saw them here, transplanted; stacks of Catholic newspapers and journals; crucifixes in every room; twee folkloric pottery ornaments. Marie-Yvonne was the crucifix-hanger. A devoted, full-time mother all her life, she also threw herself into good works in the parish. Luc's faith was quieter; he hardly spoke of it at all. The only books in their house, apart from glossy Catholic paperbacks on the spiritual life, were Victorian ones bound in half-calf by my great-grandfather, who had been an amateur bookbinder. These ornamented two shelves in the study and I doubt were ever opened. Outside, Luc had planted an olive grove, an apple orchard, plus apricot, quince and cherry trees. The grassy garden, with espaliered roses and a walnut tree near the house, flowed between low stone walls towards the looming mountain. A path took you to the bridge across the canal and into a wild countryside of rocks and scrub.

Of their seven children, five were married, with many offspring. The oldest daughter had become a nun and the oldest son a priest, joining a modern order for both men and women. They didn't wear habits. They earned their livings as teachers and social workers. Gilles had risen through the ranks to become the abbot. Last time we had visited, two years back, he invited us to lunch in the mother-house, a seventeenth-century cluster of buildings with cobbled courtyards, not far from his parents' *mas*. We ate with him in a guest parlour panelled in cherrywood. Plain-clothes nuns sped back and forth with dishes of foie gras, fried chicken and tinned veg. Marie-Yvonne, knowing they couldn't cope with vegetarians, had brought Margi some cheese in a plastic box. Gilles poured us red wine and told us about his missionary work. His order, rather than trying to reconvert the pagan Catholics in the provinces, was recruiting in the big cities among students, and also abroad, in places such as the Philippines. After lunch Marie-Yvonne insisted Gilles show us the teaching books he had written for child catechumens, dogma translated into snippets of banal prose, with equally banal illustrations in colour. I'd been fond of Gilles when we were young: he was clever, funny, passionate. Now he had a hint of smugness. I spoke to him on his terms, through an invisible grille.

Marie-Yvonne was tremendously proud of the family she came from in Normandy, rich farmers living in a nineteenth-century chateau (the one I nicked for my heroines in *Daughters of the House*) a kilometre away from my grandparents' home. She was one of fourteen children, of whom seven died young. In her turn she'd become the matriarch of a dynasty, with countless grandchildren and great-grandchildren. Now, after her heart attack, two of her married daughters were caring for her, which of course Gilles was let off doing as he was (a) a man and (b) an abbot.

On this visit, Margi and Richard and I had travelled out to Provence together. They spent the night before we left with me in London. I gave them my bed and slept in my workroom on my fold-out single grey mattress from Muji that when not in use I stowed away in the cubbyhole next to the fridge. In the morning I found a large dead spider next to me. It must have crawled in for warmth then got flattened. Sorry old dear, I said, and threw it in the bin. We caught an early bus to St Pancras, whizzing along through the dark empty city, and then boarded the 7.19am Eurostar to Marseille, as I'd done in September when I went to La Ciotat. This time we jumped off at Avignon.

I'd told Margi about Airbnb, after my trip to Paris back in July, so now she had organised an Airbnb booking for our visit to Avignon. I had agreed: it would be cheaper than a hotel and there was no reason to think there'd be problems.

Arriving at Mica's flat in an old building in a narrow street, barred to traffic, just inside the old walls, we found that the door code he'd given Margi didn't work. We stood and waited. Mica didn't turn up as promised. The sun sank out of sight behind high rooftops. The mistral howled. I'd misinterpreted Richard's assurance that it would be lovely weather in the south of France, so this morning I'd put on a thin cotton parka and was now shuddering with cold.

Margi phoned Mica: no reply. We went on hanging about. After half an hour or so, two young people, smartly dressed, smoking, strolled past with a dog on a lead. They glanced at us, turned back, said: Airbnb? We said yes. Were they friends of Mica's? They didn't explain, just punched in the door code, rapidly shouted out the numbers, adding, second floor, on the left, key under mat. They shot off. Tired, flustered, we carted up our bags, then realised we couldn't remember the door code, which meant we wouldn't be able to go out and sightsee because we wouldn't be able to get back in. I hurtled downstairs, propped the door open with a handy brick, ran along the street, but the two young people and their dog were out of sight.

Margi repeatedly phoned Mica to find out what the door code was, failed to reach him, then spent more time texting him. I climbed the corkscrew staircase to inspect the bathroom: walled and floored in concrete painted grey-green; the sink a bowl on a hollow-sided grey-green concrete cube. *Cool comme chez cool.*

At last, Mica texted Margi back. It turned out that he had indeed given her the wrong door code. It also turned out that although Margi had told him we'd need to stay a second night, we having only recently learned of Marie-Yvonne's heart attack and consequent incapacity to put us up, she hadn't organised paying him for this second night via Airbnb but had assumed she could just pay him in cash face to face. Now Mica texted again to announce he wasn't around but was very busy, collecting money from other tenants I sourly supposed. We'd have to arrange to meet him somewhere in town and pay him then. We left text messages for him, telling him where we'd be when, and went off to visit the Palais des Papes, for which Margi had pre-booked entrance tickets, before it closed. All the time we were plodding through the bleak halls, most recently used as a wartime barracks and stables before being reopened as a tourist attraction, Margi was involved in streams of texts with Mica about where to meet him and pay him, and finally Mica announced that he wouldn't be insured if Margi paid him in cash for the second night, she would have to pay him via the website, adding their percentage as before.

The *palais* seemed a vast, chilly mausoleum of emptiness and absence. What was missing? Women. Perhaps the popes had had them brought in as cleaners or smuggled in as concubines. The frescoes mainly featured men killing animals or each other. I did spot a couple of pallid Virgin Marys, a dancing Salome-temptress, a martyred queen. I liked the display of fragments of ancient stained glass, of ancient floor tiles in abstract patterns of browns and greens. Colour exploded in the artfully arranged gift shop, a single winding path forcing you through a labyrinth of popish pot-pourri sachets, herb soaps, replica tiles, bags of *herbes de Provence*, CDs, cushions, etc etc, until eventually you arrived at the popish tills.

Previously I'd visited Avignon in summer. Once with my parents, when I was twelve, at the time of the Theatre Festival. Scorching sun, canopies and café-umbrellas shading the audiences, bands playing, Algerian men dancing *en groupe* near where I sat with my parents sipping Orangina. Fired by the music, I leapt up and danced with the men and they laughed and clapped me on. The second time was in my late twenties, with a group of friends with whom I'd rented a house in the middle of a vineyard. We strolled through the crowds outside the *palais* and there, suddenly, were my parents, with Marie-Yvonne and Luc, hailing me. I'd forgotten they'd be visiting, hadn't told them I'd be in Provence too. At that time, still struggling for independence and freedom, I kept my distance a fair bit.

How bleak and forbidding Avignon seemed in winter. We

returned, shivering, to the flat. Richard and Margi spent the next hour attempting to pay Airbnb/Mica for the second night via their phones. I couldn't help as my phone was too ancient. They wrestled with the Airbnb website, with its office's unhelpful recorded messages, with online banking details that would not show up, with online accounts that refused to be activated.

I decided a drink would help. I memorised the door code and dashed out along the street, made back towards the tiny *place* at its end, in the direction of the Palais des Papes, remembering we had passed a *boulangerie* (bakery) there earlier. I nipped in just as it was preparing to close. The friendly woman serving behind the counter confirmed that yes, she also sold wine, and basic dry goods too. I bought a bottle of Côtes du Ventoux red and a bottle of Côtes du Ventoux white. Sure that Mica's flat did not boast a corkscrew, I asked the woman to open the bottles for me. She smilingly obliged. I bought food for breakfast as well, and took everything back. I'd already forgotten the door code and had to text Margi. Once upstairs, I poured us all wine. It sharpened my hunger. Margi and Richard continued wrestling with their phones. Crossly I proposed that we simply give up and go to a hotel for our second night and sod the expense. Now please could we go out and find a restaurant and have dinner? Margi and Richard agreed. They texted Mica to say that we'd be leaving first thing tomorrow morning.

Mica appeared, swinging a motorbike helmet. Tall, slim and handsome, with long brown curly hair, a stylish leather jacket. Complaining that he'd honoured our booking for the second night, which had deprived him of letting the flat to someone else, he whipped out his own phone, to prove how easy it was to contact the Airbnb website, failed in his turn, agreed with us that it was simply easier if we stayed just the one night, so that he could immediately relet the flat and not lose any money. Off he went.

I apologised to Margi and Richard for my irritability. They forgave me. The way to control my bad temper, I decided, remembering my trip to Paris with Val, would be never to try Airbnb again.

To brave the cold outside, I put on in layers all the summery clothes I'd brought with me. We walked over rain-slick cobbles through darkening, frosty streets. In the Place de l'Horloge the *marché de Noel* stalls were setting up, strung with loops of glittering lights. The old-fashioned carousel, with its gilded yellow panels and maroon horses, was still. The *tricouleur* flew above the town hall. We hopped into the hotel where we'd stayed two years previously and booked ourselves rooms. Since Margi had found the hotel's special winter deal online, via her phone, the rooms collectively cost very little more than Mica's flat.

We checked out the row of restaurants along the edge of the Place. Margi had changed her mind and decided that she felt all right about going to a restaurant after all. A week ago, she had told me on the phone she didn't want to eat out in France nor sit on a café *terrasse*. The recent massacre in Paris, two weeks ago, on 13th November, made her too scared. I sympathised, having felt similarly; I'd planned to go to La Lièvrerie for a long weekend on the 20th but had cancelled the trip, not wanting to cross Paris, wanting just to hide at home. The shootings had happened very close to where Val and I had stayed in July, at the end of the street.

Grief, both angry and stupefying, for the murdered Parisians, added to my continuing grief for Stephen and Irving. Civilians across the world were regularly being slaughtered, sometimes thanks to the military interventions of foreign governments, and I did think about them and criticise the politics that led to such killings, but I recognised that the killing of Parisians incited a deeply personal grief, and that made me ashamed, that I couldn't mourn all the dead equally.

I pored over the papers, trying to understand the nuances of the international situation. I discussed politics with friends, trying to construct an objective, rational defence of an anti-war stance. Also I suddenly decided I had to create something. I found myself making a shrine. On my worktable I spread a small lace cloth and on this I put photographs of Stephen and Irving, plus photographs torn from newspapers of the murdered Parisians, plus a large photograph from the *Guardian*: a composite portrait of the Muslims among the dead, all of them young and beautiful. I added in my statues of the Virgin and of the Holy Child, my Mexican tin candlestick in the shape of an angel. I surrounded these with candles and flowers, lit the candles, sat and looked at the faces.

A couple of days later, something strange happened. Tap, tap. Someone behind me whom I couldn't see tapped me briskly on the shoulder a couple of times. I swung round. There was Stephen, looking intently at me, smiling. He wasn't wearing his glasses. He was transfigured, somehow scoured and burnished: bronze-coloured, glowing. He was renewed and alive. I woke up. Morning in bed in my flat in London. Outside: sunshine and blue sky. Stephen was somewhere else. He was safe. He had come to tell me that he was all right. In this other state. In this other place. I wasn't to worry about him. The message was very clear.

I felt flooded with relief, even happiness. I was puzzled too. Should I write off this numinous experience as 'just a dream'? Why 'just' a dream? After my elder sister Jackie's death many years back I'd had a series of powerful dreams in which our relationship continued, in which I visited her in the post-death place where she now lived. The dreams asserted convincingly that she was somehow, somewhere, still alive. I'd eventually assumed, reluctantly, that I'd created these visitations myself, that their truth was born of psychological necessity, even though, contradictorily, at the same time I longed to believe that I'd intuited something objectively real. In some extra dimension, some parallel universe, life continued. No it didn't. Perhaps the soul did exist after all. No it didn't. Recognising that conflict, I now saw, could be another example of living with Negative Capability. I believed and also I didn't believe. I had no way of proving anything.

As a poet, as a novelist, I certainly believe in the unconscious imagination, as I've said, in the mind's power to conjure visions. Yet this place or condition Stephen was in, in which he burned and shone, seemed so utterly real I could not accept I had invented it. It seemed to have its own objective existence, as he had his within it. Close to it for those few moments I felt consoled. *Let not your hearts be troubled.* He had gone; now he had returned. My stultifying grief lifted. I could function in the world again.

I went over to Stephen's house in the East End, to help his

sister and a few friends clean and tidy, make lists for probate. I hadn't been in the house since he and I split up eight years back; once we'd begun to rebuild our friendship we met in pubs, or else he came to my flat for lunch. The fridge in his kitchen was full of jars of home-made fennel chutney and wild garlic pesto. Vicky pressed some on me, also gave me four of Stephen's books: French editions of Boulestin and de Pomiane. I'd been planning to leave him all my cookery books, in my will; now I was being given some of his. Stephen felt powerfully present: his 1970s flowery Liberty shirts that he'd preserved carefully and wore on special occasions, his rock and pop CDs, his Spanish pots and dishes. We were taking care of his house and at the same time I felt we were taking care of him, of his body, as you'd prepare a body for burial. In fact Stephen had been cremated in Spain, and his ashes would be scattered off the coast at Finisterre. I left in the early evening and went into town to meet Tom and Caroline. I took them out to supper at Zédel's, the huge, Parisian-style brasserie behind Piccadilly Circus. I wanted to celebrate Frenchness. I wanted to celebrate friendship.

In Avignon, Margi, Richard and I had trouble finding a restaurant as inviting as Zédel's. Our ideal one, for Margi, had to be inexpensive and to cater for vegetarians. I didn't mind spending money as long as the place had a certain charm, that would make you want to go in, believe the food would be OK. Margi needed to know a prospective restaurant would give her what she wanted; I, much greedier, wanted to be seduced and hope for the best. Richard got fed up with our havering and went off to find a cash point. Finally we agreed on a restaurant announcing itself as traditionally Provençal, with a red-painted door and red façade, its front windows revealing a pleasing décor of half-panelled walls ornamented with stuccoed swags, old posters, looped red curtains. The menu displayed outside promised various vegetable dishes *du terroir* as well as Meat, nothing too costly. In we went.

Local *vin rosé* in a carafe; fine. Cheery paper table mats reproduced from the old posters; fine. But *hélas!* A dish of cheese-topped aubergines in olive oil was too rich for my sister. My fish soup tasted OK but was clearly straight out of a jar. Aioli also out of a jar, just Hellmann's-style mayo with a chip of garlic thrown in. Tinned carrots and tinned green beans. Soggy overcooked cauliflower and soggy boiled potato. *Zut alors!* But the owner did give us free ice cream and polite smiles, and we did not complain about his bad food, needing to salvage some pleasure from a difficult day. Richard did better with confit of duck, out of a jar, but a good jar. Determined to enjoy himself, he praised everything. We knocked back a second carafe of *vin rosé*.

We returned to Mica's flat. I was sleeping on the sofa bed downstairs, since Richard, with his bad knee, needed to sleep on the same floor as the lav, i.e. upstairs, and not to have to negotiate the spiral staircase in the night. This was not his decision, but Margi's and mine. We kissed goodnight and went to bed.

I slept badly. At 6am I got up, made coffee inexpertly in the machine, which dribbled, sat and scribbled in my notebook. I felt tired, uncomfortable and chilly. The mistral moaned outside. Bloody hell – what was I complaining about? The people in the refugee camps further north had it far worse.

Margi had wanted a lie-in but didn't get one. At nine o'clock our cousin Josette picked us up and chauffeured us to the family house. She hadn't wanted our uncle to drive. Her husband and five children were off on a Catholic youth outing and she was taking care of her mother.

Two years ago, the industrial suburbs had extended a fair way out of motorway-ringed Avignon. Now they ribbon-sprawled non-stop: factories, supermarkets, garages and warehouses. No attempt at landscaping had been made; no trees planted to soften the ugliness. Had local farmers all agreed to these developments? Surely some had loved the beauty of their land, regretted its scarring. Now beauty was a marketing notion for tourists like me to moon over nostalgically; beauty was somewhere else, in specially designated heritage sites; here, practicality and profit-making were all that mattered. Behind the harsh outlines of industrial newbuild you glimpsed an occasional orchard, an occasional vineyard pruned for winter.

We swung off a side road and suddenly entered green countryside. We drove down a straight lane running between olive groves, with the mountain at its end. On the right, a tall green hedge; tin-backed gates opened to let us in.

Crunch crunch over the gravel to the front door. Marie-Yvonne and Luc received us fondly. Luc looked the same as ever: upright as a soldier, shoulders squared, vigorous, intelligent, his blue eyes bright. Marie-Yvonne looked blurry, somehow, her freckled face wavery in outline, softer. She and Josette stayed at home to supervise lunch. I accompanied the others to Mass.

The village church had kept its old nineteenth-century plaster statues of saints and added modern banners and posters with pious banal illustrations, sentimental slogans. As this was the First Sunday in Advent, the priest wore a green cope. Since modern Catholic teaching stressed actively involving young people as much as possible, a group of children and adolescents dressed in white robes hovered to one side of the sanctuary holding poles topped with green crêpe paper streamers, perhaps to invoke the idea of pilgrimage, *le peuple* on the road to Christmas. The dogma-writers were very keen on this image of *the people of God*. You weren't just some ordinary boring old parishioner but part of a select group: committed to holiness, aspiring towards heaven. Later in the ceremony the teenage pilgrims processed along the aisle accompanying the deacon bringing up the New Testament for the Gospel reading.

Early Western medieval theatre evolved from the Christian liturgy, I'd learned as an undergraduate, from the anguishing drama of Christ on Good Friday reproaching his followers as he hung on the cross: my people, my people, what have you done to me? Answer me! The modern rite essayed only a weak theatrical gesture: as he strode towards the altar the deacon held the sacred Book high in the air; over-reverential and pompous. Women were nowadays allowed to read the Lessons but only the priest had the authority to declaim the Gospel message. This one had a delightfully singsong Provençal accent, also a free-association attitude to sermonising: he rambled on about this and that then obviously decided he'd had enough and just stopped. Some of the shambling group of youngsters, particularly two pretty girls with heavy make-up and glistening ringlets, looked awkward and bored, and I wondered how long they'd carry on practising their faith.

At one point, when we all stood up to chant some responses, Luc, next to me, looked down and opened his hands like the leaves of a book, in a discreet gesture of prayer, very simply and straightforwardly. Tears heaved through me, surprised me. Perhaps I was moved because it was such a humble gesture. He was acknowledging need, it seemed: powerlessness, not being in control. A French Catholic version of Negative Capability.

A woman, singing into the mike with a loud soprano voice, led us in the dirgelike hymns. The ones we'd sung at convent school had much better tunes; these wobbled about all over the place. Luc said afterwards: what a screeching voice that woman had! It pierced my brain!

After Mass we queued in the bakery just opposite, an old building prettied up with lavender-blue shutters and a hand-painted sign. *Chez Lola et Violette.* Curly-haired, cheerful, friendly women, weighing out handmade biscuits and little almond cakes and *calissons* (iced oval biscuits), dishing out fresh crusty loaves, swapping badinage and jokes with the customers. Perhaps they were heretic lesbians and made passionate love on the tiled floor out back while they waited for the dough to rise. Real bread not skimpy communion wafers. Real, female bodies, warm and sensual. Priestesses.

We carried baguettes, wrapped in twists of paper, back to the car. Luc said: lovely fresh bread! At home we're always eating up yesterday's bread, so it's always semi-stale.

Exactly like his and Mum's sister, Brigitte, my beloved aunt, now dead. She only ever served yesterday's bread, which had to be finished up, while today's stayed in the bread drawer, slowly staling. Why didn't Luc rise up and demand fresh bread every morning? He could easily have driven to the *boulangerie* to buy it. No. That would have been to overturn cherished domestic precept. Thrift and religion intertwined. As Catholic children we'd been taught constantly to look out for ways to mortify the body and its evil appetites. Stale bread for breakfast might be one of them. Marie-Yvonne had always produced decent, plain food while managing to hint it wasn't really important what one ate, one didn't discuss it, and certainly one should not be a *gourmet* let alone a *gourmand*. Two years ago, Luc, after a pre-lunch tumbler of the whisky we'd brought him, had turned quite skittish, begun making jokes about sex, had got out a volume of reproductions of Renoir's paintings, pointed out the nude models' gorgeous breasts. He wouldn't be doing that this year, I could tell. He'd been quelled. His wife had been very ill and his mind was on mortality not luscious flesh.

Back at the house we sat around the huge fireplace, in which smouldered correspondingly huge sweet-smelling cherrywood logs on a thin bed of white ash. With our *apéritifs* we were served tiny cubes of foil-wrapped soft cheese. La Vache Qui Rit. Exactly the same as in childhood in Normandy. Luc drank some of the whisky we'd brought him but made no risqué jokes. Margi and the others had fruit juice. I had vermouth.

Marie-Yvonne's cleaning lady, whose name we were not told, had kindly prepared our lunch. Hors d'oeuvres of grated carrot and diced beetroot, then *civet de porc* with carrots and a few mushrooms (a piece of fish for Margi), then green salad, then two tarts, one apple and the other apricot and almond. We sipped red wine and made small talk.

Josette stayed with her mother while she rested. Margi,

Richard and I accompanied Luc on a walk around the garden, admiring all his hard work, then through the gate at the far end, across the canal, and along a rutted path, edged with scrub, that skirted the mountain. Luc wore a cap and a dark blue overcoat too wide for him. We hardly talked. We didn't need to. I felt contented just being with him. I knew he loved us. As my godfather he'd always made a special place for me, and I loved him extra for that and felt fortunate to have a godfather who was still alive. Margi's godfather, Grandpère, had died many years ago, as had both our godmothers. In our family only practising Catholics became godparents, so I couldn't be godmother to my sisters' children, since obviously I wouldn't be able to make the religious promises in good faith, but I was an aunt, and that relationship pleased me.

Returning from our walk, we had tea around the fire, Marie-Yvonne feeling strong enough to join us. Chitchat, photos of the diamond wedding last year, which we hadn't attended, photos of the grandchildren and great-grandchildren to be admired.

At one point Marie-Yvonne asked, and so what was the priest's sermon about today? I replied: oh, he just chatted. Marie-Yvonne looked shocked but Luc laughed. It was true. Later, Marie-Yvonne said: and so, Mimi, are you still writing? This question always enrages me. Of course I am still fucking writing! I replied with a brief outline of my novel's treatment of the sex trade. Silence. Marie-Yvonne produced her iPad. She'd been having trouble opening her emails. Could Richard do something? Luc had also been having trouble with his Internet connection. Richard and Luc went off together to the study to wrestle with the computer and then with the iPad.

Our priest-cousin Gilles turned up for supper. He looked not only older but also heavier than formerly (as I'm sure I did too). He sank into an armchair, put his fingertips together, answered all Marie-Yvonne's eager questions about his preaching and teaching. He looked bored, made no attempt to engage with us but waited for us to ask him questions about his work. Josette had to leave by 6pm, she hadn't wanted Luc to drive at night and so Gilles had come in order to give us a lift back to Avignon, which was certainly kind of him, and his parents were certainly delighted to see him, but we couldn't connect, we were too far outside his monastic sphere and he obviously didn't want to make the effort to enter our non-monastic one.

Josette departed to see to her own family and we sat down to supper. We ate a gratin of home-grown squash, the puree mixed with a little cream and dusted with grated cheese. Gilles talked about having visited Mexico recently, where his order had opened a house, discoursed on Mexico's intriguing culture and charming people. I asked eagerly whether he had come across the works of Sor Juana, the famous sixteenth-century Mexican poet and playwright who'd been an enclosed nun. I'd visited her convent and read some of her works. A talented musician as well as writer, the friend of the Spanish ambassador's wife, holding her own in courtly parties, she was finally regarded as too uppity, accused of heresy and punished by being sent to nurse the sick in a plague ward, where she died. Gilles ignored my question, began talking of the missions in the Philippines.

Soon after supper we felt it was time to go. Marie-Yvonne looked very tired. Luc, saying farewell, had tears shining in his blue eyes. Gilles drove us back to Avignon. He was clearly in a hurry to get back to his abbot's quarters at his monastery and say his prayers or put his feet up or just go to bed. His fast, jerky driving through the darkness, the route cluttered with diversions and roadworks, scared me so much that I shut my eyes and prayed for safe deliverance, while he made polite conversation with the other two. We said goodbye in the Place de l'Horloge. He'd been kind, yes, giving us a lift. Dutiful too: we were his relatives who'd come to visit his parents so for the sake of Mum, whom he had been fond of as a boy, he was trying to be nice to us.

We roused the hotel clerk and got into our rooms.

Tomorrow morning we'd do some food shopping for our picnic on the train home. Margi said: let's make sure we get some good fresh bread!

CHAPTER 9

DECEMBER

One Day In Dublin

Yesterday I woke up at 6am when the alarm beeped, banishing my erotic dream. Curses! Outside, the dark rain swished down. It had been raining non-stop ever since I arrived in Dublin three days previously. Each time I had left the guesthouse, a mile or so from the edge of the city centre, to find a supermarket in which to buy my picnic lunches, and to try to find a swimming pool, I had returned with soaked clothes and my umbrella blown inside out.

I had come to Dublin to teach novel-writing to a group of Americans brought over by enterprising Californian Nina G. She ran these package trips regularly, offering her participants an interesting European venue, luxury accommodation, gourmet food cooked by herself, workshop groups on different aspects of writing. I'd taught for Nina twice before, once in a manor house in Brittany and once in Lismore Castle in West Waterford in County Cork. I did it for the money, since Nina paid well, but for the extras too.

For example, the Breton trip featured a ghost. One of the writers, who'd been put up in the manorial gatehouse, was working at his desk upstairs one afternoon when he heard heavy footsteps going to and fro in the room below. A regular tramping back and forth. Since he'd been allocated the gatehouse for his sole use, he called out, then went down to check. Nobody there. The outer door locked as he'd left it. He found out afterwards from the local café owner that a Resistance fighter had been kept prisoner in the gatehouse overnight before being shot by the Germans. The plaque on the war memorial down the road mentioned the shooting. He could have seen this (though the plaque did not mention the gatehouse) then made up a story, I suppose, but in fact, on the basis of his written work I thought him not overly imaginative.

This Breton manor house, run as a posh B&B, was owned by a Dutch hippy, a tall, slender woman with long blonde hair, always casually dressed in designer clothes, and her younger companion, an Israeli artist, from whom I bought two landscape pastels. When he wasn't painting in his studio Darius tended the impressive garden, where Shetland ponies rambled about between the box hedges under the looping clematis, while the beautifully groomed older woman, in impeccable ripped jeans and skinny leather jacket, sat at her computer organising selling the jewellery she imported from India. When I left she gave me an exquisite greeny-blue turquoise necklace as a present. Part of the charm of staying in the manor was having seen it on TV years before, when it had featured in a series on house-and-garden makeovers in France that Jim and I had watched together. The previous owner had been a well-known British gardener; now I was witnessing the impressive fruits of his design. He'd transformed meadows into formal *parterres* near the house shading into woodland further away. In one episode, when he'd been ticked off by the local mayor for not bothering to learn French, he rubbed his big chin and pouted: well, perhaps he's got a point there.

The second time I worked for Nina, in Lismore, I'd been able to visit the village house where the traveller-writer Dervla Murphy had lived, and in our wing of the castle to get lost in its many-layered labyrinth when I went exploring. The décor was by Pugin. My large bathroom, gloriously not en suite but round the corner along the corridor, had linenfold panelling and stained glass, and the Gothic dining hall reared high-ceilinged and vast as a cathedral. One evening before dinner I explored down a twisting stair into the basement kitchen. Though the cook ruled over a big airy space lined with Gothic-style cupboards painted blue, the nearby servants' sitting room was cramped, chill and severe with no pictures, low ceilings, and no views. The ghost at Lismore was a huge wolfhound, which one of the students, entering her floridly wallpapered room, found lying on her bed. When she jumped and cried out, it vanished. The same student, searching for her ancestors in a nearby churchyard, noted that her watch suddenly stopped as soon as she approached a certain grave. I preferred the wolfhound story.

On both those trips it had poured with rain throughout. No change on my third Nina trip: in Dublin too the rain swept down non-stop. My rain-darkened bedroom in the guesthouse on the outskirts of the city featured salmon-pink walls and heavy floor-length curtains patterned with big pink cabbage roses on a blue and green ground. A tasselled *baldaquin* (canopy) in matching chintz projected above the twin beds; surely a double bed had stood here formerly. One of the curtains had been dragged off its hooks, perhaps by a previous occupant maddened by the rain, so I closed the gap with a large bulldog clip provided by one of the staff, a young woman from Poland. She explained that the handyman might pop in this afternoon to fix the broken curtain track, but then again he might not.

Two spoon-back armchairs and two wardrobes, tall and narrow, with open fronts faced with curtains, like confessionals, completed the furniture. I draped a silk scarf over the small, ugly TV, a trick I'd learned from Jim, who'd been a roadie in his youth and when travelling with the band always customised his hotel room to make him feel more at home. On the small narrow dressing table I put my books – four novels and Keats's letters – and my papers. Pen, pencil, rubber, pencil-sharpener.

Luxury: a large bathroom. Teak floor, a big white porcelain bath, heavy and deep, on the wall a print of a freestanding Victorian tub with curled feet, its side painted with wreaths of flowers ornamented with gilding. Fluffy white towels hung on the rail, near a dish of tiny soaps in pleated white paper packets, labels promising organic purity. I lay in my hot scented bath and relived my erotic dream and felt cheerful.

In the guesthouse dining room I had a quick breakfast: coffee, a slice of smoked salmon on wholemeal bread. I took a tray of coffee back to my room. At 7am the first student arrived for his half-hour tutorial. Americans were used to breakfast meetings but I was not; back in London I'd still be asleep at this hour.

I'd decided to offer tutorials in addition to the daily four-hour workshops I was contracted for because they benefitted the students and because as a teacher I enjoyed them. One-to-one you could focus precisely on the student's work, get to grips with his or her writing problems, explore them in depth, discover and offer possible solutions. Simultaneously you could just see where the conversation led, where it wanted to go. There was a sense of free-floatingness. A commitment to talking about the student's writing as intensely as was needed co-existed with being lightly in the conversation; not having pre-conceived notions of what the student should do. Negative Capability? Yes. Then, in a successful tutorial, we made a breakthrough: we *got somewhere*. Something similar could happen with a friend, during a heart-to-heart. Talking to Giuliana, for example, when I first knew her in Italy, we'd go on as long as we wanted, all evening if need be. There'd be a recognition, a physical sense, at a certain moment, that we'd *got there*: satisfying, like a mutual orgasm. *La jouissance*.

When you work closely with people, you often begin to love them. In the past, of course, some male teachers used to literalise loving the female students and become entranced and try to seduce them. Others felt no love and were merely exploitative. Sometimes the students fell in love with their teachers, who were older, more powerful, father figures perhaps. Some of the students, flirted with by male tutors, turned round and became stalkers. I wrote *The Mistressclass* to explore all this, retelling the story of Charlotte Brontë falling in love with her professor, Monsieur Héger, and writing him impassioned letters. At UEA, copying American practice, I used to leave my office door ajar during tutorials. It seemed ridiculous that at the age of fifty I was doing this, especially since all my erotic fantasies at that time were directed at my dear farmer away over the sea in

France, but the idea was that it reassured the students that you'd keep the correct distance. One youngish male student occasionally confided his anxiety about his girlfriend, who had severe anorexia. She was so frightened of a packet of rice cakes in their kitchen cupboard that she had to throw it away. No treatment helped. One day, answering a knock on my office door, I found this student trembling and weeping in the doorway. He blurted out his news: his girlfriend had died. My immediate instinct was to put my arms round him but I held back. Sympathy could only be spoken.

No linguistically provoked orgasm was possible with one of the students in Dublin! She barged in five minutes early, during my mid-morning break, followed by an attendant bearing her breakfast tray of coffee. She yawned and complained: I've only just got up! She banged down her cup on the table so clumsily that it spilled. She didn't notice. She hadn't submitted any work for discussion because she didn't write. She worked as a psychologist turned therapist and was just curious about writing fiction, preferring to observe workshop practice rather than participate, which I found irritating. Now she told me that in the first workshop session, when I taught the students a simple game to help us remember each other's names, she'd thought: what a pathetic game! I know much better ones! She told me that I'd come on like a schoolmarm. Because I found her unpleasant I found her ugly (another of those hags). Now I challenged her rudeness, and she apologised. She told me how very sensitive she was, and how she was attending my class to nick my ideas: she intended doing *bibliotherapy* with her clients back in the States. They'd write their stories and read them out and she'd listen. She was deeply sympathetic to her clients' problems, oh yes, but as for writing fiction and therefore trying to imagine what it was like being someone else, oh no, forget it. She lay back in her chair, chatting smugly. She tried to stay on past her time but I resisted. I pointed out the pool of her spilled coffee. Oh, she said, just fetch a cloth and mop it up.

I showed her out. Then indulged in a long silent scream. Then mopped up the coffee with a hand towel. The resulting large brown stain looked like wet shit, which would give the wrong idea to anyone coming in to do the room, although so far they hadn't bothered, not wanting to disturb me they explained, because a writer wouldn't want her flow interrupted, not that I minded making my own bed and emptying the waste-paper basket, but anyway I hastily washed the towel in the basin as well as I could in the couple of minutes before the next student arrived.

During my two-hour break, late morning, I dashed out into the rain, still trying to find a swimming pool. They were all in the process of being converted into gyms. Ever since swimming in the sea at La Ciotat, back in early September, I'd gone swimming every day, since it made me happy, as well as fitter.

Accordingly I'd brought my swimsuit to Dublin, to no avail, though I could have swum to the shops: the rain continued to pour down. I thought of Mr Jeremy Fisher perched on his lily leaf and in his house the water all slippy-sloppy in the back passage. In the supermarket I bought a boxed salad, a bottle of white wine, and a newspaper, then returned to the guesthouse, hung my sopping clothes and brolly to dry in the bathroom, lay on my bed, ate my lunch, drank some wine, read the paper, hid the bottle at the back of one of the confessional-wardrobes. Bless me, father, for I have sinned: I have indulged in hate-filled thoughts about a student, I have drunk wine at lunchtime, I have failed to take a health-giving walk. Then I had a siesta.

From one until five I taught the workshop. I followed my standard pattern: warm-up exercises of automatic writing to free the unconscious; writing exercises designed to address specific components of novel-writing such as point of view; criticism of the writing produced. Fun to work with Americans: different reference points, different histories and cultures invoked. The young men, mainly writing thrillers, were supremely polite and deferential, unlike their axe-wielding villains; the women, older and tougher, writing in other genres, less so. The women glanced at me challengingly: come on! On I came.

We'd been given the extension-cum-conservatory at the far end of the guesthouse dining room to work in, sitting around several tables pushed together. At the other end, by the entrance to the kitchen, a sarcophagus-sized fridge-freezer held all the meat Nina had ordered in for our suppers. See-through polythene packages of dark red flesh gleamed behind the see-through glass door. This close to the kitchen, despite the roar of the overhead heating system, the pounding of the rain on the conservatory's roof, we could hear Nina shouting at her sous-chefs about the right way to make caramel, coulis, ceviche. At one point she erupted, clutching her phone. The foie gras! Oh my God! They've gone and lost the foie gras! Find me a butcher immediately! Oh my God!

Most of the students equated writing novels with producing marketable commodities. They were obsessed with writing correctly to certain agent-identified, agent-approved agendas. This irritated me, not least because of my own recent unhappy experiences with Lily. These students obviously had a template for the perfect commercial genre novel in their heads. Product! They spoke authoritatively about rules and techniques, about backstory and front-loading and info dumps. They trusted literature less than self-help writing manuals. I'd come across this attitude in the UK, obviously, particularly when teaching middle-aged adult beginners who didn't read much fiction but nonetheless wanted to write, but not to this extent. I always sympathised with students; if they'd bothered joining my class then I wanted to help them all I could, but I wanted them to take risks, write something authentically theirs, not just *product*. At first I was intrigued by my Dublin group, then finally exasperated. Towards the end of one discussion I burst out in defence of making *art*, art as a vocation, writing what had to be written, experiments with form, I mentioned inspiration, imagination. The students glanced at me sympathetically, tolerantly. I tried to explain to them about Negative Capability. Nice idea, but they had deadlines to meet.

Currently, as regards my own work, I was swimming in dark water again. Just before I left for Dublin Arabella T. had delighted me by emailing that the final, final version of my novel that I'd sent her a week previously really worked, and that she'd sent it on to the Publisher. The Publisher had said she was too busy to read the novel before Christmas but would read it in the new year. Until then I just had to wait.

There was absolutely nothing I could do. I was powerless to

make anything happen. I kept telling myself this. Sometimes acknowledging my powerlessness brought peace and release; sometimes anguish. Currently it felt much easier to preach Negative Capability to the students than practise it myself.

At the end of the afternoon's lengthy and tiring workshop we moved to the sofa-stuffed drawing room for aperitifs: a choice of Irish cider or Prosecco accompanied by Nina's canapés, which she called appetisers. Tonight's elegant titbits were shredded wild mallard breast (leftovers from last night's supper) on mini oatcakes, topped by slivers of apple and a drizzle of honey. These were served from a mahogany table in an alcove lined floor to ceiling with *Reader's Digest* novels in faux-antique bindings. Mid-December: the Christmas decorations were up, tinsel and red ribbons looped along the green brocade pelmets and round the tiebacks of the swagged green curtains, a Christmas tree sparkling in one corner.

Each evening before dinner, aperitifs and appetisers to hand, we listened to readings: some by workshop participants, others by invited writers. Mostly poets, who sometimes went on far too long and over-ran their time and the room was warm and stuffy and sleep threatened and I had to doodle furiously in my notebook in order to stay awake. Under the pressure of enforced politeness, boredom and rage I drew simpering Victorian-style heroines: portraits of my own hypocrisy, perhaps, pretending I could endure hearing bad poetry by self-satisfied bad poets. Tonight a tall, slender, dramatically good-looking woman with huge, smoky eyes and short, swept-up silver-black hair and big silver earrings, a Celtic goddess in a long green velvet robe, was reciting her poems. Channelling them, rather.

The coffee-spilling student, who'd snagged a deep cosy

armchair, was blatantly fast asleep. Having chosen a seat near the drinks table, surreptitiously I refilled my glass with Prosecco. The audience had dwindled since the first evening. At the end of the workshop this afternoon I'd heard my young male students planning a night out in a pub in town that featured Authentic Irish Music. They were going to drink Guinness and scoff fish and chips and skip dinner at the guesthouse, which anyway cost seventy-five dollars a throw. Nina's gourmet cooking and fine wines did not come cheap. As one of the tutors I got free school dinners, otherwise I'd have copied the chaps and gone to the pub.

The séance ended. Bright-eyed Nina clapped vigorously. We all got up, stood about, polished off the appetisers. The Celtic goddess began talking to me about Jungian spirituality and the feminist revaluing of the Crone. No thanks; I knew about that already. Rudely I shook her off and made for the dining room.

I sat next to Susannah, a student I'd met before, on the Lismore trip, the one who'd seen the ghostly wolfhound. She was a big, lusciously pretty woman, with fresh skin, flashing dark eyes and glossy, thick black hair. She wore an elegant black cocktail frock and looked eager and young. Her eighteen-year-old daughter, similarly voluptuous and ardent, sat at a nearby table.

Susannah began telling me about the workshop she was attending on redrafting and restructuring your novel. We sipped Nina's excellent Meursault. Flushed and beaming, our hostess and her sous-chefs began serving our first course, the foie gras, which Nina had finally tracked down, stored, oh my God, in the wrong fridge. Each large white plate bore an entire goose liver. I hadn't eaten foie gras for a year or so, out of a recently born concern for the goose subjected to a fattening process some argued was cruel. Despite the mallard-breast appetisers I'd wolfed earlier I was still hungry, however, and weak-willed, and wanted to eat something delicious after a hard day's work, and so I abandoned my ethical stance and tucked in. Susannah poked her foie gras with a fork and frowned: this will be far too rich, why don't you have it? She tipped it onto my plate. The foie gras, cut open, looked and tasted like delicate, creamy curds. I ate both portions. Not only cruel, but greedy too. In my mind a child sang a song: Christmas is coming, the goose is getting fat, please put a penny in the old man's hat.

Susannah began telling me the tale of how while she was redrafting and restructuring her novel her husband had begun redrafting and restructuring their marriage: he was having an affair with a young woman of eighteen, a friend of her daughter's. Susannah was just too fat and too difficult, he was off. The young woman's mother kept phoning Susannah to ask what she should do; Susannah worked as a lay pastor and was presumed wise. My mouth full of foie gras, I tried to indicate I was listening sympathetically. Susannah's eyes glittered. She set her lips in a hard line. She said: I'm tough, I'm a survivor, I will survive this.

How heartless I must have seemed, self-indulgently munching away at rich, taboo delicacies, obviously enjoying them. I swallowed, I murmured how sorry I was. This wasn't the end of her tale. More sad, horrible details flooded out. I felt I had to go on listening. Oh dear oh dear. These characters clearly weren't lining up for a happy ending.

A woman sitting opposite ticked Susannah off: stop right there, you're upsetting Michèle too much, this is supposed to be a happy occasion!

This woman, tall and slender, with a bony, intelligent face, was apparently a patron of Nina's but in what way I never discovered. Expensively dressed in designer silk frocks, she attended the evening readings and suppers but not the workshops. She turned up always with a glass of red wine in her hand, drifted about sipping and dreamily smiling, and I admired her insouciance. She'd keep her bottle in full view on her dressing table, that one, not guiltily hidden in her wardrobe. She was right. Red wine was a good idea. I commandeered a bottle of Médoc and filled everybody's glasses.

My sister red wine lover winked amiably at me and changed the subject: we began discussing our Christmas plans. What would I be cooking for Christmas lunch? Er, a goose, actually. Though not one specially fattened for its liver. Helen, my niece, with her husband and daughter and other family members was coming to stay with me in the Mayenne and goose was what Helen wanted to eat. I'd been delighted she'd specified her preference, and had hunted around. Chantal the taxi driver thought she might be able to track one down. Then Paulette had taken over: you'll have one of my sister's, of course! She rang me to say she'd collected it from her sister's farm and put it in her freezer to await my arrival in a week's time.

I told my dinner companions about a different occasion of hunting for a French goose, a few years before. I'd left it rather late. All the neighbours had already sold theirs, but one directed me to her cousin's place, two villages away: she'll see you right. Off I drove. The cousin and her husband lived in a tiny ramshackle house in a hamlet near La Chapelle du Chêne. They gave me coffee and eau-de-vie and showed me photographs of the husband on his tractor in the 1960s, a radiant, thick-haired, handsome young man bursting with life, wearing a checked shirt rolled up over his strong forearms. Now after a lifetime's hard work he was bent and balding, stooped, moving stiffly. Our coffee drunk, I handed over thirty euros. The old couple took me out the back and opened a barn door, revealing three live geese. Which one d'you want? I picked one out at random, pointed. The old man gripped it by the neck and brought it, flapping, into the daylight. Here you are then. Off you go! Hmmm. I couldn't face driving home with a live squawking goose sitting next to me or packed into the tiny boot and squawking there. I said: please will you kill it for me? The old man raised his eyebrows, shrugged. He said to his wife: fetch a knife and some string. They knotted the goose's feet together, while it screeched, then hung it upside down from a branch of the cherry tree and slit its throat. A thin plumb-line of blood fell to the earth. I drove home with the dead bird next to me on the front seat in my basket, its head on its long flopping neck lolling over the wicker edge. Once cooked and carved, it proved tougher than old novels in manuscript. I had to make a stew with it.

Here in Dublin we'd been consuming our main course: a cube of beef on a bed of pureed potato with a leaf of frisée next to it. I don't like puddings much, so didn't eat the tarte Tatin. I felt tired of company, in need of solitude. I went back to my room, lay on my bed, and went on reading Keats's letters. As I began falling asleep I hoped for another erotic dream but knew you couldn't whistle them up, as you couldn't whistle up lovers, either, or tender geese, or swimming pools, or sympathetic agents, or Publishers keen to publish you.

CHAPTER 10

JANUARY

Another Day In Orchard Street

Yesterday the sound of men shouting close to my bedroom window woke me. 8am. Time to be up anyway. I flung on some clothes, dashed into the kitchen and opened the back door to see what was going on.

In the communal garden next door, a man in work clothes, perched on top of a ladder, was leaning over the dividing wall, feeding long thin planks across it to other workmen, standing in my area, who were carrying them through my garden and heaving them over the wall at the far end. It was raining. The men wore hard hats, shiny yellow jackets and heavy boots. They were trampling in between the shrubs across what to them probably looked like bare earth but which I knew were flowerbeds full of plants just biding their time before coming up in the spring. Their boots had made heavy dents.

I shouted: what are you doing?

It turned out the neighbour in the basement flat next door had given them permission to carry the planks in from the street through the communal ground-floor hallway all those flats share and out through the communal back garden. The workmen had assumed my back garden was my neighbour's, they improbably asserted. They were council workers, putting up scaffolding outside Mike's and Sam's back walls preparatory to mending their roofs. The foreman apologised: we had no idea!

It couldn't be much fun, heaving planks in the rain, so I let them carry on using my garden, just insisted they did not step on the flowerbeds but kept to the paving. The foreman said solemnly: if they damage the plants I'll buy you new ones. I said: well, I'll make you all some tea later on.

From the doorway I watched them for a bit, yelled a couple more times to steer them away from the budding snowdrops. Grey rain sheeted down. The garden glistened with wet: the paving stones, the flowerpots, the fence, the stems of plants. Snail tracks ran silver towards the foxgloves, their leaves reduced to lace. In this strange weather, such a mild winter, pale pink roses bloomed unseasonably, and salmon pink pelargoniums. The hostas were out, the cream-white-pale green ones and the pink ones, and a couple of white primulas.

I made coffee but didn't get on with any work. I felt too strange, couldn't settle. The previous night, arriving home late from a party, I'd found an email from the Publisher, saying that she now considered the novel 'wonderful… really wonderful' and wanted to publish it. Two years of anguish and despair were over. I sat down and cried. Like Elizabeth Bennet, I rather knew myself to be happy than felt myself to be so. I rang Margi with the good news, I emailed Nell, Georgie, Carmen, Sarah and Jenny.

The foreman declined cups of tea on his workmen's behalf: better leave them to get on with it. Restless, I decided to take the day off and go out. I began by walking towards the Elephant and Castle, pausing at a bank to get some cash from the outside dispenser. Somebody, a child presumably, had dropped a small teddy bear on the pavement. Someone else had arranged it in a sitting position, its back to the wall, and put a bottle of lager between its splayed legs. Old soak of a teddy bear. A few doors along, outside Iceland, at the shop's edge, where it abutted the twenty-four-hour Turkish grocery, a homeless man had built himself a nest. His thin mattress and sleeping bag lay behind a rampart of cardboard boxes, on which he had stowed his rucksack, a couple of bags, a mug, a radio. He sat in a folding chair and received his friends and watched the world go by. The Turkish shop assistant patrolling the pavement, guarding the racks of fruit against passing thieves, obviously accepted him, his need for shelter. He'd been there for a couple of weeks now. Nobody had moved him on, nobody seemed to be saying he was bad for business. Nobody had rehoused him either.

Further along, outside Morrisons, a white-haired woman, dressed in a long full skirt, shawl over a baggy blouse, sat cross-legged on the ground, her back to the huge black rubbish bins, her hand outstretched, muttering, please, please. Usually a young man sits there, bent over, his hood concealing his face, a folded cloth in front of him displaying his bit of cash received. Recently he's taken to drawing a fancy cross in coloured chalk on the pavement next to him, and various passers-by stop to examine it and speak to him kindly. I gave the woman some coins. Perhaps she was related to the two young men playing the accordion across the road outside M & S, perhaps they were her grandsons and had brought her out with them to make extra money, but anyway it seemed terrible that an old lady had to sit on the ground and beg.

The Groper was also experiencing the indignities of old age. He had been diagnosed with early-stage vascular dementia. This would probably get him off being punished for groping women. Back in November, coming home one night on the 45 after teaching, reading my *Evening Standard*, I had learned that he had been had up in court that morning, after some brave women had reported him to the police for groping them on the bus. As the celebrated photographer of Twiggy, back in the 1970s, he merited a report in the paper. The Groper groped! Having his collar felt at any rate. I hadn't reported him. I'd assumed that the police wouldn't care. Certainly, some of the local young men, my neighbours, hadn't understood my reaction when we'd been gardening together one Saturday, weeding the raised bed on the corner near the sheltered housing unit, and the Groper had ambled up and started trying to photograph me, whining: will she look at me, will she look at me? I kept my head down, said no, and eventually he shambled off. I explained to the young men about the groping. I could see they couldn't believe that any man would want to grope a woman of my age. Anyway, what was I making such a fuss about? It wasn't *rape*, was it? He was only trying to be friendly. Dave said earnestly: you mustn't go telling all the neighbours about him, he'll get a bad reputation, that would be so unfair. I thought, why the fuck not?

I used to enjoy strolling home via the Plum Street route, slowing to admire people's pretty front gardens, but that was the Groper's patch and every time he spotted me he made for me, waving his camera, and I had to dodge him, so eventually I'd changed my route. Now that the Groper had gone, was presumably having his dementia cared for somewhere, two months of happy strolling and dawdling had ensued. We could wander our streets in peace again, *flâneuses* not having to be bothered by that annoying *flâneur.*

I'd once read an essay by Adam Phillips in which he suggested that agoraphobia, fear of open spaces, the consequent preferring to stay at home, might mask a fear of whom you might meet or what might ensue if you went out: adventures of all sorts, sexual adventures included. Several women locally I'd talked to who feared going out either at night or into strange neighbourhoods feared being groped, mugged or raped. That wasn't a denial of their secret sexual wishes; it was grounded in reality. Yet I could see that women's reasonable fears might also conceal or jolt alongside desires for freedom, desires not to be corralled inside houses or notions of domestic virtue. Men policed urban spaces. Women used city streets in a particular, male-approved way: they could go to the shops, to the park, to the doctor's, the nursery. Gangs of drunken young women on the street were seen as far more disgraceful than male gangs. What would happen if all women freely roamed the streets? Mayhem, apparently. Yet many of us did freely roam, even if we had to cope with gropers en route. I still went walking wherever I pleased (except during the time when I chose to avoid Plum Street) and had no intention of stopping doing so. Night walking too. Pacing along through cool dark air: exhilarating; peaceful.

On this strange day of good news I felt less peaceful than bewildered. Like a child barging about and bumping into things. Nana would say: she doesn't know what to do with herself. If the not-knowing went on, the dictum changed to: she's having a funny five minutes. Five minutes turned to twenty. When it began to rain, when I had almost reached the Elephant, I jumped onto the first bus that arrived. On a whim, I sat downstairs. Normally I sit upstairs, to get the best possible view of the river as we zoom over it. Today felt different so I had to do things differently.

The woman sitting in front of me was wearing a red wool beret decorated in small chips of diamante, which spelled out Jesus is Lord. A younger woman, absorbed in phone chat, stood over a massive black buggy, longer than the usual size, coffin-shaped, all zipped up, which she had parked slantwise, blocking the way of passengers boarding at subsequent stops. She ignored them as they squeezed past her, made no effort to give them some room. At the stop on the far side of Waterloo Bridge she appeared not to notice, or not to care, that a second buggy-pushing woman had got on through the exit doors, and was trying to manoeuvre her buggy, smaller and squatter, into the impossibly small space left.

This second young woman, bending her head to keep her own phone stuck under her chin, shouted at the first woman to move, for God's sake, make room can't you. Receiving no reply, and obviously realising there wasn't room for her and she'd have to get off, and clearly feeling humiliated in front of all the watching passengers, she began screaming abuse. Why didn't you take any notice of me, why did you let me think there was room, why didn't you tell me as soon as I tried to get on? The first woman, jolted, got off her phone, and began yelling back. The bus hadn't moved. The driver came to see what the matter was, gave his opinion that the bus could not hold both buggies, the second woman would have to get off. She exited backwards onto the pavement, screaming: bitch, bitch! The first young woman, bright pink spots appearing on her cheeks, muttered after her: bitch you too! She went back to her phone. We lurched on into Aldwych.

Was there a baby or babies in that closed-up buggy? I remembered travelling on the Tube one day recently, a packed carriage, when two women pushed on, both in black robes with full face veils. They were carrying big Harrods bags and steering a sturdy buggy laden with many more. The buggy seemed just a convenience for carrying shopping. Then one woman bent right down and from the lower rack extracted a previously invisible thin swaddled baby, exactly as you'd pull a tube of Polo mints out of a slot machine. She sat down, unwrapped the baby, shook it. Like the baby in Punch and Judy. Was it still alive? Yes. It began howling.

I jumped off the bus at Holborn Tube and strolled along to the LRB bookshop in Bury Place. The window was displaying works by Angela Carter. The café next door had put a shrine in its window to David Bowie: a big photo and a candle. I bought a stash of novels and non-fiction. I chatted to the booksellers. I produced my idea for an event: an evening dedicated to Olivia Laing and her new book *The Lonely City*. The booksellers smiled and nodded towards the poster on the wall: yes, we've already organised it.

Then I wandered back southwards, across the river again, past the Imperial War Museum. Recently I'd seen the exhibition of Lee Miller's wartime photographs here, with Pete and Sousou, sharp, beautiful studies in black and white, lots of images of women at work, and then we'd driven through the south London streets, Sousou directing our progress via the map on her phone, a most exhilarating route passing lots of the inter-war vernacular architecture I so loved, to the Horniman Museum, where well wrapped up we ate lunch in the freezing stately glass pagoda. Now I turned left towards Walworth, zigzagged through backstreets. I shopped for food. In Morrisons I bought duck breasts and in East Street £1 bowls of tomatoes, courgettes and mushrooms and a couple of fat heads of celery. The Turkish vegetable seller said God bless you! I replied God bless you too! The weather was cold, the street surface greasy and wet underfoot. Few shoppers were about. What a job that man had! Standing all day in chill and drizzle. Yet he could still be sweet to people.

I walked slowly along the main road, relishing the fresh air, needing a longer pause before going home. It had been a hectic few days, bits of freelance work to finish, friends to visit, jobs to do (housework to defer), as well as get on with writing. Tonight our local supper club was meeting, and as we had just passed Epiphany and I'd told neighbours at the previous supper about the French custom of the *galette des Rois*, with the *santon* (little saint) in it and the *santon*-finder crowned king for the evening with a gold paper crown, the group had decided that tonight's meal should have a French theme. Hal would make a *galette* and I had dropped a tiny china *santon* through his letterbox and the rest of us would cook whatever French dishes we fancied. Since the community house had only one cooker, we would cook our dishes at home and transport them cold or lukewarm.

I walked to my flat via the scenic route of Plum Street. As I approached the sheltered housing unit a familiar silhouette rose up in the dusk: that big hat, that wide-shouldered coat.

Fuck! The Groper. He stood still, turning his head from side to side, vaguely looking round. He seemed slower, presumably gentled by medication. Nonetheless I crossed the road, turned the corner, got into my own street.

For tonight's group supper I was adapting a French recipe for a whole boiled duck with celery. Duck breasts would be easier to serve, I thought. I seared them in a frying pan then finished them in the oven, then carved them into coin-sized slices. I could hear my mother tutting: English people do not understand how to cook vegetables! The base of the celery is the best, the heart, so do not waste it. Take a sharp knife and pull off all the strings from the outside stalks. Chop the celery thinly and neatly, slantwise, then blanch it in boiling water, drain it then dress it as your recipe dictates.

Norman cooks blanched all green vegetables first, in order to get rid of their otherwise excessive greenness, and boiled all root ones until just done. Then you completed their cooking with a touch of butter or sauce; you never dished them up nude. Nor did you serve green beans undercooked and crisp, as was currently fashionable in England: you boiled them until plenty soft enough. Thanks, Mum. On my bed of braised celery, with a little cream, I arranged the slices of duck meat. I had cooked three breasts and now had a nice big pot of duck fat, which I'd give to my niece Helen, for her fried potatoes.

I laid the long community table with two of Mum's white tablecloths. Also tealights in little glass jars: empty antipasto pots, the sort with ears, that I'd been collecting. I tied thick hairy string around their necks to decorate them. Keri and Hal provided more tealights and several large loaves of bread. Hal's *galette* had burned, to his great distress, so although he'd brought it with him, to show us, he'd also made a pot of onion soup with tartines of toasted cheese floating on top. Other people brought salad, one person a tarte Tatin, while Dave, too busy at work to have had time to cook, brought an array of French cheeses. Word of the supper club seemed to have circulated: ten new people turned up, all young.

We drank the French wine I'd brought, also bottles from Australia, South Africa and Chile. Hal told us about attending his grandmother's deathbed in Hartlepool a few days back. He'd been her favourite grandson. He and the second-favourite grandson sat one on each side of their grandmother's bed, each holding one of her hands, and she was ready to go, she'd told us that, and we were talking to her and telling her it was all right, it was all right for her to go if she wanted to, and then we let go her hands and she just went, just like that. Keri sat quietly by, listening, looking at Hal, his face radiant with love.

I cut off the burnt top of the *galette*, like a lid, and we ate the unspoilt, delicious underneath, with its frangipane filling. The young woman who got the *santon* in her slice was unwilling to don the gold paper crown and act as monarch. Perhaps she thought it was silly and undignified, so we just carried on feasting and talking and drinking wine.

Back at home I rang Giuliana in Vicenza. We hadn't seen each other for over a year. I kept promising to come to Italy. When was I going to come? We consulted diaries and settled on a long weekend in late May. Some way off but that didn't matter. Something to look forward to. I'd begun believing in the future again.

CHAPTER 11

FEBRUARY

One More Day In Orchard Street

Yesterday, Sunday 14th February, I got up early, to finish my preparations. I was giving a lunch party for twenty friends. I called it *La Fête de l'Amitié* and made a poster on a large piece of cardboard to that effect, to prop on the table. I polished wine glasses, hoovered rugs, shoved baskets of papers (in-tray) under my bed, cleaned the bathroom, put out fresh soap and towels, removed my laptop to a high shelf, flung on a tablecloth.

Val rang. She was going shopping, did I need anything? I asked her for a copy of the *Observer*, which I had not had time to dash out and buy, and she volunteered in addition to bring crudités to serve with dips. I hadn't got any dips and wouldn't have time to make them. Never mind. The crudités could be eaten *nus*. As usual, I'd forgotten to make any kind of pudding. But Georgie had offered to bring cheese and I knew she'd include grapes, so we'd be fine.

I put on my new, olive green dress, mid-calf-length, in some sort of soft sacking, bought two weeks back from Oska off Sloane Square. The sailors' trousers Carmen and I had bought in Amsterdam were from Oska. Their London branch was calm and welcoming behind a plate-glass frontage, just a few items hung on freestanding silvery racks, high-slung ample indigo cotton curtains swishing theatrically around to create lofty-ceilinged cubicles. In five minutes I had picked out, tried on and bought two dresses and a jacket. Bliss: a shop full of beautiful clothes flattering my curvaceous shape. The new clothes cost a lot but I didn't care. I then went to nearby Peter Jones, lively with displays of periwinkle-blue and white striped china and matching crisp linen. I felt exactly as I was supposed to and longed to snap up bowls and napkins I didn't need. Escalators twined up like beanstalks inside the airy atrium. The Chelsea shoppers were thin, tanned, expensively dressed, well-groomed and heavily made up, with neat, dull haircuts, all the armour of bourgeois femininity. The slick-haired young man behind the rings counter wore a fuchsia-pink silk waistcoat and called me Madam. I swept aside his proffered trays of bling and chose a pair of gold-plated earrings set with an apple-green stone and paid £40 for them without a blink.

Ever since the Publisher had accepted my novel I had felt much more cheerful, despite the occasional *mauvais quarts d'heure* or indeed *jours* inevitable in anyone's life, and despite still waiting for Lily 2, my potentially new agent, to decide whether or not she wanted to represent me, so that dwelling in Negative Capability remained an imperative. But also the light was lingering a little longer each afternoon, thus speeding back across the river in the bus after swimming, at 5.30pm, I could catch the sunset flaming red and gold in the west behind the Houses of Parliament, and even dream of the coming of spring. I had also just been paid for three months' teaching so felt rich and hence wanted to celebrate by buying a dress. All winter I'd wrapped myself in trousers or leggings topped with tunics and scarves and shawls, perfectly nice outfits but not especially dashing, but now for a party I'd come out of my burrow and wanted to dress up.

I didn't have to buy any drink for my party: Stephen's mother Gay had sent me an entire case of wine. My friends packed in, shoulder to shoulder in a tight squeeze. No room for us to sit down to eat and no room for people to stand about holding plates and forks as well as wine glasses; accordingly I served food my guests could pick up and eat with their fingers. Elizabeth Jane Howard and Fay Maschler, in their friendly cookery book *Howard & Maschler On Food* that I'd picked up recently in Any Amount of Books in Charing Cross Road, frowned on this as too tough on the guests, but I'd decided they would cope. Hippy morsels and retro morsels and, yes, naff morsels: falafels, canapés, gem-lettuce leaves filled with prawn mayonnaise, strips of smoked salmon rolled around lengths of mozzarella, cherry tomatoes stuffed with goats' cheese, mushrooms stuffed with cream cheese and hazelnuts, plus pistachio nuts and olives. Val turned up with crudités plus tubs of dips. Georgie brought cheeses, membrillo (quince paste) and grapes. Caroline brought a big bowl of mackerel pâté. Other friends brought chocolates, bunches of yellow and orange ranunculus, pots of pink roses.

Nell acted as butler, Carmen helped pass round the platters of food, enjoying being commanding: now come on, take one! When necessary, people spilled out into the back garden for breaths of fresh air, or to smoke cigarettes. I made a speech about the little-known saint who was blessing this occasion:

Santa Valentina, her bones recently dug up at the Elephant during the excavations of the roundabout and now reposing, thanks to my *furta sacra* (sacred theft), in a shoebox under my bed, so that anybody who needed a miracle only had to go and have a little lie-down. My tolerant friends coped well with the tight squeeze, wriggling intimately to and fro, lips brushing each other's ears.

By 5pm everyone had gone. Little clearing-up to do, just washing glasses and putting the leftovers in the fridge. Despite all the drinking we'd done, twelve bottles of wine remained: exactly the number I'd started with. Santa Valentina's friendship miracle: everyone had brought wine.

One of the reasons I had wanted to celebrate friendship was because a week previously Stephen's memorial celebration had been held, two hundred friends joining his mother, sister and cousins to remember him. His sister Vicky conceived the overall plan of the day, then asked various friends to help her carry it out. The event was held at Hoxton Hall, a recently restored and re-opened former music hall in Stephen's beloved East End, now a community centre. Marie Lloyd had sung in the little theatre, which had two tiers of galleried seats, a small apron stage with steps curving down from it in front. Stephen's cousin Anne, a designer, had ordered flowers from Covent Garden market at Nine Elms. I went over early on the day to help her assistants fill with water hundreds of wine bottles which, each containing a few blooms, were arranged in massed rows across the front and a little way around the sides of the stage, giving the impression of a meadow of wild flowers. Stephen's friend the artist Julian Bell had painted a backcloth of a garland of flowers, to fit in with our foraging/wildness theme (Stephen foraged long before it became fashionable, sticking to urban spaces – the wild fennel for his chutney picked in Mile End Park, the wild garlic for his pesto collected along the edges of the canal). Other friends had made a loop of images from photos of Stephen, and a music tape: flamenco, Italian partisan songs, Dylan. At Vicky's request, I'd helped liaise between all the different people involved, also coordinated the readings of poems and other relevant texts by family and friends.

Sarah had been an important friend for Stephen. She and Chris had shared their little Stoke Newington house with him thirty years back, a time he had adored remembering and talking about because he'd been so happy living there with them. Sarah (who had been an editor at the Women's Press, founding their science fiction list) had collaborated with Stephen on several publishing projects; accordingly at the memorial she introduced and read from (among other texts) *Colours of a New Day – Writing for South Africa*, an anthology she had co-edited with Stephen, a book version of the solidarity rock concerts being held at that time, and which had a foreword written by Mandela just after his release from prison.

During the memorial preparations I felt like a lightning conductor. A great deal of pain and upset boiled around, the shock of Stephen's sudden death still resonating, and once or twice under the strain of dealing with complicated tensions I put my foot in it and people erupted and became very cross, and I just had to apologise for my clumsiness then weep in private. In the end, after all the difficulties, things suddenly simplified. Everything finally flowed and fitted together. Love took over.

The occasion became a living artwork: a crowd of people who loved Stephen both testified individually and also sank their egos to become points of colour in a massed whole like a mosaic, making both a rounded, complete portrait of Stephen and at the same time a narrative of his life as a radical publisher, political person, cook, lover of Spain, traveller, writer. Everybody was actively involved, moving about in the packed space, talking and listening and looking, eating and drinking, crying, creating an energy that composed something powerful and moving, like a strong cloud enveloping us all, breathing in and out. His mother was a tiny figure bravely walking through the crowd to talk to everyone. While he was alive Stephen knew his friends loved him, I'm sure he had no doubt about that, but nonetheless after his memorial I felt, yet again, how important to tell people while we still can that we love them. So I hosted my 14th February lunch party specifically to celebrate my friends.

Once I'd cleared up I had a sleep. Then, when darkness fell, I felt restless and went out. I struck eastwards, towards the Old Kent Road (the cheapest district for property speculators on the old Monopoly board), towards Bermondsey, a district that my neighbour Rosie remembered from her youth, when it was rough and lively, with great pubs, a thriving antique market, locals who all knew each other, not in some sentimental notion of 'community' but just knockabout real life. Bermondsey had subsequently become what estate agents call vibrant, then gentrified, now full of gourmet delis, new, expensive apartment blocks, art galleries such as White Cube, and pop-up theatres.

My beloved Elephant too was on its way to gentrification (people like me moving in and helping host supper clubs signified that), with council tenants being turfed out of the 1960s high-rise estates and these being demolished to make way for costly private housing snapped up by foreign investors, but hadn't quite made it yet. It remained endearingly ramshackle, shabby, traces of the past visible. A mid-Victorian jeweller's was still intact. A former Kennedy's the Butcher, with untouched décor of 1930s sunburst pearled glass, wood-panelled walls and green and white tiled floor, had been transformed into an Algerian café selling French-style cakes. Parts of 1890s wrought-iron-braced façades survived, also classical capitals, elaborate stucco swags and cornucopias decorating the corners of buildings; outside M & S there were patches of blue tessellated pavement. Side streets of artisanal blocks, with communal staircases open onto the pavements, remained, each building entry with its own boot-scraper, and ancient workshops built around courtyards. I'd praised these inner-city landscapes, that I so loved roving through, way back in my first novel, *A Piece of the Night*, and again, more recently, in my memoir *Paper Houses*, and my short story collection *Playing Sardines*. Part of their fascination derived from their forming part of a constantly changing, constantly evolving city. Southwark forty years ago, still a series of wildernesses in post-war semi-ruins in certain places, was very different from Southwark now, and one hadn't to regret the improvements. Austen in *Sense and Sensibility* mocks Marianne Dashwood, idealising other people's picturesque but damp cottages, mooning over romantic Gothic landscapes in the gloaming, then tripping home with wet shoes and the start of a near-fatal fever. I didn't want to be like her. Some of the proposed developments sounded excellent: for example the council was promising local people free entry to the new swimming pool it was going to build, and it did intend, it swore, to provide more social housing (the new term for council estate).

I meandered towards Tower Bridge, crossed the river, roamed the quiet Sunday backstreets empty of people, managed to get lost a couple of times, emerged near the City, turned west, kept on walking.

Reaching London Bridge I felt tired, so caught a bus homewards. I sat on the top deck, relishing the view of the river lights as we sped across. As we swooped past the Elephant, I heard the driver shouting at passengers downstairs. Stop ringing the bell over and over! Stop ringing the bell! Obviously wanting to teach his annoying passengers a lesson he did not halt at any more of the bus stops, though of course people began ringing the bell even more vehemently and shouting back at him, but he ignored our cries and whizzed all the way down to Albany Road where he halted with a great jerk and tipped us out.

I was more amused than cross. We'd been kidnapped! A young man in a chestnut-coloured sheepskin coat who got off with me unplugged his earphones and shook his head: what was all that about? The guy doesn't understand, these new bells on the buses, they go ting-a-ling three times, it's not the passengers' fault. The young man had curly black hair, a curly black beard, a fleshily handsome face. He went on: should we report him? Put it on Twitter? Oh, I don't know. Not his fault if he doesn't know about the new bells, I suppose. We walked back along the main road together and parted outside Tesco. Ting-a-ling! he cried.

CHAPTER 12

MARCH

One Day In Herne Bay

Yesterday I woke up at 5am to the sound of a blackbird singing loudly in the back garden. I lay and listened to its exquisite melody. When it stopped singing I went back to sleep.

I got up at seven. I put out food for the robins and blackbirds in the way Georgie showed me: slices of apples and halved grapes on the ground. Just hoped squirrels and rats wouldn't get there first. Did rats like fruit? Part of their five a day?

You used to spot rats only on the Underground, scuttling between the tracks. Now they followed the commuters home, attracted, like foxes, by the food rubbish dumped on the pavements. Round at Dorothy and Matt's one day, before they moved north, drinking coffee with them, gazing through the French window at the back garden, I'd spotted two rats rummaging in their compost heap. Dorothy shuddered. She said: it makes you feel so ashamed, having rats. They got rid of them eventually.

I felt complacent, never having had rats. Then last summer I had a rat of my own, which strolled in through my back door left open on a hot afternoon while I had a nap. Perhaps it had smelled the loaf of bread I'd carelessly left on the draining board. Anyway, it woke me up, rustling in the basket full of newspapers for recycling that stood near the kitchen doorway. I barricaded the kitchen and rang Dorothy: help! I put down poison, as advised by Matt. After three days, it'll begin to feel very poorly, and then it'll be done for. Bettina upstairs told me she and Angus actively encouraged their mouse, feeding it snacks of sunflower seeds. I squeaked, don't do that! Sally next door, with several mice scooting about, had summoned the man from Rentokil, who'd put down heavy-duty poisoned bait and told her to block all the holes in the Victorian skirting boards. Val warned me against using bait: you don't want to attract vermin in the first place, do you? She advised putting balls of cotton wool sprinkled with peppermint oil in strategic places such as under the kitchen sink. It seemed to have worked: I hadn't seen a rat since. Also I'd become tidier, never leaving food out. No more still lifes of fruit and veg – everything went into the fridge.

I wrapped up the housewarming present I was taking down to Herne Bay for my friends Hilary and Bill: an 1820s hand-coloured print, eighteen inches by twelve, found the previous week on a junk stall in East Street. The print showed figures in bright frocks and pantaloons strolling on the tree-lined banks of the estuary of the Cork river. Hilary and Bill had no connection with Cork that I knew of but I thought the print distinctive and pretty and hoped they'd like it. From a neighbouring stall, I bought an ornate gold frame, which back at home I customised, brushing it roughly with pale blue paint matching the blue of the sky in the print, letting the gold show through in streaks. The print inside its window fitted the frame exactly.

That morning, doing my usual Sunday prowl along the

stalls, I'd got a good haul of bargains: a first English edition (1941) of a children's book by André Maurois, with sharp, garish three-colour illustrations; a collection of ghost stories by Walter de la Mare in a rubbed slipcase; a 1950s hardback edition of selected extracts from Fanny Burney's diary; an 1830s hand-painted sugar basin bearing a twirled finial on the lid, slightly (unobtrusively) chipped; three lawn handkerchiefs trimmed with lace; a Victorian pink and gold lustre bowl. All these items would make good presents for friends. Sarah might like the ghost stories, since as a descendant of Sheridan Le Fanu she wrote them herself. Val might like the sugar basin, since she loved old china and would kindly overlook the chip on the lid. Nell liked proper handkerchiefs. Georgie liked pink lustre ware. And so on. My final bargain had been globe artichokes at fifty pence each. In Borough Market they cost four times as much. I carried them by their long stems like a posy of flowers. Two little girls, dressed in starched Sunday frocks, their hair braided and beaded, following their turbaned mother through the stalls, carried palm crosses, which they waved seriously at passers-by, blessing us. I waved my artichokes back.

Hilary loved markets too: flea markets, vegetable markets, the local Thursday market in France. I'd first met her and Bill twenty-three years back, when we were all house-hunting in the Mayenne and being shown properties by the same *notaire* (solicitor). They bought an old farmhouse ten miles or so away from Jim's and mine, and slowly we made friends. They kept their house in Stoke Newington for a while, a double-fronted early Victorian villa with a walled back garden, next to an old steam laundry. Hilary and Bill then moved to France fulltime.

They planted a big *potager*, and Hilary kept hens that she named after the nuns at her convent school: Sister Evangelina, Sister Marie-Paul, Sister Polycarp, Sister Deodata, and so on.

Hilary's first husband had been a chef, who ran The Hole in the Wall restaurant in Bath, and Hilary herself was a superb cook, with that gift for producing exactly the right dishes to suit the time of the year, in just the right amounts, everything seasonal and fresh and delicious. In summer we ate in the garden under the big walnut tree and in winter in the kitchen, whose front window sported a splendid rose-pink satin curtain with gleaming ample folds falling across the floor. Their isolated house, on top of a hill, had views all round over the countryside. An old track, its route uncovered by ex-archaeologist Bill, led down, past the clearing where beehives formerly stood, to the lane. Up this, an itinerant grocer used to travel with horse and cart, bringing the farming family supplies of matches, cooking oil, coffee, paraffin. In all other ways they would have been self-sufficient. Bill had rebuilt the outdoor bread oven, dug out a wine cellar and laid tiled floors. Hilary and Bill had integrated: they spoke fluent French, hobnobbed with their French neighbours, joined in village life. Also they were socialists, the first I'd met in the neighbourhood.

When Jim and I split up, Hilary and Bill continued our friendship. We went on inviting each other to meals and Bill very kindly gave me practical help a few times, filling up holes in walls, getting my car going, finding me a new battery charger. They gave me bottles of their eau-de-vie, as I have said, and I gave them books.

Now Hilary and Bill had decided to return to the UK at

some point and in anticipation had bought a house in Herne Bay. Hilary had memories of a Kentish childhood, a Kentish landscape. Her mother had spent her last years in a residential home in Herne Bay. It seemed an obvious choice. To begin with they'd let one of their children and his wife live in the new house, but last autumn the children had vacated it and Hilary and Bill had spent part of the winter there. They emailed me: come and visit us.

Nana, my English grandmother, had often mentioned Herne Bay, a favourite resort when she was young, easily within reach of London therefore much appreciated by working-class families such as hers, the place she and her gang of sisters went for jaunts and larks in summer, paddling, strolling along the pier, eating whelks and shrimps. Cherishing my memories of Nana's stories, having loved her so much, I was curious to see it. A bit rundown and shabby it seemed, when Hilary and Bill met me off the train and drove me around to give me a sense of the place, less than half of the pier left standing, some boarded-up shops, but on the other hand a flourishing cinema and old streets in the centre of town lined with graceful buildings.

Hilary and Bill had chosen a Victorian mid-terrace house two streets back from the sea, with a façade of stucco-ornamented red brick. The builder who put up the terrace had lived in the house himself. Built over three floors joined by a wide staircase with wooden banisters, it had a calm, peaceful atmosphere: uncluttered rooms, pale pastel walls. The big kitchen, with open shelves, where we sat to have lunch, had glass doors put in by Bill, letting the light stream in and revealing the back garden, the old buildings behind.

Hilary unwrapped the print and declared she liked it. Cork! That's where Sister Evangelina came from. She was the nun at my convent school who taught me Latin. I'll hang it up in the sitting room and every time I look at it I'll think of her.

Bill produced a bottle of Prosecco as an apéritif. Then with glasses of white wine we ate paper-thin strips of Parma ham, followed by little potato-topped fish pies bought, as an experiment, from the fish stall down on the beach, with dark green curly kale alongside, and then green salad. Red wine with the English cheeses, none of which I'd heard of, then an exquisite crème brûlée Hilary had made, and then black coffee. We talked about politics, the refugee crisis, we swapped news and gossip. They asked after my writing. I didn't dwell on the story of my search for a new agent. Too dispiriting. Three agents whom I'd approached, one after the other, Lily 2 and Lily 3 and Lily 4, had asked to see the novel. Duly, one after the other, they had subsequently declined to represent it, much as they admired its beauty and my talent blah blah blah, as actually they were terribly busy and couldn't summon the passion necessary for supporting me at this stage in my career, and didn't actually *love* the novel quite enough. Lily 3 spelled it out: it's always harder once you've had five or six novels published. (Thirteen, actually, I wanted to snarl.) Yes, I knew the younger generation of agents preferred fresh new products (otherwise known as young debutant authors). That was how capitalism worked. New! New! New! Talking to the agents felt like speed-dating: I had to accept I was too old to inspire passion. But I didn't want passion; I wanted professionalism; I just wanted someone who could negotiate a decent contract. The Lilies considered my novel too literary, not commercial enough; it wouldn't sell enough copies to give them a decent 15%, nor would they be able to sell lots of foreign rights and make money that way. Hurrumph!

Away from the agents' business world, I recognised these irritations for what they were: minor. What mattered far more was being with old friends, talking and laughing. I love being in Hilary and Bill's company; I'm equally fond of them both; we work well as a threesome, the conversation weaving easily. How happy they seemed. The Herne Bay house was a new project and they were relishing it.

After lunch we took a walk. I declined going for a proper long one across the cliffs: three weeks back I'd bashed my foot in the swimming pool and though I could manage short distances it still hurt when I stood still and put my weight on it. I'd swum too near an older woman who'd been barrelling along face down approaching me, and I had accidentally touched her leg with my foot as our paths crossed. I exclaimed: I'm very sorry! She rose up and shouted. Yes, I'm sure you are sorry, but I am very thin-skinned and if you touch me I start bleeding! She obviously wasn't bleeding, but frightened. On warfarin, presumably. Overcome with dismay, I swam away as fast as I could, misjudged the distance, struck the tiled side of the pool with my foot, thought nothing of it, then later felt pain, and saw that the foot had swelled up. I decided I'd sprained it, didn't bother going to the doctor, assumed it would heal in its own good time, just propped it up in the evenings when I sat at home reading.

I'd been swimming for too long every day, recently doing

more than my usual hour, and my hips ached grindingly. Was I trying to prove to the Lilies-in-my-head that I wasn't the old crock they'd hinted at? Caroline had ticked me off: you've overdone it again, you're so all or nothing. We'd been to the Delacroix exhibition at the National Gallery and I had to keep walking round and round rather than stay still, because that felt less painful. Afterwards we sat in nearby Terroirs and drank a carafe of white wine and talked about our work, our lives, and going home I felt happy, as I always do after seeing Caroline, she is so honest, so funny as well as serious, so affectionate. She's a few years younger than I am, slender and pretty, always beautifully dressed, an expert on where to buy nice clothes. She is kind, with that sort of kindness that never tells you to stop fretting and brace up, but just makes you feel recognised, heard, warmed. As a committed, hardworking artist she's happy to talk about art for as long as we both want, and that's part of our bond. We've made four artist's books together so far and I hope we'll embark on a fifth, because I so enjoy the process of working with her, making something together.

With Hilary and Bill I walked a little way along the rough turf of the open headland under the grey sky, the grey sea roiling down below, the far cliffs half-veiled in mist, then back inland through an old-fashioned small park set with shrubs. We made for the station, we embraced, looking forward to seeing each other soon again in France, and then I caught my train back to London.

Outside the side entrance to Victoria station a white-haired woman, leaning on a Zimmer frame, stood begging. I gave her some money. You see far more people begging in London now than a couple of years ago, certainly in poor areas as well as the usual places along the Strand: the Tories' welfare cuts have created a lot of misery. You see rough sleepers everywhere. Two days ago, for example, invited to a launch party at Daunt's in Marylebone, I'd chosen to walk there from Piccadilly, up New Bond Street, then up Marylebone Lane, relishing the way the lane bends and twists between close-packed buildings and imagining how formerly it wound through open fields, and I passed three middle-aged men camping out in the recess fronting a shop. I paused, thinking I'd never seen homeless people in this part of London. We greeted each other. They looked and sounded Eastern European. One of them gestured at the space in which they lay in their sleeping bags: this is us house. I gave them my spare change – not much. They looked pretty fed up at the meagre amount and who could blame them. The launch party was full of gaiety and jollity. I felt sure we all had homes to return to.

From Victoria I caught a 185 bus home. At my flat I checked my email and found a message from the Publisher: how are you getting on with your search for an agent? I emailed back, no luck so far, let's just go ahead with the contract, I'll get the Society of Authors to check it, let's sign and keep to your suggested publication date of spring next year.

The Publisher emailed back in agreement. She would send the contract through and then the novel could be published next April.

I poured myself a glass of Muscadet to celebrate and made myself a tomato and anchovy salad. While I sat eating it I looked around my workroom. The walls, still bearing experimental splashes of different colours from three years ago, badly needed repainting. A stack of pictures needed hanging. My CD machine needed mending. My horrible electric cooker I'd inherited when I bought the flat no longer worked properly, the knobs (stuck back on by the previous owner with blobby white glue) having fallen off, the protruding screws not amenable to pliers, therefore the front ring and the oven both blazing at high heat when you turned the cooker on at the wall, making the slow cooking of certain dishes requiring that impossible. The washing machine also had ceased functioning even though I'd paid a plumber to look at it and he had fiddled and then pronounced it fit and well. For several months I'd been taking my sheets to the launderette and washing everything else by hand in the bath. The CD player, cooker and washing machine were definitely in a state of Negative Capability. They were certainly not striving irritably after anything. They were just sitting there.

I always put writing ahead of domestic chores. In my writing I challenged the mind-body split but in my life I let things drift, mainly cleaning up just before guests arrived, then enjoying the tidiness and vowing to be tidier in future.

Negative Capability didn't have to mean negative capacity or practical ineptitude (did Keats do housework? No.).

Right. I gave myself some advice.

First: get a new cooker and washing machine in the sales, or buy used ones online, and pay someone to install them. Take the music machine in to be mended.

Second: paint the walls and hang the pictures. Wash the kitchen floor once a week. Swoosh a broom about the ceilings ditto. On the other hand: don't overdo it.

Third: strive not to be narcissistic.

I added this because recently I'd been reading M. F. K. Fisher's novel *The Theoretical Foot* with its cruelly comic portrait of an ageing, needy, self-deluded woman who moans that she's not properly loved by the female friend with whom she's holidaying. Fisher sketches a horrible narcissist. I shuddered. Writing this diary, was I like that? Oh please no, please no.

Narcissism seemed to involve a denial or distortion of the self/world, self/other balance. To function adequately as an adult, on the one hand you had to have enough self-love to survive, to make your way in the world, yet at the same time you had to care about other people, to recognise and value and enjoy your connection with them, to help them when necessary. Surely we weren't meant just to live in tiny boxes of couples; to shut out everybody else; we needed the wider group as well. The dominant, money-making culture preached the survival of the fittest, films and thrillers championed the heroic solo macho man who was invulnerable and non-dependent, but in fact we all needed each other. This year, yet again, I'd learned that. I could not have survived without my friends and neighbours, their support and affection, the pleasure we had together.

What else had helped me survive failure and wretchedness? Writing this diary. Jung says somewhere that the point of making a mistake is making something with it. Making a narrative of this past year, I had proved to myself that I could live inside time, think one thought at a time, link them in strings. My mind might often whirl like a Catherine wheel, I might often feel and think everything all at once, but I could also make patterns, make order, put one sentence after another.

Sometimes you needed the narrative and sometimes the time-less moment. You could enjoy both.

Writing: putting a shape on things. In the midst of all my depression and chaos I'd managed to rewrite my novel. I had done OK. Also, writing this diary, I'd rediscovered, recording them, the pleasures of doing ordinary things, the pleasures of living day to day.

What to make, finally, of this past year? Thoughts rushed up, leaped and danced, netting themselves together, everything was connected, there were no grand conclusions to reach. 'Irritable grasping after fact and reason' was indeed pointless. Yet again, I decided Keats was right.

However, one perception did seem to want to make itself felt. I had had to let go of my identity as a writer. At the start of the year, unable to cope with how my novel had been rejected in what felt such a brutal way, I had felt rejected too, I had fallen apart overnight. I had shattered into pieces. My identity as a writer had sustained me all my life from adolescence onwards. Not just the verb – writing – but also the noun – writer.

I remembered that Henry James story about the man who socialises at the supper table while his other self goes on writing upstairs. Perhaps, although I'd become a committed, professional, successful writer, earning a living from writing, on another level, a childhood one, I'd constructed a writerly self as a persona, as a way of coping with a difficult, often painful childhood and adolescence, a fraught and chaotic early adult-hood. Over this past year I'd had to let go of that persona; it had ceased to protect me. I had always imagined, I now discovered with embarrassment and hilarity, that a book being accepted by a publisher magically meant that I was someone my parents could love and approve of, and that a book being rejected meant I was nothing. Of course, since my books had enacted my childhood wish to rebel against my parents, they had loathed them and continually told me so. I'd remarked in *Paper Houses* how I recognised that you couldn't both rebel against the bourgeoisie and expect to be thanked for doing so. I kept on having to rediscover and re-evaluate those contradictory wishes. Here they were again, demanding to be thought about.

That childhood model no longer served. Perhaps Negative Capability could mean finally letting go once and for all of that deep, childhood need for approval by powerful others, letting go of making them the sole arbiters of whether I was any good as a person, as a writer. It is hard to believe in your own writing when it has been brutally rejected by a powerful other. Perhaps I needed to shed my need for approval. Become much bolder and braver. Strength not as a shield, but formed from the knowledge of my own capacity for weakness, my knowledge of the support of other writers, the support of friends.

These tentative conclusions felt energising. I decided, as so often, to go out for a walk, to wander through the rapidly darkening streets, taking a route I didn't know, towards unfamiliar neighbourhoods, with little idea of where I'd end up, just following Keats's friendly ghost.

Acknowledgements

Thanks to Sarah LeFanu and Jenny Newman, my first readers. Thanks to Charles Walker at United Agents, and to his colleagues. Thanks to my editor, Moira Forsyth, to Bob Davidson and all at Sandstone Press. Thanks to all my friends, and to my family.

www.sandstonepress.com

 facebook.com/SandstonePress/

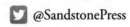 @SandstonePress